Michael Prothero

Political Economy

Michael Prothero

Political Economy

ISBN/EAN: 9783337134365

Printed in Europe, USA, Canada, Australia, Japan

Cover: Foto ©Suzi / pixelio.de

More available books at www.hansebooks.com

BY

MICHAEL PROTHERO, M.A.

BENGAL EDUCATION DEPARTMENT, PROFESSOR OF POLITICAL ECONOMY AND
HISTORY IN THE PRESIDENCY COLLEGE, CALCUTTA
FELLOW OF THE UNIVERSITY OF CALCUTTA.

LONDON

GEORGE BELL & SONS

AND BOMBAY

PREFACE.

This little work, which makes no pretensions to originality, is based upon Mill and Fawcett. It is an attempt to present in a small compass enough information to enable students to pass the B.A. or M.A. examinations of the Indian Universities in this subject. A large part of the book has been delivered in the form of lectures to students of my classes at the Presidency College. I have treated at some length the important topics of Socialism, the Gold Discoveries, Monometallism or Bimetallism, as being foremost in the minds of all thinkers on Economics in Europe or in India at the present day.

M. PROTHERO.

Presidency College, Calcutta,
April 1895,

CONTENTS.

BOOK I.—DISTRIBUTION.

CHAPTER I.

INTRODUCTORY.

	PAGE
Subject of Political Economy—Its claim to be considered a science—Political Economy in its premises a Positive, in the Conclusions drawn from them a Hypothetical Science—Methods of Political Economy—The Part played in Political Economy by Statistics—Three Schools of Political Economy—Meaning of the expression "A Law of Political Economy,"	1

CHAPTER II.

DEFINITIONS.

Wealth—Different kinds of Wealth—Money, ... 5

CHAPTER III.

REQUISITES OF PRODUCTION.

Distinction between Productive and Unproductive Labour—Definition of Capital—Nature of Capital, and the Assistance it gives to Production—Two Sorts of Capital, ... 6

CHAPTER IV.

PRODUCTIVENESS OF LABOUR.

The Greater or Less Productiveness of Labour depends on (1) the Qualities of the Labourer; (2) the Security of his Position; (3) on the Division of Labour; (4) on the Co-operation of Labour—Respective Advantages of the Large and Small Scale of Production, ... 9

CHAPTER V.

CAUSES OF PRODUCTIVENESS OF LAND.

Discussion of the Question whether Agriculture on the Large or Small Scale is most profitable—Law of Productiveness from Land and the Influences counteracting it—Future of English Agriculture, . . 12

CHAPTER VI.

CAUSES OF THE INCREASE OF CAPITAL.

On what the Increase Depends—On the Effect of the Rate of Interest on its Increase, ... 19

BOOK II.—DISTRIBUTION.

CHAPTER I.

PRIVATE PROPERTY AND INHERITANCE.

Origin of Property—Stages it has passed through—Origin of the Power of Bequest and Inheritance—Property in Land—Criticism of the Unearned Increment Theory, ... 21

CHAPTER II.

SCHEMES OF THE OPPONENTS OF PRIVATE PROPERTY.

(A) Communism, (B) Socialism, . . 23

CHAPTER III.

CRITICISM OF THE SCHEMES OF THE OPPONENTS OF PRIVATE PROPERTY BASED ON

(1) Neglect of Population Question. (2) Excessive Cost. (3) Weakening of Feeling of Individual Responsibility, and of Motives for Exertion and Self-reliance. (4) Probable Tyranny of Superintendents of Industry. (5) These Schemes put an end to Special Function of Industrial Ability, ... 37

CHAPTER IV.

METHODS OF DIVISION OF THE PRODUCE.

The English System of Division of the Produce of the Land—Other Systems—Peasant Proprietors—Slave Labour—Metayers—Cottier Tenants and Indian Rayats, ... 10

CHAPTER V.

THE INFLUENCES REGULATING DISTRIBUTION.

Fundamental Distinction between Production and Distribution—Marx on the Origin of the Capitalist—How Rent is Affected in Different Countries—Effects of Competition on Producers, Buyers, and Labourers, ... 43

CHAPTER VI.

WAGES.

Definition of Wages—Constituent Elements of Wages—Causes on which the Rate of Wages depends—The Reasons why the Rate of Wages has not increased in Proportion to the Increase of the National Wealth—Wages' Fund Theory—Socialistic Theory that Wages are a part of the Produce of the Labourer—Ricardo's Theory of Wages—Relation of Wages to Profits—Relation of Wages to High Prices and Good Trade—Adam Smith's Reasons for the Difference in the Rate of Wages—Fawcett's Criticism thereon—Remedies for Low Wages, ... 44

CHAPTER VII.

PROFITS.

The Constituent Elements of Profits—The Natural Rate of Profit in every Trade—The Relation between the Rate of Profit and the Cost of Labour—The Cost of Labour not identical with the Rate of Wages — Circumstances causing Profits to rise — Circumstances causing Profits to fall—Difference between Profits and Rent as Society progresses—Parallel between Profit and Rent—Tendency of Profits to a Minimum, and the Consequences thereof, . . 53

CHAPTER VIII.

RENT.

Reason of and Definition of Rent—Explanation of the phrase "Margin of Cultivation"—Relation of the Margin of Cultivation to the Current Rate of Profit in each Country—Effect of Improvements in Cultivation on Rent—Effect of Increase of Wages on Rent—

Effect of Increase of Population on Rent—Causes counteracting the Effect of the Increase of Population on Rent—Payments to a Landlord for the Use of the Buildings of a Farm are Interest of Capital, not Rent—Rent is not an Element of the Cost of Production or of the Price of Food—Difference between Agricultural and Monopoly Rent, ... 58

CHAPTER IX.

INFLUENCE OF THE PROGRESS OF SOCIETY ON PRODUCTION AND DISTRIBUTION, ... 62

CHAPTER X.

THE PRESENT CONDITION OF THE LABOURER AND THE REMEDIES TO BE APPLIED THERETO.

Sketch of the History of Trades Unions—Consideration of their Objects and Economic Effects—History of Co-operation and the Advantages to be gained from it, ... 66

BOOK III.—EXCHANGE.

CHAPTER I.

VALUE AND PRICE.

Definition of Exchange—Definition of Value—Macleod and Ricardo on Value—Definition of Price—Cairnes on Price—Market Price—General Rise in Values—Money, ... 83

CHAPTER II.

CLASSIFICATION OF COMMODITIES ACCORDING TO VALUE.

(1) Commodities which have a Monopoly Value—Definition of Demand and Supply. (2) Commodities, the Value of which depends upon the Cost of Productiveness. (3) Commodities, the Cost of which is regulated by the Cost of the Portion which is brought to Market at the greatest Expense, ... 85

CHAPTER III.

THE VALUE OF ACCESSORY PRODUCTS.

Joint Cost of Production—Various Examples of Joint Cost of Production, ... 90

CHAPTER IV.

MONEY.

Functions of Money—Meanings of the expressions Measure of Value and Medium of Exchange—Reasons why Gold and Silver are used as Money—Causes regulating the Amount of Money which a Country requires—Causes regulating the Value of Money—Ambiguity of the term Value of Money—Method in which the Demand is equalised to the Supply of Money—Cost of Production comparatively unimportant as compared with Quantity in regulating the Value of Money—The Value of Money more closely connected with Supply and Demand than that of other Things, . 91

CHAPTER V.

MONOMETALLISM OR BIMETALLISM AND ALTERATIONS IN THE MUTUAL RATIO OF THE VALUE OF THE PRECIOUS METALS.

Meaning of the phrase Double Standard or Bimetallism—Advantages and Disadvantages of a Double Standard—Means to secure the Advantage without the corresponding Drawbacks of a Double Standard—Ratio of the Value of Gold to Silver at different Periods—Chief Occasions on which this Ratio has been Altered, and the Causes of the Alterations—Effect of the Gold Discoveries in California and Australia—Causes of the Appreciation of the Value of Gold and Depreciation of the Value of Silver in Modern Times—Steps lately taken by the Government of India to counteract the Depreciation of Silver. 96

CHAPTER VI.

CREDIT.

Nature of Credit—Various Forms of Credit, and Explanation of their Effect on Prices (1) as a cheap Substitute for Metallic Money; (2) as increasing the Purchasing Power of the Country—Effect of an Inconvertible Paper Currency—Fallacies about an Inconvertible Paper Currency, ... 115

CHAPTER VII.

LEGISLATION RESPECTING THE CURRENCY.

Object of the Bank Charter Act—Extent to which it answers its Purpose—Use of Bank Notes at a Time of Commercial Crisis—Objections to the Act: (1) It does not secure the Convertibility of the Note, as, by the Obligation to publish its Accounts weekly, the Bank is precluded from keeping in Circulation an Excessive Issue of Bank Notes, even without the Act. (2) It causes Delay in

Advances being given by the Bank after the Collapse of the Speculation. (2) Causes Contraction of the Bank Issues on Efflux of Gold, whether Credit is affected or not. (3) Causes unnecessary Burden upon the Bank. (4) The Deposits of the Bank can be withdrawn by Means of Cheques without affecting the Note Circulation—Discussion of the Question whether the Bank of England's Monopoly of the Right of Issue of Bank Notes is advisable, ... 125

CHAPTER VIII.

THE RATE OF INTEREST.

Cause on which the Rate of Interest depends—Sources of the Loanable Capital of a country—Causes affecting the Demand and Supply of Loans—The relation of the Price of the Public Funds, of the Shares of the Joint Stock Companies, and of Land, to the Rate of Interest—Cause on which the temporary variation of the Rate of Interest and Discount depends, ... 130

CHAPTER IX.

INTERNATIONAL TRADE.

Advantages of International Trade—Mistaken Ideas about International Trade—International Trade depends upon the Prices of the two Articles traded in bearing a different Proportion to each other in the trading Countries—Equation of the International Demand—The Settlement of the Terms of Exchange—Effect on the Equation of International Demand of an Increase of the Demand in one Country for the Produce of the other—The Profit made by one Country in trading is in inverse Ratio to its demand for the Goods of the other—Effect of cheapening the Cost of Production of one of the Commodities traded in upon the Terms of Exchange—Equation of International Demand is not influenced by the number of Commodities traded in—The Trade of a Country is more profitable in Proportion to the Number of other Countries it trades with—Effect of the Cost of Carriage on International Trade—The Price of the Imported Commodity is generally lowered in the Country which imports it, and the Price of the Commodity Exported to pay for it raised—The Price of the Imported Commodity depends upon the Amount of it produced at Home in the Importing Country—The Injury to certain Classes is an Argument for Protection, but the general Benefit to Society from Free Trade countervails this—Reason why the Exports of some Countries permanently exceed the Imports, and *vice versa*—Effect of Taxation upon International Trade—Underselling, ... 132

CHAPTER X.

THE PRECIOUS METALS AS IMPORTED COMMODITIES.

Precious Metals imported as Commodities and as Money—Value of the Precious Metals as imported Commodities—Causes on which the Cheapness of imported Bullion depends—Effect of the Quantity of the Precious Metals on Prices—Any Inequality in the Distribution of the Precious Metals tends to adjust itself—Causes of exporting and importing Bullion—Law of the Distribution of the Precious Metals—Meaning of the Exchanges being "Favourable" or "Unfavourable," and of Bills of Exchange selling "at a Premium" or "at a Discount"—An Unfavourable Exchange corrects itself, . 144

BOOK IV.—GENERAL FUNCTIONS OF GOVERNMENT.

CHAPTER I.

GENERAL FUNCTIONS OF GOVERNMENT.

Limits of Government Interference—Reasons against its Extension—Cases in which the Doctrine of Laisser Faire does not apply—Mill estimates the general Merit of a Government according to (A) Its Method of raising its Revenue by Taxation. (B) Its laws of Property and Contract. (C) The efficiency of its Judicial System, by which it enforces the Execution of its Laws, . . . 150

CHAPTER II.

GENERAL PRINCIPLES OF TAXATION.

Smith's Canons of Taxation—Criticism of the First Canon, 154

CHAPTER III.

DIRECT TAXATION.

Difference between Direct and Indirect Taxation—Direct Taxes: Income Tax, and Explanation of its Incidence—House Tax, . . 158

CHAPTER IV.

INDIRECT TAXATION.

General Objection to Indirect Taxation—Malt Tax altered to Beer Tax on Account of it—Discriminating Taxes—Mill's Rules for Taxation of Commodities, ... 161

CHAPTER V.

MISCELLANEOUS TAXES.

Tax on Sales—Tax on Auctions—Tax on Contracts—Tax on the Purchase and Sale of Land—Law Taxes, ... 164

CHAPTER VI.

INSTANCES OF GOVERNMENT INTERFERENCE FROM MISTAKEN THEORIES.

Usury Laws—Regulation of the Price of Food—Monopolies—Anti-Combination Laws—Protective Duties, ... 166

CHAPTER VII.

LOCAL TAXATION.

Incidence of Local Taxation—History of the Poor Law, . 175

CHAPTER VIII.

ENGLISH LAWS OF PROPERTY AND CONTRACT.

Mill's Criticism on English Laws of Inheritance, Partnership, and Bankruptcy, ... 180

CHAPTER IX.

DEFECTS OF ENGLISH JUDICIAL SYSTEM.

Mill's Criticism—The Mercantile Law—Faults of Land Law—Uncertainty of Title—Transferability of Land—Evil Influence of the Law, ... 183

BOOK V.

SKETCH OF THE SUCCESSION OF THE THEORETIC IDEAS ABOUT ECONOMIC FACTS.

Economic Ideas in Ancient Times—Economic Ideas among the Greeks—Differences between Ancient and Modern Industrial Life—Economic Ideas among the Romans—Economic Ideas in the Middle Ages — Influence of Feudalism — Influence of Canon Law — Approximations to the Modern Order of Things—Growing Influence of Commerce—Sketch of English Trade and Agriculture

—Debasement of Money common in the Middle Ages—Nicolas Oresme, first writer on Economic Subjects — Economic Effect of the Reformation, and Discovery of America—Royal Interference with English Trade—Rate of Customs arbitrarily increased by James I.—Navigation Law and the corresponding Law in France—William Stafford—Early Italian Writers on Economic Subjects—Restrictions on the importation of the Precious Metals relaxed in Favour of the East India Company—Sir Dudley Digges—Sir Thomas Mun—Sully the first minister who paid much attention to Commerce—Sully's Measures—Theory of the Balance of Trade—Colbert's Financial Measures—Harrington's Oceana—Sir William Petty—Sir Josiah Child—John Locke—Daniel Defoe—The Bank of England—Chamberlayne's Land Bank—Law's Theories of Paper Money—His *Money and Trade, considered with a Proposal for supplying the Nation with Money*, 1705—Law's Land Bank in Scotland—Law's General Bank in France—Law's Trading Company of the Indies—Darien Company—South Sea Company—Eighteenth Century Period of Commercial Wars—Considerations of East Indian Trade, 1701—Sir William Davenant—Walpole as a Finance Minister—Josiah Tucker, Dean of Gloucester—Sir James Steuart—Pierre le Pesant, Seigneur de Bois-Guilebert—Marshal Vauban—The Physiocratic or Economist School in France—English Colonial Policy before the Time of Smith—The *Wealth of Nations* and its Contents—Interest of the Community best complied with by allowing free play to Individual Selfishness—Limitation of the Interference of Government—Errors of the *Wealth* and its Influence—Hume—Bentham—Malthus—True Theory of Rent—Ricardo and his Works—Explanation of the term Abstract School of Political Economy, and its Method—Ricardo's doctrine, that Exchange Value is regulated by the Labour necessary for the Production of a Commodity, examined—Change in English Commercial Policy—Repeal of the Navigation Laws—History of the Protective Duties on Corn—James Mill—M'Culloch—Richard Jones—John Stuart Mill—His Works and Method—His view of the relation of Political Economy to Sociology—Mill's Training—Comte's Views on Sociology and Mill's reply to them—Political Economy in Italy, France, Germany—Henry Carey, Archbishop Whately, Twiss, Thorold Rogers, Caird, Cairnes—Historical School of Political Economy in Germany—Bagehot, Cliffe Leslie, Jevons, Fawcett, Toynbee 185

BOOK I.

PRODUCTION.

CHAPTER I.

INTRODUCTORY.

> "Political Economy is the science which traces the phenomena of the production and distribution of wealth up to their causes in the principles of human nature, and the laws and events, physical, political and social, of the external world."—CAIRNES.

POLITICAL ECONOMY is a science which aims at the establishment of general principles to guide men in their action in all matters relating to wealth.

Mill says, "It is only so far as we regard action as regulated entirely by competition that political economy has any claim to be considered as a science," for only in this case are the actions of men sufficiently uniform to have a general theory formed of them.

Sir George Baden-Powell thus summarises the work of political economy :—" Political Economy unties for inspection the bundle of conditions that in its entirety is some definite effect or fact. The political economist analyses results and explains economic experience. His principles are the constants he finds in circumstances; the substantial conditions which underlie circumstantial varieties. He draws up a list of the actual conditions which must be present together if we are to have a given effect."

Political economy, as regards its premises, is a positive, as regards the conclusions drawn from them, a hypothetical science. Its premises are the facts of other sciences, but the economic conclusions drawn from them are only true if we suppose disturbing causes to be absent. This is the meaning of saying that political economy explains "tendencies" only; it asserts that, given certain conditions, certain results will follow, if other influences do not intervene.

There are two methods of political economy. The *a priori* or Deductive method considers the effect of a particular set of causes by themselves by imagining hypotheses and deducing their results and then comparing these results with actual experience. The Historic or *a posteriori* method compares economic phenomena in different stages of a nation's history, or in the history of different countries in the same stage of development, and generalises from them. These two methods are specially appropriate for different branches of political economy. Given a fully-developed industrial community, Sidgwick considers the Deductive method appropriate to the statics of distribution and exchange, that is, it will serve to investigate the phenomena of these branches of political economy in a society, which does not change, or if we only wish to investigate one stage in a nation's development independently of its relation to others. The theories of Currency, Foreign Trade and of Money are specially distinguished by Marshall as appropriate subjects for deductive reasoning.* For such a study, method is necessary. Bagehot says, "If you attempt to solve such problems as the facts of commerce present, without some apparatus of method, you are as sure to fail as if you try to take a modern fortress by common assault." Marshall points out: "Facts by themselves are silent," and some theory is necessary by which to generalise them.

In studying the dynamics of wealth—the changes in its distribution and production—we "analyse and systematise our common empirical knowledge of the facts of industry" by means of the Historical method.

Statistics are "registered observations or experiments" giving a "quantitative expression" to certain facts. They are to be compared with the conclusions which we draw from the principles of the science, and if the results do not

* *Economics of Industry*, p. 29.

coincide, we have to seek for some cause accounting for the difference.

There are three schools of political economy:—1. The Abstract or English school, of which Ricardo is the type. Writers of this school assume the universality and unlimited nature of the desire for wealth, and neglect all human passions and motives, except those perpetually antagonistic to the desire for wealth and the wish for the present enjoyment of costly luxuries. They do not consider how differently the same motive, the desire for wealth, affects different men, and the man, of whom Ricardo writes, seems so different from an ordinary human being, that he has been well described as the "abstract economic man." Ruskin stigmatises "the abstract economic man" as a mere covetous machine. Professor Marshall says of this school: "Adhering to lines of thought that had been started chiefly by mediæval traders, and continued by French and English philosophers in the latter half of the eighteenth century, Ricardo and his followers developed a theory of the action of free enterprise wonderfully complete within the narrow area which it covered, but dealing chiefly with problems relating to rent, and the value of corn, which, in the particular form in which they were worked up by Ricardo, have very little bearing on the present state of things." *

In the words of Whewell, "Certain definitions were adopted as of universal application to all countries on the face of the globe and all classes of society; and from these definitions and a few corresponding axioms was deduced a whole system of propositions which were regarded as of demonstrated validity." The "definitions" were what Cairnes refers to as "the knowledge of ultimate causes," such as the assumption that it can be always inferred how a man will act under certain given circumstances, and how he will be affected by certain motives.

2. The Historical or German school. This school traces the connection of the present social conditions of any country with the facts of its past history. The function of political economy is, according to writers of this school, wide enough to explain all the phenomena of wealth, and therefore all causes which influence men in relation to wealth must be stated and

* *Principles of Economics*, pp. 92, 93.

have their effects assigned to them. It is the Enumerative, or what Bagehot calls the All-case method, and requires that all the facts of a subject should be known before we commence to reason about it.

3. The school of Professor Marshall differs from either of the others in contemplating with equanimity a partial re-arrangement of society. They regard the character and efficiency of a man not as a constant quantity but as the product of circumstances. They question whether * " the cruelty and waste of irresponsible competition, and the licentious use of wealth," necessarily form part of the institution of private capital, or are a necessary consequence of " the services which competition renders to society, by putting the ablest men into the most important posts, and giving these in each grade freedom for the full exercise of their faculties. Whilst they agree that industrial progress depends upon getting the right men into the right place, and giving them a free hand and sufficient excitement to exert themselves to the utmost," they do not think it proved " that nothing less than the enormous fortunes which successful men now make and retain would suffice for the purpose."

" They are most anxious to preserve the freedom of the individual to try new paths on his own responsibility. They regard this as the vital service which free competition renders to progress, and desire, on scientific grounds, to disentangle the case for it from the case for such institutions as tend to maintain extreme inequalities of wealth. Economists of this way of thinking consider that the privileges of capital and wealth exceed those which necessarily attach to " the function of the undertaker of business enterprises."

The followers of Professor Marshall are distinguished from their predecessors by their opinion that economics are more closely connected with the biological than with the mathematico-physical sciences, and that physiological peculiarities, such as the food of a nation, often have important economic results. As Herbert Spencer says, " All phenomena displayed by a nation are phenomena of life, and are dependent on the laws of life." †

* Marshall, *Some Aspects of Competition*, 1890.
† *Evolution and Ethics*, p. 27.

A Law of Political Economy is "the constancy of the relation between facts and the conditions which produce them." If we can establish certain moral and physical principles, and can show that they logically result in the tendency asserted, this tendency is a law of political economy. Unlike the laws of physical science, the laws of political economy cannot be stated quantitatively, *e.g.*, Malthus's law, that population increases in geometrical progression, and the means of subsistence in arithmetical progression only, fails if looked upon as an exact statement.

CHAPTER II.

DEFINITIONS.

WEALTH consists of all useful and agreeable things which possess an exchange value, and which can be valued in money. According to Mill, "wealth is an affair of human institution only." Exchange value is a quality of a commodity depending (1) upon its satisfying some useful purpose, (2) upon its being difficult to obtain, which induces men to give other things in return for it.

Wealth can be classified under three heads:—
1. Material things.
2. Labour or services.
3. Rights and Rights of action such as credits or debts.

Money is a substance, by convention among civilised nations gold or silver, by which all other things may be estimated in value. It is also the medium of exchange as, instead of bartering one substance for another, each is exchanged for a sum of money. The mercantile fallacy confounded wealth with money; nothing was considered wealth but the precious metals, and a country was considered wealthy or poor according to the greater or less stock it possessed of them. Exports were encouraged because they brought money into the country, and imports were discouraged, as gold or silver would have to be sent out of the country to pay for the imports. The only exception to the rule against imports was that goods for re-exportation and the raw materials of industry were allowed to be imported.

CHAPTER III.

REQUISITES OF PRODUCTION.

THERE are three requisites for Production: Labour, Land, and Capital.

Labour is (A) Productive, (B) Unproductive. Labour produces utilities: (1) fixed and embodied in outward objects made by their qualities useful to man, such as the products of industry; (2) fixed and embodied in human beings. This latter class of utilities embraces all the labour bestowed by persons throughout life in improving the mental or bodily faculties of themselves or others; (3) which are not fixed and embodied in any natural object, but which merely consist in a temporary service rendered, such as the work of an actor or a showman. Labour which produces utilities fixed and embodied in outward objects or human beings is productive; all other labour is unproductive. Labour does not create any natural objects, it merely brings them into connection with each other. Man can do nothing but produce motion. The properties of matter and the laws of nature form new natural objects by combining into new forms the elements brought into connection with each other by man.

Marshall quotes with approval the divisions of labourers into the following classes:—

1. Automatic manual labourers, including common agricultural labourers and machine tenders.
2. Responsible manual labourers, who can undertake some of the duties of superintendence.
3. Automatic brain-workers, such as book-keepers.
4. Responsible brain-workers, such as the directors of production.*

* *Principles of Economics*, p. 279.

Capital is wealth saved to help future production by providing food, protection, tools, and materials for the labourers.

Capital limits industry. There can be no industries in a country but those which there is a sufficient amount of capital to support. If a government, therefore, impose a protective duty on a commodity, and so prevent its importation into the country, in order to cause it to be produced at home, they do not enrich their country by a new industry, but merely compel a transfer of capital from some other branch of trade.

Capital is produced by saving, and may be increased by economy or the increase of production, so as to have a larger fund to save from.

Though capital is the result of saving, it must be consumed to fulfil its purpose of assisting production. It is kept in continuous existence, not by preservation but by perpetual replenishment. Capital needs perpetual replenishment, and the question, whether the unproductive expenditure of a state, —*e.g.*, a war,—should be paid for by loans or taxes, is connected with this feature. If the loan is subscribed to with money taken from the capital of the country, the debt which the loan is contracted to pay is extinguished at once; but the labourers suffer, because the sum spent in wages is diminished by the amount of the loan, and the country remains charged with the interest of the debt in perpetuity.

Loans should only be resorted to:—

1. When they attract the investment of foreign capital.
2. When the capital from which they are paid would have been unproductively consumed or sent abroad for investment.

The question whether Government Loans have only absorbed the fresh accumulation of capital, which would have been invested abroad or consumed unproductively, must be answered by considering whether they have raised the rate of interest. If they have, this is because profits have risen by money having been diverted from the employment of labour to investments in these loans without any decrease in the efficiency of labour. The industrial improvements, which took place during the French Revolutionary or Napoleonic Wars, prevented this diversion of capital from the employment of labour from injuring the labourers as much as it would otherwise have done.

If the unproductive consumption be paid for by a tax, the payment is more equally shared among all classes, and if the tax be paid out of increased saving from income, the labourers do not suffer. If the tax is paid out of capital, or if the increase of a tax results in a decrease of revenue from it, it is not financially advisable, unless in a country of great annual savings in which there is a probability that the loss to capital will be quickly repaired.

What supports and employs labour is the capital required to set it to work, and not the demand of buyers for the completed produce of labour. "Demand for commodities is not a demand for labour." This demand determines only the direction in which a certain proportion of the labour of the country shall be employed; it does not determine whether the amount of this labour shall be greater or less. Thus a demand for houses will cause a certain portion of the national capital to be invested in house building, but the amount of the capital thus invested is fixed by :—

1. The total amount of capital available for investment.
2. The ratio of the demand for houses to that for other things. This ratio determines the proportion in which the capital of a country is invested in each branch of production.

Capital is of two kinds: (1) Circulating; (2) Fixed.

Circulating capital is the material which, after a single use, no longer exists in the same shape, and cannot again render the same service to production, *e.g.*, flax in making linen, or the wages which maintain the labourers. Circulating capital requires to be constantly renewed by the sale of the finished product.

The result of a single use of circulating capital must be a gain sufficient to replace the whole amount employed, and to leave a profit besides.

Fixed capital, *e.g.*, buildings or machinery, remains in use for a long time. The manufacturer is, therefore, content to wait for a long time to be completely reimbursed his expenses in production, a portion only of the cost of the fixed capital being returned to him in the price of the manufactured article each time it is made use of.

Capital is the chief economic requisite of all undeveloped countries. The low exchange has, in this respect, been useful to India by inducing the investment of European capital there, in developing the resources of the country for the production of indigo, wheat, sugar, coffee, jute, and gold.

CHAPTER IV.

THE PRODUCTIVENESS OF LABOUR.

THE greater or less productiveness of labour depends :—
    I. On the qualities of the labourer.
    II. On the security of his position.
    III. On the division of labour.
    IV. On the co-operation of labour.

I. For labour to be productive, the labourer must possess the qualities of skill, intelligence, morality, and trustworthiness : skill, that he may know the proper use of his tools; intelligence, that he may profit by instruction; morality, that he may avoid injuring his health by self-indulgence; and trustworthiness that he may save his employer the additional expense of employing other men to superintend his labour.

II. The labourer requires to be secure; this embraces both "protection by government and against government." Liberty, or protection against government, is the more important of the two. Labour is naturally more efficient in proportion as the labourer is sure that he will reap what he sows.

III. Division of labour, or the division of the manufacture of an article into several processes, each of which is entrusted to a particular workman.

This is the great difference between the industrial system of the mediæval guilds and that which at present prevails. The unit of labour is no longer an individual handicraftsman, master of all the processes of the manufacture of an article, but a group—the collection of workmen to whom the various processes of manufacture are entrusted. The workman has no longer complete control over the article he produces, which is vested in the capitalist who supplies the funds; he is reduced to a mere caretaker of a machine, charged with the duty of supplying it with materials on which to work.

Free Trade is an example of division of labour; a country confines itself to the production of those articles for which it has the greatest natural advantages and imports others.

The advantages of division of labour are:—

1. Increased dexterity of the workmen. Not having to learn each process of manufacture, they can learn the one on which their attention is concentrated more perfectly.
2. The time is saved which the workman loses in passing from one process of the manufacture to another. Fawcett regards this change of occupation as an advantage, for it prevents the labour becoming monotonous, and so inefficient.
3. If a man's attention is concentrated on one particular process, there is more chance that he may invent a machine to facilitate and abridge the labour necessary in it.
4. A labourer may be exclusively employed on that process of the manufacture which he can perform best.

IV. Co-operation of labour is: (1) Simple, when many persons work together in the same place, time, and way, as in raising a weight; (2) complex, when many persons help one another by division of labour often unconsciously. Connected with this is Wakefield's theory of colonisation, which enunciated the necessity of planting a town population near an agricultural one in a new colony, in order to provide the latter with a market for their surplus produce, and to ensure that they should not confine themselves to merely raising enough for each household.

Production may be conducted on a large or small scale.

The advantages of the former are:—

1. More extended division of labour is possible. Division of labour depends upon the demand for the commodity, and should be carried far enough to

ensure that each person to whom a particular process is entrusted should have full employment in it. There is thus greater economy of skill.
2. The employment of more expensive machinery is possible.
3. The large manufacturer can afford to experiment and to create wants by showing the public something it has never seen before, but which it wants as soon as it sees.
4. A wholesale business is conducted more cheaply than one on a small scale.
5. The large manufacturer has no need to pay attention to details, and can devote his undivided attention to the most important points of his business.

The advantages of the small scale of production are :—
1. More careful superintendence on the part of the master who can pay more attention to small gains and losses.
2. The master is less dependent on the service of hired subordinates, which is often wanting in industry and zeal. Being sure of their wages unless they commit grave faults, there is a tendency to slackness in their work.

The question which scale is most profitable really means which scale causes the produce to be in the greatest proportion to the expenses, and so allows the manufacturers working on it to undersell the manufacturers working on the other.

There are certain enterprises of such magnitude as to be beyond the power of private individuals, or the duties entrusted to those who conduct them are so important as to require the security of a great subscribed capital for their due performance. Railroads and the conveyance of mails by lines of ocean steamers are undertakings of this sort, and they are best carried out by joint-stock enterprise; one large capital being collected by the aggregation of many small sums. These undertakings also suffer by being in the hands of hired servants; but a payment of part of the wages of these servants in the form of a percentage on the profits would often make them interest themselves in the success of their enterprises entrusted to them.

The law of the increase of labour is that it is in proportion to the area of fertile land which produces food for its support. The checks on the increase of the population are:—
1. Positive.
    A. Disease.
    B. Vice, a chief cause of infertility of marriages.
    C. Enforced celibacy of certain classes, such as the clergy in Roman Catholic countries.
    D. The custom of various countries, which forbids marriage till the contracting parties have attained a certain age.
2. Moral.
    Voluntary abstinence from marriage, or, in the case of married people, abstinence from multiplication in order to retain a certain standard of comfort, and to give the children which have been borne the same position as that occupied by their parents.

In the United States the amount of fertile land is practically unlimited, and the supply of food can be largely increased without having recourse to less fertile land, and therefore raising the price. For this reason, men can multiply in the United States at the highest possible rate without check. The United States and the West Indies both require more labour, the former in order to develop the resources of the country, and the latter because the freed negroes will do no more work than will support themselves. The wants of the United States are being supplied by emigration from Europe, and those of the West Indies by coolie labour imported from India.

CHAPTER V.

PRODUCTIVENESS OF LAND.

THE productiveness of land depends on:—
    1. Fertility.
    2. Advantage of situation.

However fertile land may be, it cannot be considered productive, unless its produce can be easily and cheaply carried to a place where it can be disposed of at a remunerative rate. The vast pasture lands of Australia afford a good example of this. Before the gold discoveries, the meat of the sheep, which produced the wool, the principal staple of Australia, was valueless, and their bodies were boiled down for tallow. The gold fields brought a large emigrant population into Australia, and then there was a profitable market for the meat. The increased speed of steamers, and the discovery of the refrigerating process and the growth of the tinned meat trade, have now made it possible to export this meat to Europe.

As water carriage is cheaper than land carriage, those countries which enjoy a maritime situation, good harbours, and navigable rivers allowing trade to be carried into the interior, have the advantage over other less favoured countries of being able to carry on their commercial operations at a cheaper cost, and therefore to sell their produce at a cheaper rate.

3. Good supply of minerals.

To enable the resources of a country to be developed to the greatest possible extent it is necessary that it should have a good supply of minerals in favourable situations. We may illustrate this by pointing to the great industrial development which took place when it was discovered that iron could be smelted with coal as well as wood, and when abundant beds of coal and iron ore were discovered in close proximity to each other in the North of England.

4. A favourable climate is also of great advantage to the productiveness of a country, as it makes all industrial buildings last longer, and lessens the bodily wants of the labourers, leaving more labour available for productive employment. Closely connected with the question of the productiveness of land is the inquiry whether agriculture on the large or small scale is more productive.

On the side of farming on a large scale the advantages are :—

1. The expenses of production are proportionately less, *e.g.*, five flocks of 100 sheep each would require a shepherd apiece, but one flock of 500 sheep would not require five shepherds.

2. Increased cheapness of large purchases.

3. Machinery can be used to a greater extent as the farmers

possess more capital. It must be remembered that agricultural machines can only be used to advantage in a flat open country.

4. More manure from cattle is available.

5. Large farms generally give a greater return in proportion to the labour expended on them than small farms, as they are not farmed so highly.

The gross produce of the land is greater under small cultivation, but, as there are more people employed upon the land than under cultivation on a large scale, the net produce is smaller.

The agricultural population of France is treble that of England, but the agricultural produce only double. This would show not that small farming is disadvantageous, but that the fault of French agriculture is that agricultural properties are often too small and broken up into inconveniently scattered parcels.

There are few small proprietors in England owing to:—

1. The Laws of Entail and Primogeniture, which favour the aggregation of large masses of land in the hands of a few.

2. The English Land Law is complicated; deeds for conveying landed property from one man to another are therefore expensive.

3. The possession of land in England gives a social advantage, which raises its price above its mere commercial value.

4. The Statute of Frauds, 1677, declared that all interests in land, if created by any other process of law than by deed, should be treated as mere tenancies at will. This extinguished the tenancies of all yeomen, who had held their lands at a small customary rent, but had no written evidence to prove their tenure, and even ousted freeholders similarly situated.

5. The crops usually grown in England are, as a rule, only profitable if grown on a large scale, and the necessary expense is generally too great for small proprietors to afford.

Where small farms are possible, they enjoy the advantage of more careful superintendence on the part of the farmer. The master's eye is able to be everywhere, and greater attention is paid to small gains and losses. Peasant proprietors are, as a rule, distinguished for economy and foresight, and exercise great self-restraint in marriage and having children. They have been known to execute important agricultural works for draining and irrigating their land by means of co-operation of labour. The advantages of both systems of cultivation can be secured by associations of labourers.

It is on this account that no reform has ever contributed more to the prosperity of a country than the reform of the Prussian Land Law by Stein and Hardenberg in 1812. The peasants held the lands under certain vexatious conditions of free labour upon the estates of their lords, dating from feudal times. Stein and Hardenberg gave the peasants the absolute ownership of two-thirds of their lands, and the remaining third was given to the landlords in compensation for the loss of their feudal rights.

This brings us to the general principle that large farms pay best for crops which are grown in large masses, such as grain, forage, and pasture, and small farms for root crops, fruit, and plants, which require special care. The nature of the ground to be cultivated must also be considered. Large farming is out of place in any but a flat country, as machines cannot easily be worked except upon level land.

The Law of Production from land is that the increase of produce from land is in a diminishing ratio to the labour employed; that double the produce is not produced by doubling the labour employed upon the land, after a certain limit of productiveness is passed, but a more than proportional increase of labour is required to proportionally increase the produce. The result of this is that high farming costs more in proportion than mere superficial cultivation, and a greater price must be demanded for the produce if it is to be profitable.

Since the repeal of the Corn Laws the position of agriculture in England has entirely altered. In 1840 the expenditure per head of the population on imported food was 9s.; in 1878 it was 30s. This shows that the country has become more manufacturing and less agricultural, and that capital and labour and large areas of productive soil have been turned to more profitable uses than the production of food, since Free Trade in corn was established.

If England were to be fed by home-grown wheat, the area under wheat cultivation must be doubled; but just the contrary of this is what has been really done. In spite of the growth of towns and the conversion of land to other uses than agriculture, forty-eight out of the seventy-eight million acres in Great Britain and Ireland are already under cultivation, and of this area the proportion under wheat to that under other crops has steadily decreased since the introduction of Free Trade. Between 1873 and 1892 the area under wheat cultivation has fallen from 11·2 to 5·8 per cent. The price of wheat has fallen from 58s. to 26s. a quarter, barley from 40s. to 25s., and other agricultural produce in proportion. Mulhall thus compares the acreage that was arable and under pasture at three different periods during the present reign :—

Millions of Acres.

	1840	1870	1885
Arable	19·8	24·1	22·3
Pasture	24·3	22·2	25·6

He is of opinion that land in England has fallen 450 millions in capitalised value since 1870.

English high farming is undersold by the American system of prairie cropping, which at present yields large returns to an insignificant outlay of capital and labour. The two systems may be conveniently contrasted as "intensive" and "extensive" farming, to use Professor Marshall's terms. There is, however, reason to think that the effect of American wheat upon the English market has been exaggerated, as American wheat is only one-twelfth of the annual European supply.

It is not likely that America will continue to export as much wheat as she does at present, for the following reasons :—

1. The quantity of wheat exported from America is only about one-fourth of the total quantity grown there, and if the American population grows at its present rate of increase, it will soon require this quantity for its own consumption. The wheat-growing area of the Canadian North-West is doubly as productive as that of the American West, but the produce of this area also will probably be required to feed the increased population in America itself.

2. The prairie cropping of America is a system of "earth scratching" which necessitates the continual taking up of fresh

land, and the supply of new land which will grow wheat is not unlimited.

3. American railways have been built with foreign capital, and their construction has often been premature; they therefore failed to pay dividends and fell into the hands of mortgagees. A good deal of the capital expended on their construction thus became extinguished, and they could afford to carry wheat cheaply as they had only to pay interest on a diminished amount of capital. This advantage of cheap carriage will not be enjoyed by American wheat when once the country is fully peopled. Another cause of the cheapness of American wheat is the extremely low freight at which ocean steamers carry wheat to England from American ports. Should trade improve, this rate of freight will probably be raised. If, from either of these causes, the cost of carriage is increased, the price of American wheat in Europe must rise.*

The English farmer has the following points on his side in his competition against American wheat:—

1. He is able to dispose of the straw, after thrashing his wheat, at a remunerative price.

2. The labour he employs is 15 per cent. cheaper than American labour.

3. English wheat is generally of a better quality than foreign.

There are better times in store for the British farmer, as the price of American wheat cannot be permanently maintained at its present low figure in the European market, and the want of good communications will probably prevent South America from exporting wheat to England at a rate of cheapness equal to that of North America, though Argentina has at present come into the third rank among our sources of wheat. In the meantime, the British farmer should pin his faith on scientific dairy and garden farming and the "growth of such products as must from their nature be consumed comparatively near to their point of origin," such as dairy produce, poultry, eggs, commodities which are least affected by competition.

* It is, however, maintained by some authors that there is no reason against a still further fall in the price of wheat, as the peasants of Russia and India, who produce it, live by their wheat crop, and know no other business. The cultivation of wheat will therefore continue independently of the market price.

Another most important point for the salvation of English agriculture is the reduction of rent. One great cause of the agricultural depression is that the land has been starved. The farmer cannot invest the proper amount of capital in its cultivation, owing to the excessive increase of rent he has had to pay, often quite out of proportion to the increased value given to the land by the agricultural improvements which alone had made it possible.

In the 15th century rent averaged 6d. an acre. From 1600 to 1700 Gregory King says that rents about doubled themselves, and Jethro Tull, at the commencement of the last century, gives the average rate of rent per acre as 7s. According to Arthur Young, at the end of the 18th century this rate rose to 10s.

The Corn Laws caused the rate of rent to rise by leaps and bounds during the Napoleonic wars, whilst the rate of wages was too low to support the labourers and their families, but any deficiency was made up out of the rates. In 1830 rent averaged 25s. an acre, and twenty years later 38s. From 1854 to 1873 its increase was $26\frac{1}{2}$ per cent.

In the face of foreign competition, farmers could no longer pay these rents, and spend sufficient capital on the soil. To pay the rent required it was necessary to divert money which should have been spent upon the soil in the shape of fertilising manures. Farmers kept their accounts so badly that they did not realise that they were paying their rents out of their capital, and continued to do so rather than face the initial loss of 10 or 15 cent. of their capital, which would be incurred in giving up their holdings. English agriculture can never flourish till farmers are relieved from the necessity of doing this for the future, by a reduction of rents equivalent in amount to that by which they have been unjustifiably increased.

It would also be advisable to extend the operation of the Agricultural Holdings Act, 1883, which gave compensation to tenants for improvements unexhausted at the termination of their leases, if they had made use of fertilising manures or entered into drainage operations. A fault of the Act of 1883 was that, if a tenant did not terminate his tenancy, but continued to hold on to his farm, he was not protected against a rise in rent owing to the increase in value of the farm brought about by his own improvements. An Act for the same purpose as that of 1883 was passed in 1875, but the landlord was allowed to contract himself out of his liabilities in the matter, which rendered it nugatory.

It is necessary to grow wheat owing to its place in the rotation of crops, but many farmers in England do not grow it for the market, but only for feeding their stock.

The only exception to the law of diminished production from land is in a newly-occupied country, in which the light and poor soils are cultivated first, and afterwards the low and swampy ones, as they require more labour to fit them for cultivation.

The law of diminished production from land is counteracted by agricultural improvements, which are of two kinds.

1. Those which enable the land to yield a greater amount of produce without a proportional increase of labour.

To this kind of improvements belong the growth of agricultural knowledge which has led to the disuse of fallows, the introduction of the rotation of crops, and the growth of new products, such as the Swedish turnip.

2. Those which decrease the labour and expense necessary to raise a given amount of produce, *e.g.*, agricultural machines and the improvement of communications.

CHAPTER VI.

THE INCREASE OF CAPITAL.

THE increase of capital depends :—

1. On the amount of the fund from which saving can be made.

This fund is the surplus which remains after supplying the necessaries of life to all who are concerned in production, and is the net produce of the country.

2. On the strength of the dispositions which prompt men to save.

The desire to save depends upon the security and thriftiness of the people, and upon the profit which can be obtained in return for the use of capital, *i.e.*, upon the rate of interest.

The rate of interest depends upon the ratio between the amount of capital seeking investment in the form of loans, and the number and attractiveness of the enterprises to which this capital can be applied. If trade is brisk and the amount of money offered in loans is small, the rate of interest will be high, and *vice versâ*.

BOOK II.

DISTRIBUTION.

CHAPTER I.

PRIVATE PROPERTY AND INHERITANCE.

THE origin of private property lies in the fact that the primitive law courts, in order to prevent a breach of the peace, recognised, as owner of an article, the man who first obtained possession of it.

Even if the ownership had not, in the first instance, been lawfully obtained, the courts recognised the man as owner by prescription whose ownership had been for a long time undisputed, in order to prevent one who *bonâ fide* thought himself the owner of a property being disturbed in his possession by a long-dormant claim. Property was allowed because the desire of acquiring is the principal motive of exertion and economy, and therefore the chief incentive to progress.

It has passed through the following stages:—

Common property and common enjoyment.
Common „ and private „
Private „ and private „

The property of a village was first held in common by all the members of it. The next stage was that in which each member obtained the use of a particular piece of property, but had not the ownership of it, which belonged to the whole village in common.

The Teutonic "mark" illustrates this:—Each free member of the village had the temporary right of occupation of a particular plot of arable land, but not the ownership, as, after the lapse of a fixed period of time, he had to give up his land to some other freeman. At the same time, each freeman had the right to pasture his cattle on the pasture land of the village. This is an instance of common property and common enjoyment as regards the pasture land; common property and private enjoyment as regards the arable. So, too, the Commune or Mir in Russia is proprietor of the peasants' land; and though every adult male is entitled to an equal share, which he may cultivate for himself, periodical re-divisions are made. The system of common property in land also survives in the "almends" of the Swiss Canton of Valais, where a portion of the lands of the village is still cultivated by joint labour. After a time, the temporary enjoyment of a piece of property, which first belonged to all the freemen of the village in common, developed into perpetual ownership. Bequest was recognised, because it is essential to the idea of property for individuals to be able to dispose of what they have themselves created or acquired. Bequests were generally made to children or relatives, because they were usually on the spot at the death of the person making the bequest and could claim first occupancy, and because property was at first held in common by a family.

Mill would propose to deprive collaterals of the right of succession, and, in the absence of direct heirs, that the property should escheat to the State. He would also limit the right of bequest to a moderate competency.

Property in land is attacked on the ground that "no man made the land." Its best justification is when the landlord, by the expenditure of capital in draining or manuring, improves the quality of the land as a productive agent. Those who allow property in land maintain that the State can justifiably appropriate by taxation a portion of the "unearned increment" to the wealth of landlords by the foundation of towns near their estates or the improvement of communications by the construction of roads and railroads. Sir Louis Mallet contested this view: "The unearned increment is a value which is due to no man's exertions and therefore unearned; but no value is due to labour, only to utility and difficulty of attainment. No value is therefore earned, and if property is to be disallowed in all unearned value, there can be no property."

Fawcett argued against the unearned increment theory, that if the State appropriated all increase of value ("Betterment") accruing to estates from causes independent of the landlords, it would be bound to compensate them for any depreciation of their estates arising from causes beyond their control.

CHAPTER II.

ALTERNATIVE SCHEMES TO PRIVATE PROPERTY.

THESE schemes may be classed under two heads :—

        A. Communism.
        B. Socialism.

A. Under a system of Communism, land, capital, and the instruments of production belong to the community. The produce is divided and labour shared, as far as possible, equally, "to each according to his wants, from each according to his strength." This means that each one would consume as much as he wants and work as little as he wishes. The Shakers, Amana Society, and Oneida Perfectionists are communistic societies in America actually practising these principles. Laveleye points out that communism is attractive to reformers and workers. "The former are drawn to it by a sentiment of justice, the latter by their own necessities."

The chief writers on communism are Robert Owen, 1771–1858, who published his theories in the *New View of Society*, or *Essays on the Formation of the Human Character*, 1813; his Report to the Committee of the House of Commons on the Poor Law, 1817; and his *Book of the New Moral World*.

Robert Owen.

He carried his ideas into practical execution in his cotton mills at New Lanark, near Glasgow, at Orbiston and his settlement at New Harmony, Indiana, U.S. He recommended the establishment of communities of about 1200 paupers on spaces of land from 1000 to 1500 acres. These communities were to live each in one large building, each family in its special rooms; but the children, after three years of age, were to be taken from their parents and brought up by the community. When these communities reached the maximum number, new ones were to be created, and, if necessary, sent to colonise fresh countries. This was his answer to Malthus.

Owen was one of the first to practically realise the idea of a trades union. In 1833 he started 'the General Union of the Productive Classes,' and afterwards 'the Grand National Consolidated Trades Union,' which was intended to be a federation of various trades.

Etienne Cabet. Etienne Cabet, 1788–1856, advocated communistic theories in a work called the *Voyage en Icarie*, and acted upon them in a settlement in America, on the Red River in Texas, which he called Icaria.

Louis Blanc. Louis Blanc, 1833–82, author of *Organisation du Travail*, is chiefly known in connection with the national workshops established, at the State expense, by the French revolutionary Government of 1848. These failed from want of proper organisation, and because the workmen were employed on unproductive labour. It appears that Louis Blanc's scheme was intentionally mismanaged by his opponents with the object of making it prove abortive.

B. Socialism differs from Communism in allowing inequality of property if grounded on some principles of justice. Land and the instruments of production are to be the property of associations of workmen (Collectivism as opposed to Particularism) or the State, the produce being shared among the workers according to some definite scheme. Capital is to be held collectively, but private property may exist in other forms, and each individual can dispose of his share in the equitable distribution of the produce of himself and his fellow-workers as he pleases. "The alpha and omega of Socialism is the transformation of private competing capitals into one collective capital."* Instead of the exploitation of man by man, Socialism aims at "the exploitation of the globe by man associated to man." Its object is to replace "anarchy in production" by "systematic and definite organisation," and to do away

* Schäffle, *Quintessence of Socialism.*

with the necessity for the "struggle for individual existence." It aims at bringing about "the ascent of man from the kingdom of necessity to the kingdom of freedom."* It is a revolt against the factory system, by which the *entrepreneur* or capitalist gains "the value in use" of the labour of a vast army of workmen and pays them only in return "the value in exchange," a barely living wage. This system was rendered possible by the great industrial development of the last century, which made "collective production" general, and is, therefore, of essentially modern growth.

The word socialism was first used in describing the ideas and aims of Robert Owen's *Association of all Classes of all Nations*, 1835. As a scheme of economics, it may be divided into two principal schools: (A.) State Socialism; (B.) Anarchic Socialism.

State Socialism must be contrasted with the individualism of the older political economy. The doctrines of non-interference, freedom of contract, and *laissez faire* are given up, the functions of the State are extended, and everything must be done with its aid instead of independently of it. State Socialism wishes "to restrain the play of self-interest and egoism in the economic domain." Its ideal is extensive rather than intensive material prosperity, that a large number of citizens of a country should reach a moderate standard of wealth, rather than there should be in it a few millionaires and a large *proletariat* in the depth of poverty. Its object is "the re-establishment of a friendly relationship between social classes, the removal or modification of injustice, a nearer approach to the principle of distributive justice, with the introduction of a social legislation which promotes progress and guarantees the moral and material elevation of the lower and middle classes."

It does not, like Anarchic Socialism, propose to reduce all to a dead level of uniformity.

Capital is to be the property of the State or associations of workmen, and the State or these associations will appoint the "captains of industry" under whose control all the operations of production will be carried on. An alternative to State Socialism is Municipal Socialism. Municipalities like the

* Engels' *Socialism, Utopian and Scientific*.

London County Council will buy out the proprietors of industries like tramways and gasworks, and will work them in the interests of their constituents. Mr John Burns is of opinion that the rates could be very largely reduced by the profits which would be thus earned. The labourer is to receive for each article the price of as many hours of labour as on the average were required for its manufacture. This price is to be paid in labour notes, which are to be exchangeable for goods, as money is to be abolished as the circulating medium. As there will be no rent or interest to be paid, there will be nothing to prevent the realisation of the Socialistic principle, "to labour the full product of labour." All are to labour and to receive according to their works. More complicated labour, or work which demands higher faculties, is considered as simple unskilled labour raised to a higher power, and receives higher remuneration in proportion to the higher value attached to it.

The competition of capitalists will be abolished, and with it the destruction of capital that is brought about by the constant recurrence of periods of commercial crisis. These periods arise from over-production at a time when the purchasing power of the working classes, who are the majority of the consumers, is constantly reduced by the operation of the iron law of wages. The nearest approach to the realisation of this programme in any European country is in Prussia, where, besides the postal and telegraph system, railways are also the property of the State, and workmen are compelled by law to insure against sickness, accident, or old age, but only pay one-third of the cost, the other two-thirds being paid by the State and the employer. In Victoria also the railways are owned by the State. The English Poor Law, which gives every indigent person who likes to claim it the right of maintenance by the community, and the system of free primary education, are also Socialistic in their tendency.

B. Anarchic Socialism.

This is based on the doctrine of Proudhon:—

"The highest perfection of society is found in the union of order and anarchy; the government of man by man in any form is oppression."

"Whoever puts his hand upon me to govern me is a

usurper and a tyrant, and I declare myself his enemy."*
Man should be a law unto himself. It is the aim of this school
to do away with all central government, and to allow society
to be constituted of nothing else but a free confederation
of amorphous communes.

The Paris Commune of 1871 is the best illustration of
the scheme, in that it was the revolt of the commune or
local unit of self-government against the state or central
government. †

The history of the movement that goes by the general
name of Socialism dates from the middle of
the last century. Henri, Count de St Simon,
1760–1825, wrote *Letters from Geneva*, 1803;
Industry, 1817; *Of the Industrial System*, 1821;
New Christianity, 1825.

<small>Henri, Count de St Simon.</small>

Every individual is to be occupied according to his own
peculiar bent and capacity, his duties being assigned to him
by the central directing authority, and his remuneration being
in proportion to the importance of those duties in the eyes of
the central authority. This authority is to be popularly
elected on the ground of mental pre-eminence. The teaching
of St Simon was continued and extended by his disciples,
Bazard and Enfantin, who drew up the defence of the
principles of St Simon addressed to the French Chamber of
Deputies in 1830. The best instance of a practical realisation
of this scheme is the Jesuit settlement in Paraguay, but its
success was due to the vast intellectual interval which
separated the Indians from the Jesuit fathers, who were consequently able to exact unquestioning obedience.

Charles Fourier, 1772–1837: *Theory of the Four Movements*
through which society has passed, which are
savagery, barbarism, patriarchalism and civilisation; *Treatise on the Association of Domesticity
and Agriculture*, 1812; *The New Industrial World*, 1830.

<small>Charles Fourier.</small>

Under the system of Fourier, neither private property nor
inheritance is abolished, and private property is permitted in
capital.

The operations of industry are to be carried on by communi-

---

* *Confessions of a Revolutionist.*
† Schäffle, *Quintessence of Socialism.*

ties of 400 families, or about 1800 persons, combining their operations on or about a square league of land (*phalange*) under chiefs chosen by themselves. Every one was to reside in the same pile of buildings (*phalanstery*) to save labour and expense in building and to promote economy by having only a few persons to do all the buying and selling for the whole body. Every member of the community, whether capable of labour or not, has first a certain minimum of the produce assigned to him for his subsistence; the remainder of the produce is shared in a certain fixed proportion among the members according to the labour, capital, and talent they have contributed to the common stock. The share assigned to labour generally amounted to five-twelfths of the produce; that of capital was in proportion to each individual's share of the capital of the community, on which he was allowed the normal rate of interest, generally amounting to four-twelfths of the produce; that of talent depended upon the rank an individual occupied in each group of the labourers, which was conferred by the rank of his comrades,—this generally averaged three-twelfths of the produce. It was contended that this scheme overcame man's natural aversion to labour, as excessive toil would not be necessary where no labour was wasted and everybody engaged in some sort of labour, each choosing that kind of labour which he preferred.

Proudhon. Pierre Joseph Proudhon, 1809–65, was the author of the famous essay, *What is Property? Property is Robbery*, 1840; *System of Economic Contradictions, or the Philosophy of Misery*, 1846; *Justice in the Revolution and the Church*, 1858; *Confessions of a Revolutionist*.

Proudhon frightened the bourgeois with Anarchism, and maintained that the Second Empire favoured Socialism, hence gaining for it support which it would not otherwise have obtained. He is therefore considered a traitor to Socialism.

His socialism was of the anarchic school. Louis Blanc called his *Confessions of a Revolutionist* "the code of tyranny by means of chaos."

Lassalle. Ferdinand Lassalle, 1825–64, was the founder of the German Labour Party in 1862, the first attempt of the Socialists to gain their end by adapting to their purpose existing political institutions.

This party in 1890, under the leadership of Herrn Bebel and Liebknecht, in spite of attempts at repression, received 1,427,000 votes, and returned thirty-five members to the German Parliament, having become the strongest single party of the empire. Its chief organ is the widely-circulated journal, the *Vorwärts*.

In 1862 Lassalle published his lecture, "The Working Man's Programme, on the special connection of the present epoch of history with the idea of the working class."

In 1862 he wrote his "Open Letter" to the Leipsic workmen expounding his political and social economic programme for the Socialists, and founded his universal German Working Man's Association.

His *Bastiat-Schulze* was a controversial work written against Schulze-Delitzsch, the founder of the workmen's credit banks. Lassalle described Schulze as merely promulgating Bastiat's ideas second hand, hence the title of his book.

Lassalle thus describes the iron law of wages, which he adopts from Ricardo, and the theory of surplus value, which are the cardinal points of Socialism:—

"The iron economic law, which, in existing circumstances, under the law of supply and demand for labour, determines the wage, is this, that the average wage always remains reduced to the necessary provision which, according to the customary standard of living, is required for subsistence and for propagation. This is the point about which the real wage continually oscillates, without ever being able to rise above it or fall below it. It cannot permanently rise above the average level because, in consequence of the easier and better condition of the workers, there would be an increase of marriages and births among them, an increase of the working population, and, therefore, of the supply of labour, which would bring the wage down to its previous level or even below it. On the other hand, the wage cannot permanently fall below this necessary subsistence, because then occur emigration, abstinence from marriage, and lastly, a diminution of the number of workmen, caused by their misery, which lessens the supply of labour and therefore once more raises wages to its previous rate." "From the produce of labour so much is taken and distributed among the workmen as is required for their subsistence. The entire surplus of production falls to the capitalist. It is therefore a result of the iron law that the workman is necessarily excluded from the benefits of an increasing production from the increased productivity of his own labour."

Under the existing system, Lassalle shows, the workman cannot hope for improvement; he therefore aims at abolishing the present relations between capital and labour. Productive associations of working men using, as capital, funds the interest of which was guaranteed by the State, were to be the producers, and as such to receive the whole profits of production.

Karl Johann Rodbertus, 1805–75, called Jagetzow from his estate of that name in Pomerania, was, for a short time in 1848, Prussian Minister of Worship and Education.

Rodbertus.

His theory is that rent, profit, and wages are all parts of the national income, produced by the united efforts of the workmen. The possession of land and capital enables the landholders and capitalists to force the workmen to divide the produce with them in such a proportion that the workers have only a bare subsistence left. The producers only receive enough to support them, and therefore a smaller relative share of the national wealth, as it constantly increases. The producers are also the majority of the consumers, and, as their share of the national wealth constantly tends to relatively decline, their purchasing power also declines. Increase of production is thus met by decrease of consumption, the amount of goods purchased diminishes, contraction succeeds expansion of production, large numbers of workmen are thrown out of work and still further lose their purchasing power. He thus accounts for commercial crises by showing that the inherent laws of the present economic system contract the market, which capitalists wish by all possible means to extend. His remedy is to nationalise production by appropriating land and capital as national property. As a transition to this, the State is to fix a normal working day for the various trades, a normal day's work, and a legal rate of wages. It is the fault of Rodbertus and of his successors, Wagner and Schäffle, that their doctrines are too abstract and

ALTERNATIVE SCHEMES TO PRIVATE PROPERTY. 31

their system of Socialism is too centralised, too bureaucratic, and would require an army of Government officials to put in practice. These authors belong to the school called in Germany "Katheder Socialisten" or "Socialists of the Chair," professors whose economic doctrines are often too abstract and theoretical to be capable of practical realisation, though they have formed an Union to promulgate them.

Karl Marx. Karl Marx, 1818–83, is the most important name in the history of Socialism. Like Lassalle, he was a German Jew.

In 1845 he published his *Discours sur le libre Échange* and his *Misère de la Philosophie*, a criticism of Proudhon's *Philosophie de la Misère*, and in the same year his friend, Friedrich Engels (1822), published his *Condition of the Working Classes in England*. In 1847 the League of the Just, a league of German workmen in Paris, was reorganised and established in London as the Communist League : this afterwards developed into the International. Engels drew up the Manifesto of the Communist party issued by this body. In 1848 Engels and Marx returned to Germany and contributed to the new *Rhenish Gazette*, a paper of advanced democratic views. It is to be noted that Engels is the author of one of the most important modern treatises on Socialism, entitled *Socialism, Utopian and Scientific*, which was translated into English by Edward Aveling, 1892. In 1849 Marx returned to London and lived there till his death. In 1859 his *Criticism of Political Economy* was published, and in 1867 the first volume of his great work, *Das Kapital*. In 1864 Beesley, Odger, and Marx founded the International Association for the Emancipation of the Working Classes, a society intended for the advancement of universal Socialism. It failed on account of the antagonism of the historico-economic Socialism of Marx and the revolutionary Anarchism of Blanqui, Bakunin, and Prince Krapotkine. The governments of Europe were also at deadly enmity with this organisation, because it desired to substitute the universal brotherhood of workmen for the spirit of nationality, which it was their object to foster.

In 1870 the International protested against the Franco-German War. It was only connected with the revolt of the Commune of Paris, 1871, in so far as some of its members, such as Blanqui and the German Fränckel, took part in the Commune in their private capacity. It says not a little for the universal brotherhood theory being a reality that, in the height of the hatred for Germany at the close of the Franco-Prussian War, Fränckel was elected on the governing body of the Commune, and served as Minister of Labour and Exchange. In 1872 Marx and his party expelled Bakunin and the autonomists, who wished to overturn society in order to reduce it to a free confederation of amorphous communes. In 1873 the last congress of the International was held at Geneva.

The socialism of Marx depends upon the cardinal principle that labour is the sole source of value, and that, nevertheless, the labourers, being divorced from the means of production, are in the hands of the capitalists, who appropriate the surplus value of their labour after paying them just enough wages to enable them to subsist. In other words, the capitalists pay for labour its exchange value and obtain for themselves its value in use. The object of *Das Kapital* is to point out the contradiction between the iron law of wages and the doctrine that labour is the sole source of value. If this is so, why should the labourer only obtain barely enough wages to keep him alive? This is the anomaly for which Socialism proposes the remedy. Wages, according to the Socialists, are not paid out of capital, but are the only portion of the produce of his labour which capitalists allow the labourer to enjoy.

Under the system of capitalism, workmen are collected together in factories, and production is the result of their joint labour; but the enjoyment of the produce belongs only to the capitalist. Property is therefore the result of other men's labour, and therefore property is robbery. Capital is property, which men abstain from consuming in order to assist further production, and therefore capital is robbery and not the result of abstinence. As machinery improves, labour becomes more and more superfluous, and labourers are forced to join the "reserve army of industry," which can only obtain employment when the labourer is exceptionally prosperous. "Tools change into machines, the army of the unemployed grows ever larger. The productive agencies of society are grown too large."* The capitalists wish the reserve army to exist, in order to have an extra supply of labour to call on when necessary.

Bakunin. Michael Bakunin, 1814-76. It is not a little remarkable that Socialism has taken such a deep root in so conservative a country as Russia. It originated in England and France, but those who developed the movement were mostly German, and the most advanced school of modern Socialists is Russian in origin. The reason is that the official classes are very largely of German origin, and the Government is therefore alien to the body of the people, and that the Mir or Commune, to which Anarchic Socialism wishes to reduce society, is still a powerful institution.

The Nihilist movement, in its sympathy for the working classes, has to a great extent been set on foot by the writings of Marx and Lassalle. It is under the influence of two impulses, an impulse to Anarchism from the writings of Bakunin, and an impulse to more constitutional agitation, of which the chief exponent is Lavroff. Bakunin, in 1852, was exiled to Siberia, and, escaping nine years later, joined Herzen in editing the Socialist paper called the *Kolokol*, or *Bell*, published in London. Bakunin, in 1869, founded his Social Democratic alliance, but this came to an end the same year, and he joined the International. His principles did not commend themselves to Marx, who in 1871 expelled Bakunin and the "Autonomists" from the society. Anarchic Socialism had another opportunity, besides the Commune, of putting its principles into practice, in the Communal rebellion of 1873 in Southern Spain at Barcelona, Seville, Cadiz, and Cartagena. Bakunin, in his *God and the State*, thus defines the position of his school towards law, privilege, and authority of every description:—

"The liberty of man consists solely in this, that he obeys the laws of nature, because he has himself recognised them as such, and not because they have been imposed on him by any foreign will whatsoever, human or divine, collective or individual."

"It is the peculiarity of privilege and of every privileged position to kill the intellect and the heart of man. The

* Erfurt Congress.

privileged man is a man depraved in intellect and heart." "In a word, we object to all legislation, all authority, and all influence, privileged, patented, official, and legal, even when it has proceeded from universal suffrage, convinced that it must always turn to the profit of a domineering and exploiting minority, against the interests of the immense majority enslaved."

After Bakunin's death, the chief leaders of the Anarchist party were Prince Krapotkine, author of *Anarchist Communism*, *Anarchist Morality*, and editor of *La Révolte*; and the Frenchmen, Elisée Recluse, and Jean Grave. *La Révolte* is the journal of theoretic, *Le Père Peinard* of militant Anarchism.

A Congress held at Berne formulated Anarchist doctrines in two sets of propositions, one negative and the other affirmative.

The negative propositions were:—

1. All things are at an end. There is an end to property, war to the knife against capital, against every description of privilege, and against the exploitation of one man by another.

2. There is an end to all distinctions of country. There shall be no such things as frontiers or international conflicts.

3. There is an end to the State. Every form of authority, elected or not, dynastic or parliamentary, shall go by the board.

The affirmative propositions were:—

1. Do what you choose.

2. Everything is everybody's. That is to say, the entire wealth of the community is there, for every individual to take from it what he requires.

The chief events in the recent history of Socialism are the following:—After Lassalle's death, Socialism broke up into two parties, that of Lassalle, headed by Schweitzer and the Deputy Hasenclever, and that of Marx, headed by Bebel and Liebknecht. The latter held a Congress, which attracted a good deal of attention, at Eisenach in 1869. The retirement of Schweitzer from the presidency of the party in 1872 removed the principal obstacle to union, and the two parties coalesced as the German Socialistic Working Men's Party, which, in 1875, published the Gotha programme.

In 1877 the Universal Socialist Congress at Ghent came to the following resolution :—

"Considering that, so long as the land and other instruments of production, which are the means of life, are held and appropriated by individuals and sections, the economic subjection of the masses of the people, with all its attendant miseries and starvation, must continue, this Congress declares it necessary that the State or the Commune, representing the whole of the people, should possess the land and other instruments of labour." In 1881 the law of compulsory insurance for workmen, partly at the cost of the State and the employer, was passed by the German Parliament.

In 1883 Henry George published his *Progress and Poverty*.

Henry George. He divides the produce into only two portions, wages and rent, capital being, according to him, a form of labour. "Rent is the result of price. A number of men, no matter how, have gained possession of the soil in civilised countries, and exact a merciless toll from industry. As long as this system continues, the tolls obtained from the monopoly grow and inevitably absorb all but the bare subsistence of the labourer. Soon they grind down the legitimate profit of capital to the same beggarly condition, and the favoured idler will appropriate all wealth to himself. There is, to be sure, a remedy. No human authority has a right to give away in perpetuity what belongs to society itself, and is essential to the existence of society. The property which people possess is the mere creation of law. The analysis of the social economist proves that the recognition by the state of the sacredness of rent is a mistake. The law of rent, as formulated by Ricardo, proves that it is a danger. It is the sole and sufficient cause why the only producers of wealth, the capitalist and the labourer, toil all night and take nothing. Away with it." Mr George would therefore confiscate to the state every scrap of value in the soil, by imposing the heaviest possible taxation on rent. He denies that wages are paid from capital, but maintains that they are produced by the labourer himself, quoting Adam Smith, "The produce of labour constitutes the most natural recompense or wages of labour." The margin of cultivation regulates wages, which will be greater or less, according as the produce which labour can obtain from the natural highest opportunities open to it is greater or less. The produce is divided into two portions, that assigned to rent and that assigned to wages. The portion of wages is sub-divided into that of interest and that of wages properly so called. The tendency is for the portion assigned to rent to increase, so the share of the other items is proportionally reduced.

In the election to the German Parliament of 1890 the Socialists polled 1,427,000 votes and secured thirty-five members, becoming the strongest single party in the empire. In the same year the German Emperor invited a Congress to meet at Berlin, to discuss various questions relating to labour, thus showing the tendency of the times to attach ever-increasing importance to these points. At the last election, the success of the Socialist party was not so marked, but it still forms a powerful section in the German Parliament.

Socialists also at present enjoy considerable parliamentary power in Belgium and France. In the latter country they claim to have brought about the resignation of President Casimir Perier.

The new Parliament of 1892 saw the formation of a British Labour Party, which is the result of a movement called the New Unionism, which differs from the old Trades Unionism in the attitude it takes up towards Government. The old trades unionists held themselves independent, and thought that the workmen should settle all their own concerns themselves. The new unionists are State Socialists, and do not disdain the aid of Parliament to settle economic questions, such as the Eight Hours' Day.

They have formed a Labour Party in the House of Commons, the avowed policy of which is to obtain the modification of the English economic system to suit their views, by treating with either of the great parties in the State on the principle of *do ut des*.

The Social Democratic Federation, under Mr Hyndman, and the Fabian Society have been founded to familiarise the public mind with Socialist doctrines by means of all sorts of literary propaganda. In the United States the Association of the Knights of Labour seems modelled on the German

Working Men's Party, with the exception that it does not attempt to acquire political influence or to adapt the machine of government to its own ends.

The attitude taken up by the Church towards Socialism is an essential part of its history.

In 1848 Charles Kingsley and Frederick Denison Maurice, in *Politics for the People* and in *The Christian Socialist*, avowed their sympathy for the Chartist movement in England.

In 1864 Von Ketteler, Roman Catholic Archbishop of Maintz, published his *Workmen's Speeches and Christianity*, and recommended the establishment of productive associations of workmen with funds subscribed by Roman Catholics.

In 1868 German Catholic Socialism started a newspaper of its own, and in 1871 Canon Moufang, in an electoral address at Maintz, described the programme of this new offshoot of the Socialist movement.

In 1878 the Lutheran Catholic Church in Germany followed the lead of the Roman Catholics, and Pastor Todt published his *Radical German Socialism and the Christian Body*, advocating the abolition of private property and the wages system, and the establishment of productive associations of workmen. Court-preacher Stocker, the head of the anti-Semitic movement, also gave in his adherence to these schemes. Recently in England Cardinal Manning showed a considerable leaning towards Christian Socialism, and Bishop Westcott of Durham is the president of an association to promote its objects. This association is called the Christian Social Union, and is based upon the principle that religion is concerned with man's actual state in this present world as well as his possible state in the next.

CHAPTER III.

CRITICISM OF THE SCHEMES FOR SUBSTITUTES FOR PRIVATE PROPERTY.

CRITICISM of these schemes is based on five main points:—
1. Neglect of the population question.
2. Their cost would probably be so great that the schemes would involve commercial ruin.

3. Weakening of the feeling of individual responsibility and of the motives to exertion and self-reliance.
4. It is very probable that the tyranny of the superintendents of State industry would be as intolerable as that of the capitalists under the present system.
5. It puts an end to the special function of industrial ability.

1. It is argued that, whilst human nature remains what it is, if a labouring man is ensured a maintenance for himself and as many children as he chooses to bring into the world, all restraints on multiplication would be removed, and population would press much more hardly than at present on the means of subsistence.

2. Fawcett estimates the cost of the nationalisation of the land of England at £4,500,000,000. This sum could not be raised at less than 4½ per cent., so that the annual interest would be £202,500,000; but land or house property does not yield more than 3¼ per cent. interest, therefore there would be an annual deficit in the payment of the interest of the loan of 1¼ per cent., or £50,000,000, which would have to be made up by taxation. If the State were to let the land at an uniform rate, some, especially building sites, would be under-rented and some over-rented, and an easy method of political corruption would be placed in the hands of those charged with the letting of land.

If taxation had to be resorted to for payment of interest on the loan, it is not to be easily understood upon whom this taxation would fall, as it is the essence of the scheme that the State should be owner of all the means of production in it. The only way out of the difficulty would be to tax the compensation paid to the landowners and capitalists on the appropriation of their property.

Fawcett also points out that if the means of production were nationalised, the plant of co-operative societies and all the tools and money of a thrifty working man in the Savings Bank would be appropriated too, and so all the advantages of economy would be lost. The peasant proprietors would naturally object to an appropriation of their property by the State. Peasant proprietorship is, therefore, a great obstacle in the way of Socialism; to such an extent is this the case that the German Socialist leaders are said to contemplate abandoning the agitation for the nationalisation of the land out of deference to it.

3. By Socialism, State help is substituted for self-help. A man would feel that he had no longer to depend upon his own exertions for the improvement of himself and his family, in the event of Socialism coming into force. There would be no motive for saving, as no economy could enable a man to acquire property or rise to a superior class, so that one of the principal incentives to progress would cease to operate. All men would be driven to conform to the standard set by the superintendents of production, and all individuality of character would cease to exist.

4. All unchecked authority is dangerous, and Socialistic authors have hitherto neglected to suggest any checks upon the authority of those superintendents to whom the charge of the national production is unreservedly committed.

5. Socialists ignore the distinction between labour and ability. Ability is the chief constituent in the production of wealth, as it is necessary for the purposes of invention and the management of complicated industries. Labour affects one man's task only, ability the tasks of the many workmen who are all under the control of the head of the business.

Socialism puts an end to the "wages of ability," and it will never be exercised if it is only to be remunerated on the same scale as labour. So much for the difficulties of detail in putting Socialistic schemes into practice. The theory of Socialism is based upon a fundamental error. In confining their conception of labour, as the basis of all value, exclusively to manual labour, the Socialists have neglected the fact that the labour of the capitalist in initiating and superintending the operations of industry is just as much labour as the work of the artisan. This labour of the capitalist is rather what Mr Mallock, in his *Labour and the Popular Welfare*, calls ability, but it is more essential for the creation of wealth than mere manual labour.

If we do not accept the Socialistic theory of the origin of value, but prefer to find it in utility and difficulty of attainment, there is not so much necessity for nationalising the instruments of production, and it seems preferable to look to the principle of co-operation as the best means of terminating the present divorce between capital and labour.

Socialism has been of immense service to the world:—

1. As a protest against the idea that the good of the community is best promoted by the play of "enlightened selfishness." It has enforced the importance of the "ethical factor" in all economic questions and brought before all men's minds their duty towards their neighbour, especially towards the poor. It has encouraged interference with the freedom of contract in cases where the parties to the bargain were not on an equality. The moral well-being of the people is to Socialists of more importance than the productiveness of the resources of the State.

2. It has called attention to the fact that capitalism exposes the commercial world to anarchy at the time of strikes and commercial crisis. This anarchy causes waste of the products of industry, and compels the industrial forces themselves, such as ships and machinery, to lie for a long time idle. Competition is an essential feature of capitalism, and is the equivalent of the struggle for existence in the physical world. The competition of the capitalists makes them try to reduce the expenses of production, including wages, to a minimum, and strikes are the retaliation of the labourers. Capitalists have themselves seen that excessive competition causes their profits to tend to a minimum, and they have formed the system of Pools and Trusts in America to regulate it. These Pools or Trusts correspond to Syndicates or Rings in England and France and Cartels in Germany.

CHAPTER IV.

DIVISION OF THE PRODUCE.

ENGLAND and Scotland are the principal countries in which the three requisites of production belong to different owners, and the produce is divided into wages, rents, and profits. In other countries the produce is divided differently according to the ownership of the requisites of production.

The case in which the same person owns all three requisites of production—land, labour, and capital—embraces the two extremes of the labourer's condition in existing society.

1. Where the labourer owns the land he cultivates, and himself provides the capital he uses, as do the peasant proprietors of the United States, Scandinavia, France, and part of Belgium. The marvellous fertility bestowed upon the land by the "petite culture" of the peasant proprietors of France is proverbial. It was of them that Arthur Young, Secretary to the English Board of Agriculture, wrote in his pre-Revolutionary *Travels in France*, "The magic of property turns sand into gold. Give a man a secure possession of a bleak rock and he will turn it into a garden; give him a nine years' lease of a garden and he will turn it into a desert."

2. In slave countries the master owns all three requisites of production. Slave labour is described by Cairnes in his *Treatise on the Slave Power* as reluctant, unskilful, and wanting in versatility. In the United States it was only profitable when the labourers could be collected together in gangs, so as to be easily watched, and centred on a small area, as in the cultivation of cotton, tobacco, sugar, and rice, and when the planters had at their command a large reserve of fertile virgin land. This reserve was necessary, as the carrying on of agriculture in the old States by slave labour had to a great extent exhausted the fertility of the land.

We must next consider the case in which the same person owns the land and capital, and supplies the whole or part of the stock necessary for the cultivation of the land by the labourer.

The principal examples of this tenure are the metayers of Italy and the cottier tenants of Ireland.

The term Metayer is properly only applied to the tenure when the landlord's share of the produce is half, but the division of the produce between him and the tenant, and the share of the capital each contributes, vary. The peculiarity of the tenure is, that the rate of division of the produce and the share of the capital contributed by each is fixed by undeviating local usage, and so long as the tenant performs his part of the bargain, he is not liable to have his rent arbitrarily raised or to be ousted from his holding.

The inefficiency of the system is due to the want of capital; neither the landlord nor the tenant like to invest their own money to a greater extent than the tenure obliges them. They know they will not be able to reap the whole benefit of the increased produce, but will each have to give a share of it to his partner in the undertaking, who has contributed nothing to bring it about.

The cottier tenants of Ireland differ from tenant farmers in that they do not farm for profit but for a subsistence. The rent of cottier tenants is fixed by a competition, not of capitalists like rack rent, but of labourers, and it may be forced up in nominal amount to more than the annual produce. The tenant knows that, whatever the rent nominally amounts to, the landlord must leave him enough for subsistence, and that, if he improves the land himself, his rent will be raised by a corresponding amount, so he has no motive to be industrious. Under this system the land is badly cultivated and will always be so till the tenants get security of tenure and compensation for unexhausted improvements.

The rayats of India resemble the cottier tenants of Ireland, and rarely own more than the cattle employed on the land. The State is theoretically the landlord, and it has been the object of much legislation to give security of tenure to the cultivators. In Bengal the zemindar is the middleman between the cultivators and the State, and the causes for which he is allowed to increase a rayat's rent or oust him from his holding are strictly limited. In Madras and Bombay the rayats pay their rent directly to Government, and in the North-West Provinces, Government makes the settlement of the revenue with village communities, the members of which are all conjointly liable for the shares of defaulters. In all these provinces there is a tendency to increase the number of years for which the settlement of revenue is made.

CHAPTER V.

INFLUENCES REGULATING DISTRIBUTION.

There is this fundamental distinction between production and distribution, that the former is regulated by the laws of nature and various physical conditions which are independent of human control, whilst the latter is entirely a matter of human regulation. It is only since the revolution in industry of the last century that competition has been of much importance, and it is only so far as the action of men in the field of economics is regulated by competition that political economy can be called a science at all. Competition and the gradual weeding out from trade of those devoid of business talents is the industrial counterpart of the Darwinian struggle for life and the survival of the fittest.

In the Middle Ages the weak could not make terms for themselves by competition, but custom was the source of such rights as they possessed, and these rights gradually developed into law. Karl Marx, in *Capital*, has been the first to point out that "the economic structure of the present capitalist society has grown out of the economic structure of feudal society," the capitalist taking the place of the chieftain of feudal times. Even now rent is, in different countries, affected by different influences, by competition in the case of rack rent, and by custom in the case of metayer rent. The influence of custom on prices is overcome in modern times by improved facilities of communication and by the greater cheapness offered by large capitalists, who undersell the retailers. It is only true of the wholesale trade that there cannot be two prices for one commodity in the same market, for in the retail trade custom and vanity often make people buy at a dearer price than they need.

Professional fees, such as those of doctors, are strictly regulated by custom; competition only diminishes each man's chance of obtaining patients, it does not lower the fees the patients pay.

Competition cheapens prices. A producer cannot obtain more than the ordinary rate of profit for his goods, for if he demanded a price for them which allowed him more than this rate, other producers would readily undersell him.

On the other hand, buyers compete among themselves to buy goods, and will thus be forced to give the highest price the goods are worth. The competition of labourers lowers wages, but cannot lower them below the normal rate of wages in each district, as, if it did, the labourers would cease to multiply, part of the capital of the country would thus cease to be employed for want of labour, and wages would return to their former rate, owing to the competition of capitalists for labour.

CHAPTER VI.

WAGES.

WAGES have been defined as "the reward of those who are employed in production with a view to the profit of their employers, and who are paid at stipulated rates."

They consist of the following elements:—

1. Interest on capital expended in training the labourer. Clergymen are often gratuitously educated by means of scholarships, and so the capital expended in their education is small. This partly accounts for their professional incomes being generally so limited.

2. A sinking fund to replace the wealth extinguished by the growing age or declining strength of the labourer.

3. Insurance against premature death or loss of work.

The rate of wages depends upon the ratio between the number of people working for hire, and that part of the circulating capital of the country which is expended in the direct purchase of labour, excluding that part which is expended in the purchase of unproductive labour, such as domestic servants or actors.

Mr Mallock, in his *Labour and the Popular Welfare*, shows that the income of the labouring classes has risen so quickly

that, in 1860, it alone was equal to the income of all classes taken together in 1800. Mulhall estimates the increase of wages from 1840 to 1880 as 50 per cent., but since that time the rate of increase has fallen to from 25 to 20 per cent. Great as this increase has been, it is less than in proportion to the increase of wealth in England owing to :—
  A. Increase of population which lessens wages—
    1. By increasing the supply of labour.
    2. By increasing the price of food, so that the money wages of the labourers have less purchasing power, according as the real wages or wages in kind (the commodities necessarily consumed by the labourer as food) have gone up in price.

The wages of labour are a compound result of two causes— real wages or wages in kind, that is, the quantity the labourers obtain of the ordinary articles of consumption, and the money price of these articles.

The tendency of the price of food to rise is counteracted by importation from abroad, and occurs chiefly in articles which cannot be easily imported.

  B. The increased use of labour-saving machinery has the same effect on wages as if an addition of a number of men, equal to that of those whose labour has been saved, had been made to the labouring population.

Machinery increases the return to capital, and hence allows the produce to be sold at a lower price, or allows the manufacturers to obtain a higher rate of profit. From either of these sources a fund is set free for the increased employment of labour, which soon counterbalances the loss of those who were turned out of employment by the setting up of machinery. Labourers profit by cheapness as workmen, because the more products there are to be exchanged for their equivalents the more will consumption grow, the greater will be the demand for labour of various kinds, and the higher will be wages.

Though labourers as a body do not suffer by the setting up of machinery, the labourers of a particular trade often do, and this suffering is in proportion to the higher wages which they formerly drew, owing to the possession of some special skill or dexterity. Marshall points out in this connection,

"Machinery decreases the demand for general intelligence."*

C. The investment of money abroad.

On this account an increase of wages without increased efficiency of labour can seldom be really profitable to the labourers, as, if the rate of profit is diminished, more capital will be sent abroad for investment, and the amount spent in the payment of labour is proportionally lessened.

The wages fund theory is that there is a fixed amount devoted to the payment of labour in each country, irrespective of the number or "industrial quality" of the labourers, and unalterable by the force of law or public opinion, or by employers or under the compulsion of strikes. If wages are forced up in any trade, other trades must lose an amount equal to the extra wages gained by the trade, the wages of which have increased. Mill states it thus:—

"There is supposed to be at any given instant a sum of wealth which is unconditionally devoted to the payment of the wages of labour. This sum is reasoned on as at any given moment a predetermined amount. More than that sum it is assumed that the wages-receiving class cannot possibly divide among them; that amount and no less they cannot but obtain. So that the sum to be divided being fixed, the wages of each depend solely on the divisor, the number of participants."

It is argued that, if the amount to be given as wages were a predetermined amount, wages in England would not have increased and pauperism diminished, in spite of the increase of the population. This is because English manufactures have expanded and new industries have been set on foot. At the same time, England, through Free Trade, can draw her supplies of food from countries where the law of diminishing return is not yet felt. Since the potato famine in Ireland, the population has decreased, but there has been no rise in the rate of wages. This is because of the decrease in the amount of capital invested in Ireland.

The truth is, that raw material and fixed and circulating capital must all be employed in certain proportions to each other for the purposes of manufacture. If the manufacturers desire a certain amount of production, they know that wages

*Economics of Industry, p. 165.

will form a certain proportion of their expenses. To this extent only is the amount which will be spent on wages fixed and certain. The theory apparently owed its origin to the fact that, in the years 1830–40, the amount available for the payment of labour appeared to be fixed, as the conditions enabling masters to raise wages were never realised. Wages are paid out of capital, they are not, as the Socialists suppose, part of the products of industry; if they were, how could a navvy on the construction of a railway be paid his wages? The railway may not come into operation for years, it may even be abandoned before opening, but yet the navvy receives his wages; these cannot come out of the produce of his labour, as nothing has been as yet produced. The wages must therefore come from the produce of past labour, which has been saved to assist future production, *i.e.*, from capital.

The relation of wages to profits is said to be that the rate of profits can never be increased but by a fall in wages, and is never increased by a better distribution of labour, by the invention of machinery, by the establishment of roads or canals, or by any means of abridging labour either in the manufacture or the conveyance of goods—Ricardo (M'Culloch, p. 75); that "profits are the leavings of wages," but wages and the cost of labour are not identical, though often confused, as in the following quotations: "There can be no rise in the value of labour without a fall of profits"— Ricardo (M'Culloch, p. 23), and "profits vary inversely as wages; that is, they fall as wages rise and rise as wages fall" (M'Culloch). This is because the produce of a manufactory is divided into profits and wages; if wages increase, there is less left for profits, and *vice versa*. But if the total produce be increased by the increased efficiency of the labourer, improvements in the management of the factory, or in the process of production, the rate of wages may remain the same as before, and yet the share of the produce allotted to profits be increased. The rate of profits is more properly described by Mill as depending on the cost of labour. The cost of labour is arrived at by comparing the labourer's wages with the amount of wealth his labour produces. If the labourer becomes more efficient, the cost of labour will fall, because more produce will be raised with the same wages as before, or an equal amount with less wages. The efficiency of labour, which regulates its cost, depends upon the existence of an abundant supply of fertile land on which to raise the necessary food at a low cost. Where this abundant supply of fertile land exists, as in Australia, wages may be higher than in England and yet the rate of profit be also higher.

High wages and high profits indicate a low cost of production, as they are the direct results of a high industrial productiveness. General high money wages show that bullion is plentiful in the country in which wages are high, or that its labour is so efficient that bullion can be imported cheaply in exchange for its exports.

The relation of high wages to good trade is that capitalists can afford to give high wages for a time when trade is good, as their capital is momentarily more productive than usual, and they are realising more than the ordinary rate of profit. This abnormal rate of profit, and with it the opportunity for higher wages than usual in the trade, soon disappears owing to the action of other capitalists, who withdraw their money from other investments, and hasten to invest it in the trade which pays for the moment a higher rate of profit. This investment from outside sources often reduces profits as much below as they were formerly above the normal rate. The more skilled the labourers are the greater is the advantage they derive from a particular trade being exceptionally prosperous, as they enjoy a temporary monopoly which corresponds in duration to the time it takes to train the additional supply of labourers required for additional investment of capital in the trade.

General high prices and general real wages or wages in kind have no connection, as the food, shelter, and comforts of the labourer are not affected by the causes which produce the abundance or scarcity of money. The fact that general prices are high shows that money is plentiful in the country.

Prices in a particular trade depend upon the cost of production, and the cost of production depends upon—(1) Profits of capital; (2) Taxes; (3) Cost of labour. Both the former elements might increase and so bring about a rise of prices without affecting wages.

Ricardo's theory of wages is that there is a certain minimum of wages, the lowest subsistence allowance on which the labourers will consent to keep up their numbers by marrying and having children. This minimum depends upon the price of food. If, by improvement in agriculture or by repeal of the Corn Laws, the price of food is permanently cheapened, wages will fall, unless the labourers require the same standard of comfort as existed before the change, and restrain their rate of multiplication accordingly. The standard of comfort of the labourers being given, money wages will depend on the price, and therefore on the cost of production of the articles consumed by the labourers. The price of these articles depends upon the productiveness of the least fertile land in cultivation or the least productive agricultural capital in use.

Adam Smith assigns five causes to account for the difference in the rate of wages between different trades.

1. Agreeableness or disagreeableness of the employments themselves. A collier or a grinder of cutlery gets high wages to compensate him for the danger and disagreeableness of his trade. In the same way professional dancers are looked down upon and have to be compensated for this by high wages.

2. Ease and cheapness or difficulty and expense of learning the trade. Any trade which requires a man to be bound apprentice to a master workman to serve for a long time without wages, will not be undertaken, unless there is a probability that the man will eventually earn enough wages to compensate him for having kept himself for a long time whilst learning his trade. It is this inability to support themselves whilst learning a trade that generally prevents unskilled labourers from ascending into the ranks of skilled workmen.

An unskilled workman often earns as much as he ever will soon after he begins to work; the wages of a skilled workman, on the other hand, are progressive, and proportional to the skill he exhibits. The higher wages of the skilled labourer represent the return to the capital spent in training him, and if the skilled labourer attains to any exceptional skill, his remuneration is often of the unlimited nature of the price paid to the possessor of a monopoly. It is the object of trades unions to maintain this monopoly by restricting the admission of fresh labourers into the trade they represent.

3. The constancy or inconstancy of employment. A bricklayer or mason, who cannot work in bad weather, requires to

be compensated for the long period he may be out of work by earning extra wages when he is at work.

4. The small or great trust placed in the workman. If the workman be trustworthy the employer is saved the wages of superintendence and can afford to give him higher wages. In this case the superior reward is the effect of the absence of competition, it is the fruit of the rarity of the desired quality, and represents the price of a kind of monopoly, as do the extra wages paid to a workman of exceptional skill.

5. The probability or improbability of success in the employment. It is almost certain that a boy trained to shoemaking will be able eventually to work at the trade with a fair amount of success, but in the profession of law or medicine, the few who are successful should gain the income which would otherwise have fallen to the unsuccessful majority. This is analogous to the element of Risk in Profits.

Fawcett considers that this cause has not much effect even in the learned professions, because success depends upon causes which are out of an individual's control, as for instance in the case of barristers upon acquaintance with solicitors.

Men often enter a profession for the sake of the position it confers, or for the sake of duty, as some men enter the Church, and then they do not mind drawing an income from it inferior to what they might obtain from other sources. Fawcett adds that ignorance and the expense and difficulty of travelling often prevent a man from moving from one district to another where he might obtain higher wages. He instances the Wiltshire or Dorsetshire labourer, who, if he moved to Yorkshire, might obtain wages amounting to sixteen or seventeen shillings a week instead of eleven or twelve. In Yorkshire the wages are higher because of the number of other trades there which compete for the labour of the agricultural labourer.

In districts like Wiltshire or Dorsetshire, the labourers of which will not readily move from one part of the country to the other, wages are more affected by a change in the ratio of capital to population in the district itself than by any such change when it affects the whole country at large. The following remedies have been proposed for low wages :—

1. To have a minimum of wages fixed by law, but if this was more than the capitalists could afford to pay, they would

cease to invest their money in the business, as it would no longer return the rate of profit to which they consider themselves entitled, and they would send it abroad for investment.

The change would also stimulate an increase of population, so that the condition of the labourers might soon be as bad as it was before the minimum was fixed, owing to an increased rate of multiplication.

2. If the working day were fixed by law at eight hours instead of ten, and if the labourer did not become more efficient, the employer would have to pay as much for eight hours' work as he does now for ten, and so his rate of profit would fall, and he would probably seek some other mode of investment for his capital.

If, on the other hand, the employer raises his prices to recoup himself for this fall in the rate of profit, he runs the risk of being undersold even in the English market by foreign producers. If all prices could be raised without fear of foreign competition, the labourer would not be benefited,—he would get greater money wages for a given number of hours' work. These money wages would possess less purchasing power owing to the rise in prices.

If the State is called on to permanently find work at the ordinary rate of wages for all the unemployed, it must have the power of checking the increase of population, as all prudential checks on population would cease to operate. In the case of a number of workmen thrown out of employment by some sudden unavoidable cause, it is justifiable for the Government to temporarily find work for them, and if the increased taxation necessary were paid from increased personal saving or from capital which would otherwise have been invested abroad, the labourers would be benefited by the employment of an increased amount of capital productively.

3. The Allotment System. If the labourers are given allotments of land, they are helped by their own industry, and the productive powers of the country are at the same time increased by the greater care and attention bestowed by the labourer on his allotment than would be bestowed on the same piece of land if farmed by a capitalist farmer. The gross produce of a piece of land cultivated as an allotment is greater than that of an equal area of land cultivated on a large scale. The

Allotment Acts, 1887 and 1890, the Small Holdings Act, 1892, and the clause in the Parish Councils Act, 1894, which allows compulsory hiring of land for allotments by County Council order, have all been passed with this object of helping the labourer by means of his own industry. The danger is that it will stimulate population, and that the labourers will multiply so largely that their wages, with the allotments thrown in, may become soon only equal in amount to their former wages before the allotments were given.

The effective remedies for low wages are those only which increase capital or diminish the pressure of population.

1. An efficient scheme of national education renders the labourer more intelligent and so more efficient. It renders the moral restraint upon over-multiplication operative, by teaching parents the sin of bringing into the world more children than they can hope to bring up in at least as good a position in life as their own. It teaches the labourer the duty of foresight and of laying by for a rainy day, thus indirectly benefiting the community by diminishing the number of those who have to be maintained by the Poor Rates.

2. Emigration. This would be doubly effective :—

    A. By relieving the congestion of population in the mother country. It is, however, the most intelligent workmen who generally emigrate, and these the mother country can least well spare.

    B. The emigrants will be able in the process of time to relieve the necessities of the mother country by exporting cheap supplies of food.

3. Co-operative associations of working men, who would become owners of the instruments of production, providing the necessary capital by small subscriptions from their own body. They would thus be able to divide among themselves the whole undivided product of labour.

CHAPTER VII.

PROFITS.

The constituent elements of profit are:—
1. Reward for saving. This is calculated according to the prevailing rate of interest in the country on the best security.
2. Insurance against the risk incurred by the loan of the capital or its investment in business.
3. Wages of superintendence.

The reward for saving is an invariable quantity for all occupations at the same time and in the same country.

The insurance against risk and the wages of superintendence are variable quantities, and vary according to the comparative danger or safety of the employment and the "social dignity" attached to it. Farming, for instance, is a healthy employment in which a gentleman may occupy himself without loss of social prestige. Those who employ themselves in farming therefore do not expect so large wages of superintendence as in other employments. When the profits of an employment are sufficient to give the amount of reward for saving, insurance against risk, and wages of superintendence that are required by the peculiar circumstances of the trade, then the natural rate of profit is said to be secured. The circumstances of each trade differ: if there is greater element of danger in one trade than in another, the rate of profit in that trade will be permanently higher. On the other hand, Fawcett points out, "the natural profits of farming are low because English tastes are such as to make farming a pleasurable occupation."

When the rate of profit in any trade rises above or falls below the normal rate, a tendency is at once put in motion to cause it to revert to that rate.

If profits are raised above this normal rate, manufacturers invest as much capital as possible in the trade, withdrawing it from other investments and raising loans from bankers and bill brokers. This increase of profit to be made by capital invested in the trade has the following effects:—

1. It increases the demand for, and therefore the price of, the raw material.

2. It diverts capital from other investments to the trade enjoying these temporary high profits.

The supply of produce is thus much increased, often more than in proportion to the demand, and prices fall till the rate of profit returns to its former level or even falls below it.

A trade cannot be quickly extended beyond its normal limits by the investment of capital diverted from other trades; till this is done those already in the trade enjoy abnormally high profits. The supply of labour also cannot be quickly increased; till this is done the labourers already working in the trade enjoy exceptionally high wages owing to the competition for their labour.

In the same way, if the rate of profit in a trade has fallen below the normal level, production is restricted and the supply of goods falls off. The supply becomes less than the demand, and a tendency begins to operate by which prices, and with them profits, are restored to their former level.

The general rate of profit depends upon the excess of the productive power of labour over the cost of its support, *i.e.*, upon the cost of labour. The rate of profit does not depend upon wages, for, if labour becomes more efficient, the amount paid in wages may be the same as before, and yet, the total amount of the produce being increased, there will be more allotted to the share of profit.

The cost of agricultural labour depends upon its cost when applied to the least fertile land in cultivation; the least fertile land in cultivation in Australia is better than the least fertile land in England, therefore the cost of agricultural labour is less there than in England, and so, in spite of wages being higher in Australia than in England, the rate of profit is also higher because the efficiency of labour is greater. Agriculture is the staple industry of Australia, and the rate of profit in other trades is regulated by it. If labour be inefficient, wages may be low and yet the cost of labour be high.

"The cost of labour, and therefore the rate of profit, is a function of three variables," which are—

1. The efficiency of labour: this depends upon the supply of fertile land.

2. The wages of labour: this depends upon the proportion which population bears to capital. The rate of increase of the population depends upon the price of food, and the rate of the increase of capital depends upon the security, foresight, and disposition to economy of the people, and upon the rate of profit obtainable.

3. The greater or less cost at which the articles composing the real reward of the labourer can be produced or bought. Fawcett points out that £400 of every £1000 spent in agricultural wages is spent in buying bread. He supposes bread to be reduced one-fourth in price, so that £300 will now buy the quantity of bread needed. The labourers, therefore, will be as well off as before, if they receive £900 instead of £1000, for they will be able to buy just as much bread. The employer will thus have £100 more to spend in employing more labour or in some other form of productive investment. The labourers thus share with their employers in the advantage of cheap food, and they also reap the benefit of the additional sum set free for employing them.

Profits can only rise—

1. If the labourer becomes more efficient without being more rewarded.

2. If, without becoming less efficient, wages fall, and no increase takes place in the cost of the articles composing the remuneration of labour.

3. If the articles of which the labourer's wages are composed become cheaper without the labourer obtaining more of them.

Profits can only fall—

1. If the labourer becomes less efficient, from worse education, diminished strength, or the destruction of fixed capital, such as machinery.

2. If wages rise without increased cheapness of the articles composing them or greater efficiency of labour.

3. If, without any increase of the labourer's wages, the articles composing them became more costly.

As society progresses, there is this difference between profit and rent, that the former falls, the latter rises. The rate of profit attains its minimum and the rate of rent its maximum in old societies. A rise in agricultural prices would imply a rise in rent but a fall in profit. A tax levied on agricultural profits would raise prices and thus indemnify producers, a tax on rent would fall on the owners of the soil.

Walker draws this parallel between profit and rent. In the same way as rent is due to exceptional natural advantages, so the rate of profit is due to exceptional natural abilities. Just as there is some land which returns no rent, so there may be, from absence of business qualifications, a theoretical no-profit stage of production. All profits are drawn from a body of wealth created by the exceptional abilities or opportunities of those employers who receive profits, measured from the level of those who receive no profits. If the demand for goods is so great as to require a certain amount to be produced under the management and control of those whose efficiency in organising labour and capital is small, the cost of production will be large and its price correspondingly great, and yet not enough to yield that class of capitalists more than that scanty subsistence which may be considered as no profit. The price of goods produced by men of higher industrial grade will be the same as those produced at the greatest disadvantage, but, as their cost of production is less, there will be more divisible as profits in a ratio corresponding to the business talents of the capitalists. Both classes have to pay the same wages, and the more skilful man makes profits only in proportion to his greater skill. Any cause keeping unsuccessful people in the trade increases the profits of the successful trader, by enhancing the cost of production, and consequently the price of that portion of the supply which is produced at the greatest disadvantage; the difference is therefore greater between the cost of production of the commodities which they produce and that of the commodities produced by successful traders, who enjoy this difference in the shape of extra profits.

As a nation progresses, profits tend to a minimum, because—

1. An increase of population brings less fertile lands into cultivation, and hence raises the price of food. The cost of labour becomes increased and the rate of profit proportionally diminished.

2. People become more prudent, and can be induced to save by a smaller return to capital than before. A larger amount of

capital will thus be accumulated, and the average rate of profit proportionally lessened. Fawcett notes that the amount of wealth saved in any country at any particular time is partly the cause and partly the effect of the average rate of profit.

The greater the amount of capital accumulated, the less will be the rate of profit, and the less the rate of profit the less will be the amount of fresh capital accumulated. In each stage, therefore, of a nation's social and economic history, there is an average rate of profit depending upon the amount of capital which will be saved in the hope of obtaining the current rate of profit. The tendency of the accumulation of capital to lessen the rate of profit is counteracted by:—

1. The exportation of capital for foreign investment, thus enabling food to be imported for an increasing population without any diminution of cheapness, and at the same time making room for more capital to be accumulated at home at the current rate of profit. All the capital saved in a country, but invested elsewhere, has no influence upon the average rate of profit in that country.

2. Agricultural improvements, such as the use of artificial manures and the growth of the turnip on corn lands, enable additional food to be produced without additional cost, and so prevent the cost of labour from increasing.

3. The conversion of circulating into fixed capital, by setting up machinery and constructing railroads, absorbs a large mass of capital, and thus makes room for more capital to be accumulated without lowering the rate of profit. Machinery and railroads decrease the cost of labour and so raise the rate of profit. They enable a country to possess a constantly increasing capital without reducing profits to a level at which saving would cease.

4. A commercial crisis destroys capital and so prevents the rate of profit being lowered, as generally happens when there is a large mass of capital seeking investment. Loans levied by Government for unproductive purposes absorb capital in the same way and have the same effect upon the rate of profit.

The "Stationary State" is when the rate of interest has fallen so low that there is no longer sufficient motive for saving, and the accumulation of capital therefore ceases.

The causes which prevent the rate of profit from being lowered by the accumulation of capital keep a country from falling into the " Stationary State."

The consequences of the tendency of profits to a minimum are :—

1. The argument, based on the danger of lessening the capital of a country by Government expenditure on valuable though unproductive purposes, is no longer so important, as the loss to capital will soon be repaired. If a loan were raised for colonisation or education, the money subscribed to it would probably be taken from capital which would be sent abroad for investment or unproductively consumed, and thus the loan would not injure the labourers.

2. The argument against emigration, that it can do no good to the labourers if it diminishes the capital of the country in the same proportion as it relieves the congestion of the population, loses its force when we see how soon the loss of capital is made up.

3. The introduction of permanent improvements of land and the setting up of machinery, in a land of great annual savings and low profits, only makes room for more capital to be accumulated at the current rate of interest, and therefore does not do the injury to the working classes, by the diminished employment of labour which it brings about, that is commonly supposed. The amount spent on railways in 1844–45 probably saved the country from a depression of profits and interest, which would have occurred if the accumulation of capital had not thus been checked.

CHAPTER VIII.

RENT.

THE reason of rent is that land is a necessary instrument of production, which is wanted by many but which cannot be obtained except from those who have appropriated it, namely, the landlords.

The quantity of land which possesses an advantage of position or fertility over the worst land in cultivation, which pays merely a nominal rent, is limited, and therefore a payment is demanded for its use. The rent of any land is the excess of the value of its net produce over what would be returned to the same capital if employed on the worst land in cultivation, which pays only a nominal rent, as it returns no excess over the ordinary rate of profit. The worst land in cultivation, which returns only the ordinary rate of profit to the farmer, is said to be on the "Margin of Cultivation." The position of the margin of cultivation depends upon the current rate of profit in each country. As this gradually decreases, lands of inferior fertility can be cultivated consistently with returning the current rate of profit. Any decline in the rate of profit raises rent, because it brings inferior land into cultivation, and therefore the difference between the return to capital expended on the worst, and the return to capital expended on the best land under cultivation is greater.

It is a law, that if the product of any, even the smallest, portion of the supply of agricultural produce, requires as a necessary condition a certain price, that price will be obtained for all the rest, so the natural value of agricultural produce is determined by that portion of the supply which is grown and brought to market at the greatest expense. The owners of those portions of the produce which are grown and brought to market at a less expense than the most expensive, enjoy more than the ordinary rate of profit. It is this surplus over the ordinary rate of profit which they are compelled by competition to give to the landlord as rent. Improved methods of cultivation, such as steam tillage, diminish the cost of agricultural labour and increase the net produce of land. The farmer has therefore a larger surplus, which he can pay over to the landlord as rent, and yet realise the ordinary rate of profit. Rents will thus rise and the margin of cultivation descend, as inferior land can be cultivated and yet return the ordinary rate of profit. The benefit of improved machinery or agricultural improvements to the farmer is only temporary, and lasts till the rent is raised, and thus the surplus over the ordinary rate of profit absorbed. The effect of an increase of wages is to increase the cost of agricultural labour. Some of the least fertile land in cultivation ceases then to return the ordinary rate of profit, the margin of cultivation rises, and rents fall as the difference of the return from the worst and best land in cultivation becomes reduced.

The increase of population has a tendency to cause rent to rise, because it brings land of inferior fertility into cultivation. Farmers must obtain the ordinary rate of profit from these inferior lands, and so the price of food rises to compensate them for the increased cost of production. The share of produce allotted to rent increases in amount, because the difference between the return from the worst and the best land in cultivation is increased. The increased share of the produce allotted to rent has also risen in value owing to the rise in the price of food.

The effect of the increase of population in causing rent to rise is counteracted by—

1. The importation of the required additional supplies at cheap rates.

2. Agricultural improvements; these provide the country with increase of food without extending the area of cultivation, and so prevent one cause of the rise of rent. They, however, contribute to the raising of rent in another way by increasing the net produce of the land.

The buildings of a farm are furnished by the landlord's capital, and all payments to him for their use are to be considered as the interest of capital, calculated upon what it would cost now to erect others as good. When capital is invested so as not to require repeated renewal, as in giving a permanent increase of fertility to the land by draining, the payment to the landlord for the use of the land so improved is rent.

Rent is no cause of value, but the measure of the advantage which the inequality of the return to capital invested in land of varying degrees of fertility confers on all but the least fertile land under cultivation. The price of agricultural produce must be such as to enable the ordinary rate of profit to be realised from land on the margin of cultivation. If all rents were remitted, agricultural prices would decline, and land on the margin of cultivation would cease to return the ordinary rate of profit, and therefore go out of cultivation.

This it cannot do, as the population remains the same, and therefore just as much food is required as before. Even if the land became rent free, the price of agricultural produce would not be less, as the conditions upon which it depends are not altered. The cultivator who pays rent gets in return an instrument of production, the superiority of the value of which, over that of the land for which a merely nominal rent is paid, is in exact proportion to the greater amount of rent paid for it. Rent thus equalises the profits of different capitals by enabling the landlord to appropriate all extra gains caused by the superiority of natural advantages. The case of ground rent paid for a manufactory is the only case in an old country in which the expense of rent enters into the cost of the manufactured article. Another case is monopoly rent in a new colony.

The following objections have been raised to the above theory of rent.

1. It fails when applied to new colonies when only lands of the best fertility are cultivated, and corn is raised at a uniform cost; there is therefore no surplus value available as rent.

2. It fails to account for the rent paid by the worst land under cultivation as well as by that which is not cultivated at all. In a new colony, where property in land is a monopoly of Government and the land is leased from the Government, the holder of a grant pays rent for the whole area of land in his grant, even though he may not yet have brought some of it under cultivation. These are instances of monopoly rent.

In new colonies farmers will not raise agricultural produce without receiving the ordinary rate of profit. All the surplus in the price of agricultural produce over the ordinary rate of profit is necessary, because the Government exacts a rent, and can do so owing to the State monopoly of land. Agricultural rent, the price of produce being given, will vary directly with the productiveness of agricultural industry (the natural fertility of the soil and the skill exhibited in the application of labour). The productiveness of agricultural industry being given, rent will vary with the price of produce. Monopoly rent, unlike economic rent, produces an increase of the price of the produce in proportion to the rent exacted, and is not regulated by the different prices of agricultural produce, but by demand and supply.

CHAPTER IX.

INFLUENCE OF THE PROGRESS OF SOCIETY ON PRODUCTION AND DISTRIBUTION.

In early times, the guild system of production was individualistic. This prevented the ready transferability of capital from one form of investment to another which is so marked a feature of the modern industrial system. Every master workman was acquainted with all the processes necessary for manufacturing the article in which he dealt, and he preserved his right of property in the produce of his hands till he parted with it to some purchaser. The right of entry into any trade was jealously confined to the apprentices who had been trained by some master workman of the guild of that trade. "Each craft tried to be and was very much a mystery, except to those who carried it on." *

In modern times, the workmen's tools have become machines, and the system of production is collective. The operations of industry are conducted on too great a scale to permit of an individual carrying on all the processes of the manufacture of an article. By division of labour, each process of the manufacture is entrusted to a different workman, and the industrial unit becomes not an individual but a group of workmen combining their operations in a factory. These workmen contribute only their labour, they do not, as under the guild system, work with their own funds, but with funds contributed by the capitalist. The workmen have therefore no right of property in the goods produced by their labour; this right is vested in the capitalist. The times are favourable to production on a large scale, and the workmen are in general divorced from the land and other instruments of production

* Bagehot, *Postulates of Political Economy*, p. 94.

by their poverty. Increased physical knowledge showing itself in greater power over nature, greater personal security exhibiting the fruit of greater production and accumulation of wealth, the growth of the principle of co-operation shown in the rise and progress of joint-stock companies, and the ready transferability of capital from one means of investment to another are further marked points of contrast between the modern and the old industrial systems.

The question how production and distribution are affected by the progress of society has been called the Dynamics of political economy as opposed to the Statics; the one deals with society as being in a constant state of motion towards improvement or decay, the other deals with society as if it were in a constant state of stable equilibrium.

Let us now consider the effect on wages, profits, and rent of the various ratios in which capital can stand to population.

Increased wages, when common to all descriptions of productive labourers, and when really representing an increased cost of labour, must be at the expense of profits. The rate of profit and cost of labour varying inversely as one another, the farmer is compensated for cultivating under less advantageous conditions than before by a rise in prices, else he could no longer secure the average rate of profit; he is not compensated for having to give higher wages owing to a rise in price of the labourers' necessaries—this must be at the expense of his profits. If a simultaneous improvement took place in all branches of production, values and prices would remain unaltered and profits would rise because the cost of labour would be lowered.

If capital be advancing and the rate of the increase of the population stationary, wages will advance, and if the labourers do not become more efficient, the cost of labour will be increased and the rate of profit will fall. In the case of agriculture, as the farmer must receive the ordinary rate of profit, the increase of wages will be at the expense of rent, which will fall. If the cost of labour is increased in any greater ratio than its real remuneration, by an increase in the cost of the articles on which the wages are spent, there will be an additional fall of profits corresponding to the rise in price of the articles on which the wages are spent. If population and capital increase in equal proportions, and the labourer receive the same real wages and spend them upon the same articles as before, then the food for the increased population must be produced at a greater cost; but its rise in price extends over the whole supply, whilst the increased cost affects only a portion of it; so rent will rise, as there will be a greater surplus than before, after giving the farmer the ordinary rate of profit. The money amount of wages will be the same, but as the produce upon which they are spent has increased in price, they will not go so far as before in the purchase of the labourers' necessaries; and the profits of the manufacturer will therefore fall as he will have to make up the difference if the labourers maintain their customary standard of comfort.

If population increase and the rate of the increase of capital be stationary, only wages will fall and the price of agricultural produce rise. Rent will also rise, both in the amount of produce assigned to it and in the money value of that produce.

If the cost of wages to the capitalist be decreased as much as the real reward of the labourer, the rate of profit will be increased, but not if wages, though decreased in amount, cost as much as before.

If an improvement takes place in the production of a commodity not consumed by the labourers, and the rate of the increase of capital and population remain stationary, the capitalists will be benefited by the increased cheapness of the article as consumers only. But if the improvement takes place in any of the necessaries of life, either by decreasing the amount of labour necessary to raise a given amount of produce on a given area of land, or by enabling the same area of land to raise a greater amount than before, there will be a fall of prices, because the cost of labour is less than before, and in the latter case an additional fall, because the margin of cultivation has receded to land of greater fertility. If there be three qualities of land yielding on the same area and with the same expense 100, 80, and 60 bushels of wheat, the price must be such as to allow the least fertile land to be cultivated with the ordinary rate of profit to the farmer, who has a surplus of 60 bushels available as rent.

If one-fourth less labour be required than before the improvement, all the three qualities of land must still be retained in cultivation, but the money value of the landlord's rent of 60 bushels will fall one-fourth, as the money value of the produce has fallen in that proportion, owing to the cost of production being less than before. If, however, the produce required can be grown on one-fourth less land than before, the least fertile quantity of land will go out of cultivation, as on the best land can be grown $100 + \frac{1}{3}$ of 100 or $133\frac{1}{3}$ bushels, and on the second best land $80 + \frac{1}{3}$ of 80 or $106\frac{2}{3}$ bushels. The whole produce of the second best land will be required to meet the expenses of cultivation, therefore the rent will be $133\frac{1}{3} - 106\frac{2}{3}$ or $26\frac{2}{3}$ bushels instead of 60, and the money value of this rent will be reduced in the ratio of 60 to $106\frac{2}{3}$.

The reason why agricultural improvements seldom actually lower rent is, that they seldom cheapen food, they only prevent its becoming dearer. They seldom throw land out of cultivation, but only allow it to be cultivated consistently with returning the current rate of profit. Their effect is to do away with the necessity of resorting to less fertile land by enabling that already under cultivation to yield more produce with no increase of proportional cost. They thus at first prevent the increase of rent by counteracting the rise of price, which would otherwise be necessary when inferior lands are taken into cultivation to provide food for additional population, but eventually cause it to rise higher than before by enabling an inferior quality of land to be cultivated, and yet return the ordinary rate of profit. Their effect in lowering rent is counteracted by the increase of population.

If the labourers could live on a cheaper produce, such as maize, rents would be lowered, since the food for the whole population could be raised on much less land than before. The consequence to the labourer of the introduction of maize as an article of food would be that wages would remain the same, and the labourers would enjoy the benefit of the increased cheapness of food if they maintained their customary standard of comfort.

If, however, increase of the population was stimulated, the cheaper food might be grown on land too barren for wheat, and then the margin of cultivation may descend lower and rent rise higher than if corn were the usual food, as then the land would support a much larger population without reaching the limit of its powers. The Irish potato famine of 1848 shows that the cheaper the food the worse is the economic condition of the population, as they have no cheaper article of diet to fall back upon in the event of scarcity.

Given the habits and requirements of the labourers, rent profits and money wages are the result of the "composition of forces" of the increase of population and agricultural improvement. If the first be superior, either the labourers will submit to a reduction in the quantity or a deterioration in the quality of their food, or if not, rent and money wages will rise and profits fall. If the latter be superior, rent and money wages will tend downwards and profits upwards, as the cost of labour to the capitalist will be reduced.

CHAPTER X.

THE PRESENT CONDITION OF THE LABOURER AND THE REMEDIES TO BE APPLIED THERETO.

THE labour movement advances towards its object—the improvement of the condition of the working classes—by three paths:

1. Trade Unionism.
2. Co-operation.
3. State and Municipal Socialism.

The most remarkable phenomena of our present industrial system are trades unions and strikes on the part of the labourers, and locks-out on the part of the employers.

Present (1892) statistics as given in Webb's *History of Trades Unionism* state the number of Unions as 594, with a membership of 1,232,993 members, and an income of £1,790,842. The percentage of trades unionists to the rest of the population is 5·89.

Trades unions first come into notice in a royal proclamation of 1718 against those "lawless clubs and societies, which had illegally presumed to use a common seal, and to act as bodies corporate."

Mr and Mrs Webb notice a Woolcombers' Union in Yorkshire in 1741, and the Clothworkers' Society at Leeds is alluded to by the committee of the House of Commons on Woollen Manufactures in 1806.

By the Act of 1799, as amended by that of 1800, all combinations of workmen for trade purposes were declared illegal. This was the more unjust, as the jurisdiction of the magistrates to fix the rate of wages, in the event of a dispute between the masters and workmen, had fallen into disuse. In 1811 a select committee of the House of Commons resolved that "no interference of the legislature with the freedom of trade, or with the perfect liberty of every individual to dispose of his time and his labour in the way and on the terms that he may judge most conducive to his own interest, can take place without violating general principles of the first importance to the prosperity and happiness of the community."

This principle of even-handed justice to the workmen was only theoretically observed, as will be subsequently seen. In 1813 the provisions of the Statute of Apprentices, 1563, empowering the justices to fix the rate of wages in a neighbourhood, were repealed. In 1814 the provisions of the same statute were abolished which forbade masters to employ any workmen who had not been formally admitted and served as apprentices in the trade.

This did away with the last restriction on the factory or collective system of production, as the choice of the masters what workmen they would employ was no longer limited. In 1824 the law forbidding combinations of workmen was repealed, mainly owing to the labours of Joseph Hume in the House of Commons. This was followed by a large number of strikes. In 1825 a further liberating measure was passed, which allowed the right of collective bargaining, and of withholding labour from the market by concerted action. In this year the right of emigration was first allowed to artisans.

The first important trades union was the Builders' Union, or union of the seven building trades (joiners, masons, bricklayers, plasterers, plumbers, painters, and builders' labourers), which came into existence about 1830. The cotton-spinners of Manchester and clothiers of Leeds also formed unions about this time.

The first union of the coal-miners of Northumberland and Durham lasted from 1830 to 1832. In 1833 Robert Owen had a vain idea of a "general union of the productive classes." He also originated a Grand National Consolidated Trades Union, but this was premature, as, though the workers of each trade had learned to act together, the various trades had not yet learned the advantage of concerted action.

In 1834 the spread of trades unionism so alarmed the Government that it was in contemplation to revive the Combination Acts, but the general agitation carried on throughout the country by the trades unions defeated this.

In 1834 there was a general outcry against the sentence of seven Dorsetshire agricultural labourers, who were condemned to seven years' transportation for administering unlawful oaths. On admitting members to the Grand National Consolidated Trades Union, Owen's idea was that the grand lodges of this body should be the head offices of large joint-stock companies, owning the entire means of production in their industry. The weak point in his scheme was, that he provided no means for the admission of new members, but apparently would have allowed these bodies, as they stood at the time, to close their ranks and refuse to admit any fresh workers, except as labourers on fixed wages.

In 1835 Nassau Senior was appointed to report to Government on the working of trades unions; he recommended the severe enforcement of the common law prohibitions against conspiracy and restraint of trade, and the absolute forbidding of picketing.

No action was taken upon these recommendations.

In 1836 the plumbers, bricklayers, carpenters, and operative stonemasons formed separate unions.

From 1837–42 the energies of the trades union agitators were diverted into a political channel by their combination with the Chartists.

In 1841 was formed the Miners' Association of Great Britain and Ireland. This collapsed after the great strike of 1844, but was revived by Alexander Macdonald in 1863.

In 1845 Thomas Slingsby Duncombe, M.P., formed his National Association of the United Trades for the protection of labour. The efforts of this body were to be seconded by the

National United Trades' Association for the employment of labour, which was intended to raise capital for the employment of labourers on strike.

At this time the trades unions also formed a fund to assist emigration as a means of diminishing surplus labour.

In 1851 William Allan finally constituted the Amalgamated Society of Engineers, composed of the following trades :— smiths, millwrights, ironmoulders, engineers, and boilermakers. This was not merely a fighting union, but gave its members the advantages of a benefit club, and proved the model on which the later unions formed themselves.

In 1852 occurred the great strike of the engineers in London and Lancashire on the question of abolishing overtime. The objects of the strike were approved of, and material assistance given by, Frederick Denison Maurice and Charles Kingsley, the "Christian Socialists."

In 1855 the Friendly Societies Act was passed; and it was supposed that any society which deposited its rules with the registrar, acquired thereby the right of having disputes among its own members settled summarily by the magistrates, and of proceeding against its officers for breach of trust.

In 1859–60 occurred the London building trades' strike. The Engineers' Union greatly increased its reputation by giving three weekly donations of £1000 each to assist the strikers. This strike is important, as its strike committee was the germ of the London Trades Council, 1861. The first permanent committee of the nature of a trades council was the Liverpool Trades Guardian Association, established in 1848 to protect trades unions from suppression by the employers' use of the criminal law. Permanent councils were also in existence, at this time, in Glasgow, Sheffield, and Edinburgh.

In 1859 a small concession was made to trades unions, by the exemption from the penalties attaching to molestation or obstruction the mere agreement to obtain alteration of hours or wages, or the peaceful persuasion, without threat or intimidation, to cease or abstain from work in order to obtain these wages.

In 1860 Robert Applegarth constituted the Carpenters' Union. Allan Applegarth and George Odger, member of a union of ladies' shoe manufacturers, were the prominent members of what Mr and Mrs Webb call the Junta. This body managed the operations of trades unions from the time of the formation of the London Trades Council down to the passing of the Trades Union Act in 1871. Their chief lieutenants were T. J. Dunning, a bookbinder, author of *Trades Unions and Strikes, their philosophy and intention*, 1860, an able defence of trades unions from a working-man's point of view, and Alexander Macdonald, among the coal-miners.

The chief organ of trades unions during this period was the *Bechive*, 1861-77, edited by George Potter, and contributed to by Frederic Harrison and Professor E. S. Beesly. Its place was subsequently taken by the *Labour Standard*, edited by George Shipton, Secretary to the London Trades Council.

In 1864 the International Society of Working-men was formed, and the English leaders of trades unionism took a prominent part in its deliberations.

The law of master and servant at this time was exciting considerable discontent. The employer who broke a contract of service could only be sued for damages, but a similar breach of contract on the workmen was a criminal offence punishable by imprisonment. This arose from the fact that the law on the subject dated from the Statute of Labourers, 1349, and the Statute of Apprentices, 1563, when the labourer was legally forbidden to withhold his services or bargain for his wages, the obligation to labour being a duty arising out of status and enforced by statute. Lord Elcho's Master and Servant Act, 1867, was the first attempt to remedy this inequality of treatment.

In May 1864 the Glasgow Trades Council summoned a national meeting of trades unions in London.

In 1866 another similar meeting was summoned by the Sheffield Trades Council at Sheffield to concert measures against locks-out by employers.

In 1866 occurred the Sheffield trade outrages, of which the cutlers were especially guilty.

In 1867 a Royal Commission on Trades Unions was appointed, and the outrages at Sheffield specially inquired into. The accusations of violence proved exaggerated, and the Commissioners reported that four-fifths of the Sheffield trades were free from crime.

In 1867 the position of trades unions was further complicated by a declaration of the Court of Queen's Bench that the power which trades unions believed themselves to possess, of prosecuting their officers for breach of trust under the Friendly Societies Act of 1855, did not legally exist.

The Trades Union Commission of 1867 recommended that no combination should be liable to prosecution for restraint of trade except those formed to do acts which involved a breach of contract, and agreements not to work with any particular person. Registration, and thereby the securing of legal protection for their funds, was only to be allowed to those societies whose rules were free from restrictions on the number of apprentices, the use of machinery, and the customs of piecework and sub-contract. The minority report (of Messrs Frederic Harrison, Thomas Hughes, and the Earl of Lichfield) recommended that no act should be considered illegal if done by a workman, unless it was illegal if committed by any other person, and that no act of a combination of workmen should be considered illegal unless it was criminal in a single person.

This period is remarkable for several important books on the subject of trades unions:—*Measures for putting an end to the Abuses of Trades Unions*, by Frederic Hill, 1868. *The Trades Unions of England*, by the Comte de Paris, 1869. *Thornton on Labour*, 1870. *Trades Union Defended*, by W. R. Callender, 1870.

In 1871 the Trades Union Act was passed. No union, however wide its objects, was to be illegal merely because it was in restraint of trade. Every union was entitled to be registered if its rules were not expressly contrary to the criminal law.

The registration, by which the unions secured legal protection for their funds, and power to prosecute its officers for fraud or embezzlement as regards their corporate property, was so devised as to leave untouched their internal organisation, and to prevent their being sued or proceeded against in a court of law. There was considerable agitation on the part of the trades unions against the express prohibition contained in the bill of violence, threats, intimidation, molestation, or obstruction on the part of unionists. Picketing was to be severely punished, "watching and besetting" by a single man being made as grave an offence as by a multitude. The most the trades unions could obtain was the embodiment of these criminal provisions in a separate bill, the Criminal Law Amendment Act.

The practice of assembling great meetings of union delegates at some central place continued. In 1868, thirty-four delegates met at Manchester, representing 118,000 trades unionists, and in 1869, forty-eight representing 250,000.

The first National Trades Union Congress was assembled in 1871, to agitate against the criminal section of the Trades Union Act.

In 1871 the first Trades Union of Women which survived for any length of time was constituted in the Edinburgh Upholsterers' Sewers' Society.

In 1874 the Trades Union Congress held at Sheffield was attended by the representatives of 1,100,000 organised workmen, including a quarter of a million miners, the same number of cotton operatives, and 100,000 agricultural labourers.

In 1873 the employers of labour recognised the importance of trades unions by organising themselves in the National Federation of Associated Employers of Labour. In the same year Joseph Arch constituted the National Agricultural Labourers' Union.

At the general election of 1874 Alexander Macdonald (Stafford) and Thomas Burt (Morpeth) were returned as the first labour members of the House of Commons. They were both coal-miners by trade.

In 1875 the new Conservative ministry took up the labour question. They repealed the Criminal Law Amendment Act of 1871, and, by the Conspiracy and Protection of Property Act, they limited the application of the Law of Conspiracy to trade disputes. The Masters and Servants Act of 1867 was replaced by the Employers and Workmen Act of 1875. Masters and workmen became two equal parties to a civil contract. Imprisonment for breach of engagement was abolished. Peaceful picketing was allowed. Collective bargaining was legalised. No act done by a combination of workmen was to be criminal, unless the same act done by an individual was criminal.

It is noticeable that Trades Unionists are sometimes as inconsistent as their employers. The latter could not complain against factory legislation that it was interfering with industry, and at the same time call on the Government to prevent free combinations of their workmen. The Trades Unionists, on the other hand, whilst demanding freedom to combine, cannot consistently refuse to work with non-union men, or compel their employers to expel such men from employment, in spite of the fact that they embrace within their ranks but a small fraction of the adult labourers of the country.

In 1876 Henry Crompton published his book on *Industrial Conciliation*, which is the chief authority for boards of conciliation between employers and their workmen. Another work of a similar tendency was L. L. Price's *Industrial Peace*.

In 1880 the Employers' Liability Act enforced on employers the duty of insuring their workmen against the risks of their trade. The fault of the Act was that "contracting out" on the part of the workmen was allowed, and the employers escaped liability provided that an insurance fund was kept up partly by their own subscriptions, and partly by those of their men.

In 1894 a bill was passed through the Commons making void any agreement on the part of the workmen to "contract out," but the Lords struck out this clause.

The depression of trade which began about 1878, produced a large number of strikes against reduction of wages, but generally in vain. The activity of the unions was consequently greatly diminished till they were galvanised again into life by new unionism in 1888-89.

The Royal Commission on Labour of 1894 has, by a majority report, recommended that trades unions should be vested with complete personality, allowing them to sue and to be sued, and that they should be made liable in their corporate property for any breach of contract made on behalf of the workmen with their employers. The undertakings of the trades unions would thus deserve more confidence than they have hitherto met with, if this guarantee of their being strictly adhered to were insisted on. This proposal has not commended itself to those members of the Commission who are drawn from the Socialist party.

Another highly commendable proposal of the Commission is that no workshop should be carried on without a certificate that all proper sanitary precautions have been complied with, especially in the matter of overcrowding. Not only occupiers but owners of workshops are to be responsible for the breach of this regulation.

The most powerful separate trades union is that of the Amalgamated Engineers with a membership of 72,221, a yearly income of £189,774, and a balance at the end of 1891 of £237,251.

Next to it is the National Union of Boot and Shoe Operatives (established 1874) with 43,000 members, boilermakers with 39,000 members, and the Amalgamated Society of Railway Servants, 31,000.

Webb's *Trades Unionism* gives the following statistics of trades unionists in the year 1892 in some of the most numerous trades:—miners' federation of twenty organisations, 318,500; cotton weavers, 83,000; shoemakers, 49,000; railway servants, 48,000; carpenters and joiners, 38,000; compositors, press and machinemen, 33,250; cotton cardroom operatives, 31,000; bricklayers, 27,000; tailors, 23,900; Eastern Counties Labour Federation of Agricultural Labourers, 17,000; iron founders, 15,000; and shipwrights, 14,000.

Trades unions, in their capacity of friendly societies, are not economically important, but it is in their capacity of combinations to raise wages, by limiting the number of labourers and by placing various restrictions upon the employers' method of conducting their business, that their action must be considered.

Many unions limit the number of apprentices which a master workman can take; the effect of this is to deprive the public of the reduction in the price of goods which follows the fall of wages consequent on the number of workmen in the trade being increased. This amount of labour of which employers are compulsorily deprived is thrown as a burdensome surplus upon other trades which are not so protected by unions, and the wages in these trades are proportionally depressed. The trades unions thus confiscate a part of the wages which would otherwise be paid to the labourers whom they debar from choosing their own trade.

The trades unions forbid labour-saving machinery in pursuance of a policy of "making work," though there is no connection between the amount of work a country has to perform and the rate of wages prevailing in it, *e.g.*, California, with less working hours and less work, has a rate of wages double that of England.

Another object of trades unions is to arbitrarily diminish the hours of labour. The effect will be that, unless the labourer grows more efficient by working shorter hours, the employer will have his rate of profit diminished by the falling off in the scale of production, and because the expense of keeping up the plant falls upon a diminished amount of goods. If he raises his prices to compensate himself for the increased cost of production, he runs the risk of being undersold by foreign producers; if the employer can raise prices without this danger, the labourers, who are the majority of consumers, have the benefit of shorter hours of labour for the same pay neutralised by the increased dearness of goods.

The unions dislike piecework and extra payment for working overtime, as in these cases labour is paid more according to its value than when wages are reckoned by the day. They dislike the payment of higher wages to the better workmen, but, unless this is done, the standard of work will be lowered, as no one will do more work without getting more pay for it, and all money paid to the worse workman above the value of his work acts like a compulsory poor law in his favour. They do their best to prevent a workman from showing any superiority over his fellows; this is called "besting one's mates" and is forbidden by the rules of many trades unions.

By insisting that a rise in profits should in all cases be followed by a rise in wages, they destroy the average rate of profit, the surplus of the good times needed to meet the deficiency of the bad.

They clamour for a minimum rate of wages, but this is only possible with a due regard for the interests of the employer, if the labourers are reduced in number down to a point at which there is a demand for their labour at the minimum rate of wages.

It is legitimate for the labourers to combine to sell their labour on the best terms, and trades unions provide the organisation which alone makes a strike possible. Strikes can only succeed when the operation of competition can be prevented, e.g., the agricultural labourers of Dorsetshire were already receiving the minimum rate necessary to support life, so they could not be replaced from other districts, and the farmers were compelled to yield to their demands.

No advance of wages that is extorted by a strike can be of lasting benefit to the labourers if it is liable to be neutralised by other labourers instantly forcing themselves into the trade from a wish to share in this rise. Competition acts only gradually, because the labourer is often too ignorant to see the benefit of migrating to another place or is too poor to do so, and the new labourers cannot be quickly trained to a new trade. The rise of wages which the trades unions secure is therefore of benefit to the labourers till the ratio between the workmen and the capital employed in the trade can be altered. Such a rise has a tendency to divert capital from the trade and so reduce the demand for labour in the trade.

Trades unions place the labourers in a better position to sell their labour. If the employers know that the workmen are organised, and that a strike may take place at a time when trade is exceptionally prosperous, they will be more inclined to grant their demands. They enable workmen to hasten, by combined action, the rise of wages which would in any case follow on the increased competition for labour when trade is exceptionally prosperous. Another way in which trades unions may act most beneficially is by the formation of Boards of Conciliation in union with the employers.

Such Boards of Conciliation in the iron and coal trades have arranged the Sliding Scale system of wages. A normal rate of wages is fixed for a normal condition of trade, and any fall or rise of price of the commodity below or above this normal level is followed by a fall or rise of wages in a corresponding proportion. Marshall is of opinion that " the direct influence of unions on wages is small relatively to the great economic forces of nature." He points out that the rise of wages has been greatest in occupations which have no unions, such as domestic service and employments for women and children. This is because there has been an increase of the demand for labour in these occupations accompanied by a diminution of the supply. The most Marshall will allow is that, "other things being equal, wages in trades in which there are strong unions are likely to be higher than those in which there are not."*

Such action is legitimate, but any attempt of a trades union to compel workmen to join it, or to exclude them from employment if they do not, or to prevent them from selling their labour in the way they deem most advantageous to themselves, should be severely punished.

The New Unionism of the present day differs from the old Trades Unions in putting pressure on the workmen to join its ranks and in its attitude towards Government. It no longer preserves the independent attitude of the old pioneers of labour, but has attempted to capture the political machine for its own ends, and has formed a party in the House of Commons, which is ready to barter its support in return for the compliance of the Government with the labour programme. The new unionism is Socialistic, and aims at using trades union machinery to further its programme. At the Belfast Trades Union Congress of 1893 it was carried that all Members of Parliament who received aid from trades union funds in their elections should bind themselves to support the Socialistic labour programme. The Norwich Trades Union Congress of the next year confirmed this resolution. A split on this point is probable in the labour party. As long ago as 1851 Laborde said "the force of Socialism lies in the suppression of the corporations" (trades unions). Unless this is done, we may take it for granted that the prosperous workman will resist to the utmost the nationalisation of his own individual property. He will hardly agree with the cry of the French Socialists, "l'ouvrier qui épargne est un traitre," "the workman who saves is a traitor." A further point of difference is that the new unionists wish for an aggressive policy on the part of the trades unions, and they should not degenerate into mere mutual insurance societies. They also protest against the exclusion of lowly paid trades, like the dockers, from the benefits of organisation of labour. The formation of the Gasworkers' Union, and the great London

* *Economics of Industry*, pp. 405, 406.

dock strike of 1889, gave a great impulse to trades unionism throughout the country.

Under our present industrial system, the interests of masters and men are antagonistic, because the labourers are divorced from the means of production. We have discussed the remedy proposed by the Socialists for this grievance, and it remains to consider that of co-operation or profit-sharing. This is based upon the principle that the labourers should not work simply for hire, but should share in the profits raised by their industry. Its great advantage is that it substitutes self-help for the State help of the Socialists.

Co-operation may be in (1) production; (2) consumption or distribution; (3) societies of credit or banking.

Co-operation in production originated in France and has chiefly flourished there. Its originator was M. Leclaire, who divided a certain percentage of his profits among his workmen in the ratio of their wages. This example was followed in 1865 by Messrs Briggs of the Whitwood and Methley Junction Collieries near Leeds. The United Coal-Miners of South Yorkshire in 1874 bought the Shirland Collieries for £70,000 (£31,000 paid down and the remainder raised by debenture bonds), but they failed to pay the interest on these bonds, and the undertaking failed.

The Ouseburn Engineering Factory was established by some Newcastle engineers, on strike for the Nine Hours' Day in 1871, on a co-operative basis; it failed in 1876, but has been re-established.

This bonus from the profits, being distributed according to the aggregate amount of wages, falls generally in larger proportion to the best workmen, who are thus given an interest in the prosperity of the business. It is contended that the bonus is not a sacrifice on the part of capital, but a measure of the increased efficiency given to both capital and labour. It is essential, however, that there should be profits to share. The workmen are ready enough to share in profits, but are not so ready to accept partnership in losses, and a strike at Methley Colliery was the result of the withdrawal of the bonus during a period of bad times of the coal trade.

Other co-operative productive societies that have at various times existed are the Leeds Flour Mill and the Associations of

Co-operative Shoemakers in Northamptonshire. In 1887 there were twelve co-operative productive societies in the North of England, employing more than 3000 workmen. The Oneida Perfectionists, who manufacture silk twist, and the Amana Society, who produce woollen stuffs, are communistic societies in America engaged in production.

The Sun Cotton Mill at Oldham, the metropolis of co-operation, had no share of its profits assigned to the workmen employed, but its shares were issued at £5, so they might be held by people of the labouring class.

The principle of co-operation in farming was first put into practice by Mr Gurdon at Assington in Suffolk in 1830. He let a farm to an association of labourers at the ordinary rent, and also advanced the association money to provide the necessary stock and implements. This advance was soon repaid, and the labourers became the owners of the stock and implements on the farm, and carried on the business so successfully that a second farm was let in the same way. The agricultural depression ruined the second and larger farm in 1883, but it paid the original shareholders £16 a share, the landlord and other creditors were paid up in full, and only the later shareholders lost money. The farm was eventually started again with the help of the London Co-operative Guild, and up to 1888 was able to pay its rent and the current rate of wages to its labourers, though it made no profits. The smaller farm remained on the same basis as when originally started.

The Shakers in America are a communistic society owning land on co-operative principles.

Co-operation in production was assisted by the French revolutionary Government of 1848, which made a grant of three million francs to assist fifty-six societies. Of these the Associations of the Co-operative Masons and Pianoforte-makers met with most success, but the grant of Government subsidies did not succeed in strengthening the movement. In 1887 there were forty-seven co-operative associations of workmen existing in Paris.

Co-operation in production has generally been less successful than co-operation in consumption, on account of the vicissitudes of trade and the rareness of business talents among the working classes. Professor Marshall acknowledges this.

"The managers of a co-operative association seldom have the alertness, the inventiveness, and the ready versatility of the ablest of those men who have been selected by the struggle for survival, and have been trained by the perfectly free and unfettered responsibility of private business." *

Co-operation in consumption originated in England, where the Rochdale Equitable Pioneers' Society was founded in 1844. Its members clubbed their means (£28) to buy goods from the wholesale shops, and purchased goods from the common stock thus accumulated with ready money at ordinary retail prices. Interest at 5 per cent. was first paid on capital, and the surplus of the profits was divided among the customers in the ratio of their purchases.

This example was followed on the Continent by the Zurich Consumers' Union and the Co-operative Union of Milan. The Civil Service and Army and Navy Co-operative Stores in London adhere strictly to the principle of selling their goods for ready money, but, instead of giving back to the customer his share of the profits in a lump sum each quarter, they spend their profits in selling their goods some 20 per cent. cheaper than the retail merchant. This they can do, as their ready-money system enables them to turn over their capital many times in the year. They can thus do a maximum of business with a minimum of capital. They give no credit, and therefore require none from the producers, who sell to them cheaper in consequence, and they make no bad debts. Mulhall gives the following statistics of the growth of co-operative stores :—

Year.	Members.	Capital.	Sales.
1861	38,000	£365,000	£1,100,000
1884	898,000	£10,480,000	£30,400,000

Those stores are not really co-operative in which no share of the profits is allotted to the persons employed by the concern, but the profits are given away to the customers, who buy more cheaply than at the ordinary retail price. They do an important service to production in getting rid of a large number of retail dealers, who all have to get a living out of the commodity they sell and therefore raise its price more than in proportion

* *Economics of Industry*, p. 191.

to its cost of production. Mill believed that nine-tenths of these retail dealers were superfluous, Rogers four-fifths.

The Rochdale Pioneers' Society have supplemented their operations by establishing the Wholesale Co-operative Society, the object of which is to give facilities for purchasing goods in the best market to various small struggling co-operative societies. In 1887 it supplied goods to 790 retail societies holding shares in it; and a similar wholesale society in Scotland supplied goods to 231 retail societies. It has been proposed that the co-operative productive societies should unite themselves to these wholesale societies, and so secure a certain and steady market for their produce.

Co-operative banking was set on foot in Germany by Herr Schulze-Delitsch (the *Bastiat-Schulze* of Lassalle) in 1851. Herr Schulze-Delitsch was a leader of the Progressive Party in the Prussian Parliament, and he established credit banks which lent money to their own members, thus enabling a workman to provide himself with capital. The funds for the purpose are partly subscribed by the members, partly borrowed on the credit of the association, every member of which is jointly and severally liable for the debts of every other member. In the credit banks on the system of Schulze-Delitsch there are shareholders who need not be members; in the banks on the system of Raffeisen the members alone are responsible for making and collecting loans.

The proportion of subscribed capital to borrowed funds may be as 10 to 90 at the commencement of a society, but afterwards must be brought up to 50 per cent. All members must hold one equal share of the capital of the society, which must be increased in proportion to its business. The shares may be paid up in full or in regular instalments, but till they are so paid up, no dividends are paid on them. On the other hand, it is only the fully paid-up capital that is liable for deficits, the principle being "in proportion to the share of gain the risk of loss." The liability for deficits is in the following order: (1) Reserve Fund, (2) Fully paid-up capital, (3) Private property of members. In 1885 there were 1,500,000 members of these credit banks, owning a capital of £15,000,000.

Co-operative banking is forbidden by law in England, and the only institutions it has been found possible to set on foot are the bank established by Dr Rutherford at Newcastle in 1871, and the bank connected with the Wholesale Co-operative Society, in which co-operative societies have shares.

Co-operation has had to overcome the following obstacles in England. Before 1852 no co-operative society of workmen could legally constitute itself. In 1852 Mr Slaney's Industrial and Provident Societies Act admitted associations of working men to the statutory privileges of friendly societies, exempting them from the formalities applicable to joint-stock companies. Up to 1867 no co-operative society could have more than £200 invested in any commercial concern. Up to 1871 no society of this sort could buy or sell land except for purposes of its trade.

BOOK III.

EXCHANGE.

CHAPTER I.

VALUE AND PRICE.

EXCHANGE is the means of converting the produce of labour into its most convenient form, *e.g.*, a hunter has more deers-flesh than he can eat, and wants bread, so he converts part of his flesh into bread by means of exchange.

To exchange for anything else, an object must possess—

1. Value in use or general purchasing power. This depends upon its capacity to satisfy a desire or serve a purpose. Aristotle bases the cause of all value on χρεία (demand). Utility is no inherent quality, it arises out of the relation of things to man's requirements, and its origin is the desire of the consumer, not the labour of the producer. It is not the measure of exchangeable value, though essential to it, *e.g.*, water, though most useful, is generally valueless, because the other essential element of value, namely, difficulty of attainment, is absent. When once the element of difficulty of attainment is present, as in large towns to which water is brought by human labour, water will possess a value.

2. Difficulty of attainment, *e.g.*, air, though a requisite of life, has no value, because it can be freely obtained by all.

"Labour was the first price, the original purchase money paid for all things." This does not mean that the labour with which a thing was or can be made is the cause of its value, but that the quantity of labour it will exchange for or purchase shows what its value is, and how much it has varied from time to time or from place to place. Ricardo, and after him the Socialists, however, are of opinion that the quantity of labour required for producing a thing is the sole cause of its value.

Macleod points out that, if this is so, it follows that—

1. All differences or variations in value must be due to differences or variations in labour. The enormous value of land in great cities cannot be attributed to labour.

Land has a special value as the site of fairs; when the fairs remove its excess of value ceases, but this would not be so if labour were the sole cause of value. Labour cannot be said to be the cause of the value of a diamond, which we may pick up without any exertion.

2. Things produced by the same quantity of labour must be of equal value, but then the rubbish in which a diamond is found would be of the same value as the diamond itself. If a man shot a pheasant with one barrel of his gun and a crow with the other, both birds should be of the same value.

3. The value must be in proportion to the labour. Then a nugget of gold, found after six months' labour, should be more valuable than one of equal weight found on the commencement of the labour.

4. A thing produced by labour must always have value and the same value. If this were so, fashion could not make things, especially articles of dress, valueless when they go out of fashion, and gold or legal attainments could not be valueless among savages. If value depended upon labour, it could never be, as it really is, purely local.

Price is value estimated in money. Every article has generally two prices, its normal price and its market price. Its normal price depends upon its cost of production. Its market price is the price prevalent in a certain market. A market is defined by Cairnes as a district in which competition is fully and freely operative, and in which all sellers know the terms of other sellers and all buyers those of other buyers. The causes which make market price differ from normal price are—

1. Temporary local alterations of the ratio of demand to supply.

2. Custom, which sometimes makes people buy from the

shop which they have been accustomed to, even though they might get things cheaper elsewhere.

The relative market prices of different articles vary according to the estimates formed by people, not of the total utility of the amount of each article they buy, but of the final utility. The final or marginal utility means the utility to the buyer of just the last portion of the commodity for which he will give the price asked rather than go without it. Marshall points out, "The marginal utility of a commodity to anyone diminishes with every increase in the amount of it he already has."* This regulates the normal price to the buyer. Cost of production regulates normal price to the seller.

There is no such thing as a general rise in values, as all things cannot rise in value relatively to each other. Prices may rise, but if they rise equally, it is of no consequence to anybody's rent, wages, or profits, as, of all that is bought with money, they get neither less nor more than before. Money is the only thing which has altered (fallen) in value. The producers of money, and those who have to receive or pay fixed sums of money, are the only persons affected.

CHAPTER II.

CLASSIFICATION OF COMMODITIES ACCORDING TO VALUE.

1. CERTAIN things have a monopoly value, as the supply of them cannot be increased. To this class belong pictures by deceased artists, and rare wines, the produce of particular vineyards in special years. The value of this class of commodities depends upon the equalisation of the supply to the demand: this is effected by raising the price till only those continue to demand the article who can afford to pay the price required. If the supply is naturally or artificially limited, as was the case with tea before the East India Company's monopoly of the trade to China was abolished in 1834, with the produce of the Spice Islands under the Dutch East India Company, who often destroyed part of the crop to

* *Economics of Industry*, p. 78.

keep up prices, with opium in India and tobacco in France, as they are Government monopolies, the price of the commodity is often only limited by the buyer's estimation of its worth to himself. Demand is defined as the desire for goods or commodities seeking its end by the offer of general purchasing power. Supply is the desire for general purchasing power seeking its end by the offer of specific commodities or services.

2. Things which can be produced by capital and labour to any extent, without increased cost, are always sold at a price which will repay the manufacturer the capital he has laid out in wages and in the ordinary expenses of production, together with the ordinary rate of profit on his advances. This price is called the cost of production. All manufactured articles belong to this class. The market value of a commodity results from the local ratio of the supply to the demand, and must be such as to create a market for the existing supply. The market value of a commodity only remains constant during a period which cannot exceed the length of time necessary for altering the supply. If competition be active and the power of production indefinite, manufacturers will only be reimbursed the cost of production. If, for any temporary cause, a thing exchanges for more than its normal value, additional capital will quickly be invested in the trade, and so may increase the supply to an extent even more than in proportion to the demand. The value of the article may then even fall below its original amount, in which case over-supply will be corrected by total or partial suspension of production. If there are buyers at the market price for a greater amount of the commodity than is offered for sale, its price will rise till those who cannot pay the additional price cease to wish to buy it. If a greater amount is produced than people wish to buy, the supply is equalised to the demand by increased cheapness, which either calls forth more buyers or induces those who have already bought to take more. General high wages, profits, or taxation do not affect values, but if the wages or profits of an employment, or the tax levied on it, exceed the average rate, its value will correspondingly increase.

A general increase of the cost of labour lowers profits, and therefore lowers relatively the value of things made by machinery, as the element of profits enters more into their value than into that of other things. Profits also enter more largely into the cost of production of some things than of others if they are required to yield a profit during a longer period of time. Cloth is as valuable as it ever will be as soon as it is manufactured, but wine is improved by keeping. The wine and the cloth are originally of the same value, but the wine will not be kept for five years unless saleable at the end of that time for an amount equal to the value of the cloth and five years' profit thereon at compound interest. The difference in value between the cloth and the wine at the end of five years will be larger the higher the rate of profit.

A rise in general profits, therefore, affects the value of those things in which profit is a large element much more than the value of those things in which it is a small element, and to this extent may be said to have an effect on values. The greater the proportion of the whole capital, which consists in buildings, machinery, or in anything which must be provided before the immediate labour can commence, and the more durable these are, the more largely will profits enter into the cost of production. A commodity is made by £1000 worth of real labour; its cost of production will be £1200, being £1000 repayment of capital and £200 profit at 20 per cent.

A second commodity is made by £500 worth of real labour and an imperishable machine worth £500; the owner does not want to be repaid the price of the machine, as he still has it, and it is undeteriorated in value, but he requires a profit on it. The cost of production will therefore be £700 (£500 to replace capital advanced in wages and £200, 20 per cent. profit on the whole £1000). Profits in this case will be in the ratio of £200 to £700, or $24\frac{4}{7}$ per cent. If the machine deteriorate in value 20 per cent. yearly, then £100 must be added to the cost of production to reimburse this, and it will be £800. Profits in this case will be in the ratio of £200 to £800, or 25 per cent.

A rise of profit demanded in the preliminary stages of a manufacture exerts an influence, like that of compound interest in accumulating debt, in raising the price of a commodity, as that part of the capitalist's expenses which consists in the profits of previous capitalists is increased.

If a squatter in Australia demand a higher rate of profit, say 5 per cent., on the wool of his sheep, he increases his price to the wool merchant, who pays him £105 for every £100 paid before. The wool merchant will demand from the cloth maker to be repaid this sum with a profit, so his price will be £105+5 per cent. on £105, or £110, 5s. The cloth manufacturer will demand repayment of this advance with a profit from the tailor, and his price will be £110, 5s.+5 per cent. on £110, 5s., or £115, 10s. 3d. The price of a coat to the wearer will be calculated on the basis of the tailor receiving £115, 10s. 3d.+5 per cent. on £115, 10s. 3d., or £121, 10s. 9d., and will represent a certain portion of this sum. Thus each man expects to be repaid the cost of production with a profit, and the price of the coat to the wearer is increased more than in proportion to the original increase in the rate of profit demanded by the squatter: an increase of 5 per cent. in the price of the wool causes an increase of more than 20 per cent. in the price of the coat.

It is asserted that there sometimes arises an excess of supply over demand, with the result of a fall of prices and a depression of trade.

If the word demand be used as equivalent to the power of payment, when the supply is doubled the power of payment is also doubled, as this only consists in commodities.

If the word demand be used as equivalent to the wish to buy, though those who have an equivalent to give might have all their wants satisfied, yet the fact of their going on adding to their production shows that all their wants are not yet satisfied. Production is not excessive, but ill-assorted, if one thing is produced when the demand is for another. A glut of one commodity takes place when there is a deficiency of some other commodity to be offered as an equivalent.

If people go on investing their savings from habit, they make them over to labourers in payment for labour. When the labourers have all their wants satisfied, they will shorten their hours of labour and so diminish production.

It is erroneously supposed that periods of commercial crisis are due to excess of supply, as also that it is the cause of the tendency of profits to a minimum.

When the supply is in excess of the demand, the profits of

the manufacturers are lowered, but consumers can generally be found for the commodities if the price be lowered sufficiently.

Professor Marshall has been the first to emphasise the contrast between the parts which nature and man respectively play in production.* Capital and labour invested in land obey the law of diminishing return. On the other hand, given an increased investment of capital and labour in a trade, improved organisation generally follows, and the produce can be increased in direct proportion to the capital and labour invested. Thus the law which capital and labour obey when they are invested in a manufactory is diametrically opposite to that which they follow when invested in land. The return to an increase of the capital and labour invested is in the former case proportionally greater, in the latter case proportionally less.

3. The third class of commodities are those of which only a limited quantity can be produced at a given cost, and if more is required, it must be produced at a greater proportional cost. Agricultural produce is the chief example of this class, the value of which is regulated by the cost of that portion of the supply which is brought to market at the greatest expense. The produce of mines or fisheries has its value regulated similarly to that of land; all the most productive mines or fisheries cannot be worked at once, owing to physical causes, and the value of the produce of each mine or fishery is proportional to the superiority of its productiveness over that of the worst in use.

The price of fish is especially subject to fluctuations, as its production depends upon conditions which are out of men's power to control, and it is so perishable that a market must be found for it almost at any price. Mines and fisheries, like land, yield a rent which is fixed by the same considerations as agricultural rent. Rent is the price paid for a differential advantage in the production of a commodity and does not enter into its cost of production. The gains of a patentee resemble rent, and do not, any more than it, affect values. The patentee's profit is the difference between the cost of his improved process and the ordinary one; this profit will remain

* *Economics of Industry*, pp. 200, 201.

so long as the market is not fully stocked with articles manufactured by the improved process. Anyone who, by superior talents or better business arrangements, can bring his produce to market at a lower cost, whilst its value is determined by a higher rate of cost of production, enjoys a similar differential advantage, but it does not affect the value of his goods.

In a new colony the values of arable and pasture land alter their mutual relation as society progresses.

The value of easily portable commodities is regulated by their cost in the mother country plus the cost of carriage. Corn is grown for export, and arable land is more valuable than pasture, as there is no sufficient market for the meat of the cattle. As the colony progresses and the population increases, there is a greater demand for meat, and, as it cannot be imported, the value of pasture land rises.

CHAPTER III.

THE VALUE OF ACCESSORY PRODUCTS.

Some things have a joint cost of production, being both produced by the same operation. The expectation of the joint profit of both causes money to be laid out upon them, and the outlay would have to be incurred for the one even if the other were not used or wanted. Wool and mutton, beef hides and tallow, gas and coke belong to this class.

A given quantity of coke with the gas resulting therefrom must exchange for other things in the ratio of their joint cost of production. Suppose there is a good market for the gas but not for the coke at the price offered, the price of the gas will be raised and that of coke lowered, till the demand for each fits so well with the demand for the other, that the quantity required of each is exactly as much as is generated in producing the quantity required of the other, and there is therefore a market for each at the price required by the joint cost of production. Rotation of crops is an instance of joint cost of production: the farmer bases his expectation of profit on the combined produce of each of the two crops on the same field in two successive years, and the value of both must be such as to allow an equal quantity of each to be sold.

CHAPTER IV.

MONEY.

GENERAL WALKER'S definition of money is that it is "that which passes freely from hand to hand throughout the community in final discharge of debts and in full payment for commodities, being accepted equally without reference to the character or credit of the person who offers it, and without the intention of the person who receives it to consume it or enjoy it or employ it for any other use than in turn to tender it to others in discharge of debts or payment for commodities."

The possession of money shows that the holder of a coin has done society a service, the value of which is proved, measured, and registered by the coin, and for which he expects an equivalent when he parts with the coin. Money is a measure of value and a medium of exchange. It is the standard by which future obligations are determined. It is also a form in which capital can be held in suspense without loss, till the precise form of investment can be decided on. A measure of value is something by comparison of which with two other things we may ascertain their value relatively to each other; thus, if the price of a pint of ale be threepence and the price of a loaf of bread be sixpence, we say that the bread is twice as valuable as the ale. Money is not a perfect measure of value. "To enable the money price of a thing at two different periods to measure the quantity of things in general which it will exchange for, the same sum of money at both periods must correspond to the same amount of things in general, *i.e.*, money must always have the same purchasing power," which is not the case, as its value constantly varies.

Money is the medium of exchange or the substitute for barter. If a baker has bread to sell and wants tea, instead of waiting till he can find some one with tea for sale who wants bread, he sells his bread for money, thus obtaining a medium of exchange which is desired by everybody, and with the money he buys bread. The adoption of some one commodity as the standard renders the comparison of values easy. Mr Jevons says: "The chosen commodity becomes a common denominator or common measure of value, in terms of which we estimate the values of all other goods."* Money renders exchanges possible by acting as the intermediate term in each exchange, and also makes them more definite. Money is also the standard by which future obligations are determined; thus, when a contract is made for a payment in the future, such as rent, it is generally agreed that the payment should be made in gold or silver, as being less variable than other commodities in value. It is also a form in which capital can be held in suspense without loss, till the precise form of investment can be decided on. We thus sum up the functions of money. Money is—

1. A medium of exchange.
2. A measure of value.
3. A standard of value.
4. A store of value.

Gold and silver are chosen as the materials of money because—

1. They possess high intrinsic value in a small bulk.
2. The amount of labour necessary to produce a given amount of the precious metals does not vary much, therefore their cost of production is fairly constant.
3. They are indestructible under ordinary conditions of atmosphere.
4. They can be easily divided, so that a number of small pieces of money will be worth no more and no less than an aggregate piece of equal weight.
5. They are easily distinguishable, and there is no trouble in ascertaining their value.

The amount of money which a country requires for circulation varies directly with prices and depends on—

1. The amount of goods to be sold for money. When prices are high, a greater amount of the precious metals is

* *Money*, p. 5.

needed to perform a given amount of buying and selling than when they are low.

2. The number of times goods are bought and sold for money before being consumed.

3. The extent to which cheques, bills of exchange, and other paper substitutes for coin are in use. In England the banking system has been brought to such perfection that it has been calculated that there are only 226 sovereigns in use in every nominal £10,000.

The natural value or general purchasing power of money is the value of the bullion of which it is made in addition to a value equivalent to the cost of coining when not borne by the State. The value of the precious metals principally depends upon their employment as the material of money, as the value of the amount of them used in the arts varies very little from year to year. The charge for coinage is called a seigniorage. In England there is no such charge, and the mint gives coin of the same weight as the bullion it has received. Where a seigniorage is charged, this is generally done by returning coin somewhat less in weight than the bullion, and the mint retains the difference to reimburse the cost of coinage. This has the effect of a debasement, as the nominal and bullion value of the coin no longer correspond. It checks the tendency to melt the coins for exportation, for coins are more valuable than bullion in proportion to the amount taken out of them as seigniorage.

If the precious metals are imported, the value of money will be the cost of the labour and capital expended in producing the equivalent exchanged for it.

The English mint is compelled to buy all the gold bullion offered to it at £3, 17s. 10½d. per ounce, but this is because three sovereigns and exactly that portion of a sovereign which is equivalent to 17s. 10½d. can be coined from an ounce of gold. The price of gold is thus constant, but this does not show that the value of gold estimated in other commodities is constant also. That quantity of money will be in circulation in any country which will enable it to perform all the required exchanges consistently with its maintaining a value equal to its cost of production.

The precious metals are the produce of mines, and therefore

their value is proportional to the superiority of the mine from which they are produced over the least productive mine in existence. If the cost of money is above this its natural value, prices will be low, if the cost is below its natural value, prices will be high. The average price of commodities thus depends upon the cost of production of gold. As the precious metals are largely used for jewellery and ornament, besides being coined into money, and as they are so durable that a comparatively small annual production keeps up the supply, the adjustment in value to the cost of production is slow, and even if the annual production were stopped, it would be long before prices were affected. The supply is more easily increased than decreased; and it must be much increased, as on the discovery of the silver mines of Potosi or the gold-fields of California, before its effect can be felt in lowering prices all over the world. The cost of production is thus comparatively unimportant as compared with the quantity of money in fixing its value or purchasing power. Any increase of the quantity of money decreases the amount of goods it will purchase and raises prices in the ratio of the increase.

If each sovereign of £10,000 changes hands ten times in a given time, £10,000 can perform as much work in buying and selling as £100,000. The average number of times each piece of money changes hands in order to perform a given amount of buying and selling is called its rapidity of circulation, and the stock of money in the country is considered as multiplied by the figure which expresses its rapidity of circulation. The value of money is thus inversely as its quantity multiplied by its rapidity of circulation. The cost of production being given, the quantity required will depend upon its rapidity of circulation, and the rapidity of circulation being given, the quantity required will depend upon its cost of production. The value of money means its purchasing power over goods. The term is ambiguous, being sometimes used as equivalent to the current rate of interest. The supply of money is the whole amount in circulation at one time, and the demand for money is all the goods offered for sale. The demand for money increases with the cheapness, the quantity needed being in inverse proportion to the value.

The ratio between supply and demand temporarily regulates

the value of money. If the supply of money be small, its power of purchasing goods will be high and prices will be low; if the supply be large, its power of purchasing goods will be low and prices will be high. If the demand for money increase, owing to the growth of a nation's population or wealth, and if the supply be not increased, the value of the precious metals estimated in commodities will rise, and prices will fall. If the supply of money be increased, and no cause arise, in the increase of business to be transacted, for requiring more money, its value estimated in commodities will fall and prices will rise. But, at a time of a low value of money and high prices, a greater amount of the precious metals is needed to perform a given amount of buying and selling than when the value of money is high and prices low; the demand for money is thus increased in exact proportion to its depreciation in value. The demand, which was less than the supply of money, is thus equalised to it. When the value of gold is low, more will be used in the arts, and the supply will be decreased, as the less productive mines will cease to be worked. These two causes will also contribute to equalise the supply to the demand of money by lessening the quantity in circulation.

So, too, when the value of gold is high, more will be produced, as gold-mining will be more profitable; but this very increase of quantity tends to lower the value of gold and so equalise the demand to the supply. The value of the precious metals is more closely connected with supply and demand than that of other things, for any alterations in their cost of production will not act upon their value unless they actually increase the supply in existence, whereas the value of other things may be altered by a potential increase of the supply.

The following cases are exceptions to the rule that increase of the quantity of money in a country causes prices to rise:—

1. If, by being brought into a country and placed out at interest, it increases the stock of money to be invested, and so lowers the rate of interest, it will cause some of the capital hitherto invested in the country to be sent abroad for investment. It may do this without having acted up the market for commodities.

2. If the increase of money be only proportional to the increase of transactions usual at different times of the year,

e.g., the accumulation of money necessary for the quarterly payment of dividends at the Bank of England.

CHAPTER V.

MONOMETALLISM OR BIMETALLISM AND ALTERATIONS IN THE MUTUAL RATIO OF VALUE OF THE PRECIOUS METALS.

EITHER gold or silver may be used as the only legal tender in a country (Monometallism), or the circulating medium of the country may be composed of both metals indiscriminately (Bimetallism). The country which uses both metals as a legal tender, or considers a debt to be legally discharged by payment in either metal, is said to have a double standard of value. Professor Jevons thus explains the meaning of a " standard of value ":—

" All that a standard of value means is that some uniform unchangeable substance is chosen in terms of which all ratios of exchange may be expressed and calculated without any regard whatever to the feelings or mental phenomena which the commodities produce in men." *

Up to 1874, the Latin Union (France, Belgium, Italy, Switzerland, and Greece) had such a double standard, gold and silver being legal tender to any amount for debt at a ratio of $15\frac{1}{2}$ to 1. In 1874, this system came to an end, as the Governments limited the amount of silver they would coin. From 1803 to 1874, however, the French metallic coinage was sufficiently large to retain this ratio of $15\frac{1}{2}$ to 1 against other countries. Mr Giffen denies this, and says the Bimetallic law was virtually inoperative, as at one time during this period, silver was *de facto* the sole standard, and in the latter part of this period gold, the other metal only emaining in use at a premium.†

From 1878–1890, the United States had a partially bimetallic monetary system, as by the Bland Act the Treasury

---

* *Case against Bimetallism*, p. 126. † *Money*, p. 68.

had to coin not less than two or more than four million dollars worth of silver a month, these dollars being legal tender at a ratio of 16 to 1 of gold.

The Sherman Act followed the Bland Act, by which the Treasury bought 4½ million ounces monthly and issued notes in payment for them, exchangeable for sterling. The treasury was empowered to coin as much of this silver as was required into "Bland" dollars and use them to redeem the notes. These "Bland" dollars enjoyed a nominal value about double their intrinsic value, and were exchangeable for gold at par. The Sherman Act was repealed in 1893, mainly owing to President Cleveland's action.

In Java and Holland gold and silver are both legal tender, at a ratio of $15\tfrac{5}{8}$ to 1, and the currency of either country circulates in the other.

Most nations use gold for their higher and silver and copper for their lower payments, establishing a ratio between the metals according to their relative value, and allowing payments to be made in either metal according to convenience. England is practically a monometallic or single standard country, as silver is only a legal tender up to forty shillings and copper to one shilling. The monometallists prefer gold as the sole standard of value, because—

1. The cost of obtaining gold, and therefore its value, varies less than silver.

2. If a double standard of value were adopted, its uniformity would be affected by the variations in value of two metals instead of one.

The advantage of a double standard is that the circulating medium of a country can be replenished by drawing on the stock of both gold and silver in the world, and the consequent tendency to a fall of prices on the increase of wealth or population in a country can be thus arrested. The disadvantage lies in the consequences which arise, if the value of the two metals relatively to one another no longer agree with their rated proportion, owing to some cause affecting the cost of production of one of them. If the value of silver relatively to gold be depreciated 5 per cent., all who had payments to make would make them in the cheaper metal, and all who had money to receive would thus lose 5 per cent. of their debts. Twenty shillings are a legal tender for a debt of £1, and the debt would be paid in silver, as silver convertible into twenty shillings can be procured for less gold than that contained in a sovereign. All the sovereigns would be melted, as they would buy more shillings in bullion than they would exchange for as coin, gold coin being rated in silver at below its bullion value.

If gold were depreciated in value relatively to silver, a sovereign would no longer be worth twenty shillings; all debts would be paid in gold, and shillings would be melted to be exchanged for gold, since they would buy more sovereigns in the form of bullion than they would exchange for as coin, silver coin being rated in gold at below its bullion value.

Bimetallism has thus a constant tendency to depreciation of the currency. Though the currency would nominally consist of two metals, only the one which was depreciated in value relatively to the other would be really current, and the other would be melted for exportation, being worth more as bullion than as current coin. Locke thus states the case against bimetallism: "Two metals, as gold and silver, cannot be the measure of commerce both together in any country, because the measure of commerce must be perpetually the same, invariably keeping the same proportion of value in all its parts, but so only one metal does and can do to itself. An ounce of silver is always of equal value to an ounce of silver, and an ounce of gold to an ounce of gold; but gold and silver may change their value one to another, and one may as well make a measure, namely a yard, as a measure of trade of materials that have not always a settled invariable value to one another. One metal therefore alone can be the measure of account and contract and the measure of commerce in any country."*

The advantages of a double standard can be secured without its drawbacks by—

1. Making the least costly metal the only legal tender, and allowing the more costly one to be bought and sold as an article of commerce, it being coined and allowed to pass current at whatever value the market assigns to it.

2. The English method of fixing a limit, above which silver is not a legal tender. This is fixed for silver at forty shillings

* *Tract on Money.*

and for copper at one shilling. The English silver coins are tokens, that is, they have a value assigned to them by law in excess of their bullion value and may be considered as depreciated to that extent. By the law of 1816 they are coined at the rate of 66 to the troy pound of silver. In the case of a shilling this excess over bullion value is about 6 per cent. This excess of value is given to silver coins in order to prevent it being profitable to melt them down and exchange them as bullion for gold, in the event of any rise of the value of silver relatively to gold. It was desired to prevent what occurred in France, where the silver in the five-franc piece was of such an amount that four of them were as nearly as possible equal in value to the gold in a napoleon or twenty-franc piece. When silver was greatly in demand to send to India to pay for cotton during the American War of Secession, these five-franc pieces were melted and replaced by gold. Precaution is taken in England against the loss which would arise by paying debts in silver, to which a fictitious value has thus been assigned, by limiting the value of debt which can be paid in it to forty shillings.

The bimetallists maintain that if the great commercial countries in the world would agree, it would be possible to maintain the value of silver relatively to gold by fixing a legal ratio. If the value of silver were to fall below this legal ratio, it is maintained that the competition of people anxious to pay their debts in the cheaper metal would create an increased demand for it, which would arrest its decline in value. There would be no motive to export the undervalued metal if the same ratio of value prevailed universally. They also argue that the State has the power of deciding what substances shall be money and what the value of these substances shall be, by means of its power of deciding what substance shall be deemed legal tender and discharge all debts. Government cannot fix the value of the precious metals as commodities, but only with regard to their use as money. They consider the quantity of money has more effect in regulating its value than the cost of production. On this account bimetallism is by some called the Quantitative theory of Money.

The effect of the currency reform adopted by the Indian Government in 1893 would seem to some extent to confirm the theory that the quantity of money acts powerfully upon its value. The new scheme has not indeed raised the value of the rupee to the desired limit of 1s. 4d., but has prevented its fall in sterling price to about 10d., which would otherwise be its price at the present value of silver—28d. per ounce. The monometallists, on the other hand, argue that nothing can arrest the ultimate conformity of a coin in value to the cost of production of the bullion it contains.

At various periods the value of silver relatively to gold has varied as follows:—

Just before the discovery of America, it was fixed in Spain by the Edict of Medina, 1497, at $10\frac{3}{4}$ to 1. This would represent a value of silver per ounce of about 7s. 9d. After the discovery of America, and before the value of the silver mines of Potosi was known, the value of silver, as compared with gold, fell to about $13\frac{1}{3}$ to 1. Adam Smith considered that prices in England were not sensibly affected by the American mines till 1570. In the period 1681–1700 it fell to 15 to 1, and 1871–75 to 16 to 1, in 1876 it was 17·8 to 1, in 1879 18·39 to 1. The ratio of 16 to 1 was first fixed in Spain on the 17th July 1779, and remained in force for a little less than a hundred years. The year 1876 was the year in which the great fluctuations in the price of silver commenced. In 1875 the average price of the year for silver per ounce was $57\frac{7}{8}$d., and in June 1876 it fell to a monthly average price which fluctuated between 52d. and 50d. per ounce. In 1888, with the price at 42d. an ounce, the ratio fell still further to 22 to 1; at present the price is about 28d. per ounce and the ratio nearly 33 to 1.

In the years 1852–57 twenty million pounds' worth of gold was produced annually from the mines of California and Australia, whereas the whole annual yield of gold from all sources just before this time was only half this amount; the total output of gold was therefore trebled. In the last three years of this period the value of the gold produced was treble that of silver.

Professor Leone Levi in his *History of Commerce* gives the following table to show the comparative amount of gold and silver produced from the principal sources of supply in the world before and after the gold discoveries:—

	1846.		1852.	
	Gold.	Silver.	Gold.	Silver.
N. and S. America	£1,300,000	£5,250,000	£13,300,000	£7,250,000
Russia	3,500,000	1,250,000	3,500,000	...
Europe	...	...	...	1,250,000
Austria ⎫ Borneo ⎬ Africa ⎭	1,200,000	...	1,200,000	...
Australia	...	...	12,000,000	...
Total	£6,000,000	£6,500,000	£30,000,000	£8,500,000

The reason that this enormous increase in the amount of gold exercised so little influence upon its value as compared with silver, or upon prices in general, was that contemporaneous with a great increase in commerce consequent on the adoption of Free Trade and the repeal of the Navigation Laws. Without this increase in amount of the precious metals, there must have been a heavy and sudden fall in prices.

Mulhall thus compares the state of English imports and exports at various periods during the reign of the present Queen:—

	Yearly average in Millions of £.	
Period.	Exports.	Imports.
1837–40	50	59
1841–50	83	75
1851–60	153	121
1861–70	270	213
1871–80	371	278
1881–86	395	291
1891 Value of Trade of the Year	309	435
1892 " " "	291	429

The increase of commerce was therefore so great as to enable this vast additional amount of gold to be absorbed without producing a rise in prices of more than from 10 to 15 per cent., according to Professor Jevons.

Fluctuations in price are not a trustworthy means of testing changes in the value of gold, unless we make allowance for changes in the circumstances of the production of each of the commodities under investigation. Thus Free Trade and improved means of communication, extending the sources of supply of corn, account for a fall in the price of bread since 1848, in spite of the increase of population. Trade was very active, and all the means of production were extended to the utmost in the period 1872-74, and when trade returned to its wonted condition, there was an augmented supply to meet a diminished demand, prices had therefore to fall independently of any changes in the value of money. The fall in the value of gold cannot have been very large, else some of the least productive mines would have been no longer worked; but we do not find this to have been the case.

The increased production of gold depreciates the value of the metal and raises general prices in two ways:—

1. Those into whose hands the increased supply of money comes spend more of it and prices naturally rise. Production is extended to meet the increased demand; this cannot be done without increased employment of labour, but, when all the labourers in a trade are fully occupied, the competition for labour necessitates a rise in wages, and prices must rise if profits are to be maintained at the former level.

2. Wages cannot rise in any of the principal trades without affecting the rate of wages in others, so wages in some trades may increase without the commodities they produce having risen in price. The rate of profit in these trades must decline, and production be contracted, till the consequent increase in demand allows prices again to rise.

The effect on prices of the increased production of gold cannot be correctly estimated without deciding the two following points:—

How far are the precious metals used for the purposes of art in the country?

How far are paper substitutes for money in use?

Accordingly as either of these conditions arise, the tendency of the increased supply of gold to raise prices will be proportionally counteracted.

The advance in prices thus depends: (1) On the direction of the new expenditure. As the increased supply of money will be mostly in the hands of the labouring classes, it will be expended mostly upon their necessaries.

(2) Upon the facilities for extending supply. If production cannot be easily extended, the price of the commodity rises.

The supply of raw produce, especially raw animal produce, can be least easily extended to meet the increased demand, as the production depends upon natural agencies requiring time to accomplish their ends. Thus it happens that animal products, such as meat, milk, and, in a less degree, mineral and agricultural produce, are most affected by the rise in prices. The supply of agricultural produce cannot be increased till the next season, so, if the value of gold falls, the price of corn will tend to rise, unless this tendency is checked by importation. The production of manufactured goods, on the other hand, can be easily extended to meet the increased demand, and therefore their price does not rise so much. Spun and woven fabrics are the only things which have fallen in price with the progress of society, as in them there have been improvements in production greater than in that of the precious metals.

(3) Upon the facilities for contraction of the produce. If much machinery is employed in a trade, it is not easy to diminish production, in case the wages of the trade have risen without a corresponding increase of the price of the commodity produced.

Prices in the different markets of the world tend to an equality, because—

1. Different nations, producers of the same commodity, compete with one another as to which can sell at the cheapest price in neutral markets.

2. The reciprocal demand of commercial countries for each other's produce is affected by their price. Thus, if prices rise more rapidly in England than in India, more Indian goods are bought in England and less English in India. The precious metals have to be imported into the countries of Asia to pay for the excess in value of their exports over their imports, and, by increasing the supply of money in the country into which they are imported, tend to make prices rise there proportionally.

The effect of the increased production of gold in Australia itself has been as follows :—

1. General rise of money wages. This was fourfold during the most productive period of the gold-fields, but has now declined to double. The rate of money wages was formerly regu-

lated by the average earnings in the gold-fields, but now by the earnings of agriculture, which has replaced gold-mining as the most profitable industry of the Colony.

2. The price of Australian produce and the rate of general prices in Australia rose. This rise in prices was easily effected, as the amount of the precious metals previously in circulation in Australia was small. The price of Australian wool in Europe could not rise without a damaging effect upon the trade, but the growth of the meat trade from Australia saved the producers from being obliged to increase the price of wool.

3. The gold-fields handicapped Australian agriculture, for the farmer only cultivated the best soils owing to the abnormally high wages he had to pay. In spite of large tracts of fertile land which remained unoccupied, more than half the increased food supply required for the gold-fields had at first to be imported. It was only when the gold-fields became less productive that the labour which had been attracted to them began to devote itself to the more generally profitable trade of agriculture, and also to the production of tin, antimony, and cotton. California, unlike Australia, had a special fertility, which enabled agriculture from the first to maintain its ground against gold-mining, so much so as to permit of the export of food.

4. Australia, by her advantage in the production of the precious metals, gets her agricultural imports at a less cost than the cost to the original producers, and is a gainer in proportion to the increased cheapness (50 per cent.) of the gold with which it buys foreign produce. This gain will last till the gold prices in other countries are raised proportionally to the decline in the cost of gold in the countries which produce it. It is this decline of the cost of gold and the consequent high prices in Australia that keeps up the value of its exports, such as wool. The industrial development of Australia will never prosper till prices in Europe rise so much that it is no longer profitable for Australia to import commodities from Europe, but she will produce them herself instead of devoting herself exclusively to the production of gold, wool, and meat, things in which she has the greatest natural advantage.

The rise in prices has affected the countries of the world in the following order :—

1. England and America. These countries possess the greatest facilities for supplying the markets where gold is given in exchange, England as the great manufacturer, and America as the great producer of food stuffs and raw material, therefore they obtain gold at the cheapest price and attain more quickly to the higher level of prices and incomes produced by the cheapened cost of gold. England and America only benefited by cheap gold in so far as it is spent on commerce with foreign countries, the gold price of whose commodities has not risen as much as in England or America.

2. The perfection of the banking system in England and America provides non-metallic substitutes for money, so the greater amount of the precious metals imported from California and Australia flows from England and America to the Continent of Europe, and thence, in the form of silver, to the countries of Asia, to pay for the excess of value of the exports from these countries over their imports. This excess arises from the higher level of prices in England and America, on which account the Asiatic countries purchase less European goods, and the difference in value between their exports and imports becomes increased. The Asiatic countries have parted with their commodities for this extra supply of money and cannot replace them, so, as their stock of money increases, their means of well-being decline. The precious metals which are superfluous in England and America thus pass from them in a constant stream, which saturates the currencies of Europe, and then loses itself in the hoards of Hindustan and China, the money systems of these countries being more passive and absorbent than those of Europe.

Mr Goschen considers that gold has appreciated in value during the period 1878–88, basing his opinion on—

1. The general fall of prices. Since 1873 gold prices have steadily declined owing to the increased supply of commodities and the increased share of the duty of money thrown on gold by the demonetisation of silver. It must be noted that there are large reserves of gold in all the principal banks of the world, but these have no effect in preventing

the fall of prices, as they do not act on the market for commodities.

2. Gold was wanted to fill the void left in the silver currencies of France and Germany, which were melted to supply the silver sent to India, to pay for cotton during the American War of Secession and also for the cost of public works such as railways and irrigation canals.

3. The increased demand for gold, the resumption of specie payments by the United States and Italy instead of paper money, the demonetisation of silver by Germany in 1871 and the restriction of silver coinage by the Latin Union in 1875. The Latin Union in 1875 agreed to concert certain financial measures, limiting the amount of silver which each country would coin, and arranged for the joint use of a decimal coinage of francs, &c. This increased demand for gold was contemporaneous with a falling off in its production. In estimating the effect of these causes upon the value of gold, we must consider how far banking facilities, providing substitutes for money, have been extended in these countries, as in that case the increased demand would not have had so much influence in raising the value of gold.

The balance of argument seems to support Mr Goschen's view that gold has appreciated. Mr Fawcett considers that, though the depreciation of gold has been arrested, there has been no great appreciation of its value. Mr Macleod considers the fall of prices since 1873 to be due not to appreciation of gold, but to decline of speculation following on the commercial failures of 1873. The tendency of the increased production of gold is to alter the proportion of the distribution of money throughout society, hence an addition of some 40 per cent. to the currency of England has been absorbed without a corresponding increase of prices.

The increase of wages of the labouring classes causes the demand for gold to increase more rapidly than their numbers would lead one to suppose, because the labourers cannot be paid by credit, and the field for credit is contracted in proportion as the wages of the labourers were increased.

The alteration in the value of silver has taken place since 1870; before this time the production of silver had not varied much for twenty years.

From 1852 to 1862 between £8,000,000 and £9,000,000 worth of silver were produced.

1862 to 1870 from £9,000,000 to	£10,800,000.
1875	£15,000,000.
1876	£20,100,000.
1877	£16,600,000.
1878	£19,500,000.
1879	£19,800,000.
1880	£19,900,000.
1881	£21,000,000.
1882	£22,600,000.
1883	£23,400,000.

In 1884 the value of amount produced was £23,000,000, and thus was treble that of the silver produced in the ten years 1852-62.

The following table shows the comparative amount and value of the gold and silver produced of late years:—

Year.	Tons.		Value in millions of £.	
	Gold.	Silver.	Gold.	Silver.
1851–60	2018	8,956	282	78
1861–70	1885	12,201	264	105
1870–80	1715	22,347	241	178
1881–88	1067	21,960	148	154

These figures prove that the amount of silver produced has greatly increased relatively to that of gold, but, owing to the fall in exchange, its sterling value has not increased proportionally.

The silver of the Nevada mines, especially the Comstock lode, has an additional effect in depreciating the value of silver, for the reason that it is found in combination with so much gold (45 per cent.) that the mines would yield a very large profit, even if the silver were sold at a quite nominal price. This is partly the explanation of the fact that the production of silver shows no signs of falling off, in spite of the fall in its sterling price. This is proved by the statistics given below.

Year.	Average annual production of Silver in ounces.	Average price of Silver per ounce.
1876–80	78,776,000	$52\frac{3}{4}$d.
–81–85	90,435,000	$50\frac{5}{8}$d.
–86–90	111,213,000	$44\frac{5}{8}$d.

	Annual production in ozs.	
–90	133,237,000	$48\frac{11}{16}$d.
–91	144,453,000	$45\frac{1}{16}$d.
–92	from 152,102,000 to 157,535,000	$39\frac{13}{16}$d.

Production has almost doubled itself between 1878 and 1891, the figures being 73,476,000 oz. and 144,453,000 oz. These figures seem to show that even a further fall in the sterling price of silver would not materially diminish the output.

We have to ask ourselves, therefore, why an increase in the amount of silver, which is not greater than the increase in the amount of gold from the Australian and Californian mines, has produced a fall in the value of silver from 60d. per ounce to 42d. in 1888, and at the present time to about 28d. Gold has not fallen in value proportionally to the increase of its production, owing to the following reasons :—

1. The rapid development of commerce.

2. The export of silver to the East, 1860–70, to pay for cotton during the American War and for labour employed on the Public Works of India. This silver was replaced by gold.

3. Displacement of silver by gold in Germany and the Scandinavian kingdoms, in Austria, 1872–75, Holland, and partially in the countries of the Latin Union, 1875.

Silver, on the other hand, has depreciated so much in value because the supply has so much increased at a time when demand has fallen off, owing to—

1. Demonetisation by Germany and Austria and the Scandinavian kingdoms, which has both increased the supply of silver to be disposed of and decreased the demand for it, thus doubly lowering its value.

The amount of silver in circulation in Germany before the demonetisation was sixty million pounds; about half this amount was required for the subsidiary silver coinage, but thirty million pounds worth were thrown upon the market. The Scandinavian kingdoms in the same way disposed of two million pounds and Austria of four million pounds.

The amount of silver set free by Germany was required by the United States on resumption of specie payments, and France temporarily increased the quantity of silver required by purchasing, 1872–76, about three million pounds worth each year, and Italy slightly added to the demand by resuming specie payments in 1883. With these exceptions, the amount of silver demonetised by the European kingdoms was thrown upon the silver market and had a great effect in depreciating its value.

2. The demand for silver in India has decreased, owing to the increase of the home charges necessitating a permanent excess of exports over imports, and the substitution of Government bills for silver as a means of paying for the balance. In the period 1859–67 the annual average import of silver into India in excess of the exports averaged fifteen million pounds. This fell off between 1868–9 and 1871–2 to about £10,000,000 and again between 1872–3 and 1875–6 to £4,100,000. In the seven years ending 1887–88 the net average annual import of silver into India was Rs 77,000,000, or 770 lakhs, which was worth, at 15 to the pound, about five million pounds, and the continued depreciation since 1888 has still further diminished the value of the silver imported into India as compared with the total amount produced in the world.

In the period 1860–70 India absorbed £101,000,000 worth of silver, or more than was produced in the world, and the demand was met by drawing upon the silver currencies of France and Germany. In the next decade this amount fell off by more than 50 per cent. In 1888 India only absorbed about a quarter of the annual production of silver, assuming the value of the amount annually produced to be about twenty million pounds.

We give below the value of the annual importation of silver into India in tens of rupees for 1889 and the four subsequent years.

Year.	Tens of Rupees.
1889	10,725,872
1890	12,338,474
1891	15,433,654
1892	10,603,733
1893	15,228,021

In the years 1890–91 the import of silver was abnormal, owing to the temporary rise in the sterling price of the rupee brought about by the passing of the Sherman Act in the United States. In 1893 the currency changes introduced by the Indian government produced a similar result.

Though the exports of India exceed the imports by from seventeen to twenty-one million pounds a year (average nineteen million pounds), yet about sixteen million pounds worth represents the amount due from India to meet the home charges, and the balance only (averaging, 1878–88, from four to five million pounds) has to be liquidated by silver sent to India, and Government bills are to a great extent substituted for even this amount. The debt due from India to England is not lessened by much investment on the part of the natives in Government securities, or by the practice of "open loans" which prevailed under the East India Company, by which money could be at any time brought into the treasury and deposited there at a fixed rate of interest, even though not immediately required by the Government.

The increase of the home charges and therefore of Council Drafts is thus one of the principal causes which check the importation of silver into India and diminish the demand for it, thus depreciating its value.

It is maintained that the purchasing power of the rupee in India, in relation to purely Indian goods, has not declined since 1873, and that the rise in rents, country food, and the wages of domestic servants, may be accounted for by the increase of the European population in India and by the extension of railways providing facilities for the transport of food produce to the great cities.

There was a rise in prices of from 30 to 40 per cent., owing to the importation of silver after the Mutiny down to 1870, but the common opinion is that this rise was arrested, and prices have slightly fallen from their pre-Mutiny level, when the importation of silver into India fell off after 1870. The evidence of Mr O'Connor's Indian Prices and Wages Statistics for 1893, and the diagrams of the prices of food grains compiled from it for the new Indian Statistical Atlas, is decidedly against the opinion that the purchasing power of the rupee in India has remained stable since 1873. It appears that the prices of food grains remained stable during the period 1873–85, allowance being made for seasonal vicissitudes, but from 1885 to 1893 rice has been from 50 to 60 per cent., wheat 30 to 40, and millet from 10 to 20 per cent. higher in price than they were twenty years ago. This is probably due to the great exportation of rice and wheat from India which has been brought about by the low rate of exchange. Bad seasons and the practical impossibility of much extending the area of cultivation have also adversely affected the yield of rice. It is probable that this rise in the price of rice will reduce the profits of the Indian tea trade, as in many districts the tea garden coolies, finding that their wages do not go so far as they did in the purchase of rice, are beginning to demand an increase of wages.

The competition of Indian wheat (Panjab) in the English market, which is rendered possible by a low exchange, is one of the causes of the depressed condition of English agriculture. India is the third of the sources from which wheat is exported to England, and the quantity she exports is increasing—4,700,000 quarters in year ending June 30, 1894, against 3,000,000 in 1893 and 1,500,000 in 1892.

The dependence of the Indian wheat trade upon the low rate of exchange is shown by the following figures:—

Year.	Tons of Wheat exported from India.	Rate of Exchange per Rupee.
		s. d.
1881–82	993,176	1 7·895
82–83	707,202	1 7·525
83–84	1,047,824	1 7·536
84–85	901,538	1 7·308
85–86	1,053,025	1 6·254
86–87	1,113,166	1 5·441
87–88	676,908	1 4·898
88–89	880,504	1 4·379
89–90	689,961	1 4·566
90–91	706,024	1 6·09
91–92	1,515,349	1 4·7

In the year 1891–92 the demand for Indian wheat was abnormal, owing to bad harvests in other countries, from which it is generally exported.

The argument that a low exchange is favourable to the industrial development of India is based on the fact that it encourages the investment of European capital in the country. It is principally however, one class—the export merchants—who are benefited by a low exchange. The loss to Government on the home charges and to private individuals, in remitting money to Europe, and in paying for European goods consumed in India, must be set against this, as the sellers of European goods of course raise the prices in rupees to compensate themselves for the loss by exchange.

The report of the Herschell Committee on Indian finance shows that a falling rate of exchange was not so favourable to the expansion of Indian exports, as a whole, as had been commonly supposed, but that trade had prospered more when the rate of exchange was steady.

From 1871-72 to 1876-77 the gold value of the rupee fell from 23·126d. to 20·508d. ($11\frac{1}{4}$ per cent.), but the exports of the latter year were actually less than those of the former, their rupee value being about 10 per cent. greater. In this period the imports increased 17 per cent.

From 1878-79 to 1884-85 exchange was steady, only varying from 19·961d. to 19·308d., the exports in this period increased $36\frac{1}{2}$ per cent., and the imports 17 per cent.

From 1884-85 to 1888-89 the sterling value of the rupee fell from 19·308d. to 16·379d. (15 per cent.), but the exports only increased 16 per cent., and the imports 25. In the year 1888-90 there was a slight improvement in exchange, but the exports only increased $6\frac{1}{2}$ per cent., and the imports were less than in the previous year.

A noticeable result of the low rate of exchange is that the share of the United Kingdom in the trade of India has fallen from 57 to 48 per cent., but that of Austria has doubled itself in the last twelve years, and the imports from Germany, France, and Holland have proportionally increased. The reason is that on account of the fall in the gold value of the rupee, Indian purchasers cannot afford to pay English prices for goods, but buy inferior articles from other countries at a cheaper price.

The land revenue for permanently settled districts, and even of those settled for thirty years, worth in 1888 about

£5,000,000, is a more or less fixed amount, and is constantly declining in its power of satisfying the demands upon the Government. The revenue is not spent in India, and gold to pay for remittances and the fixed interest on debt has to be bought by payment in constantly depreciating rupees. All possessors of fixed incomes in India equally suffer. A gold coinage is unsuitable to India, on account of its cost, as it would have to be paid for in depreciated silver, and because the majority of the people are so poor that their purchases are chiefly conducted with annas and pice.

The following proposals have been made for the relief of the Indian Government from the difficulty into which it has fallen owing to the depreciation of silver.

1. To declare that rupees were henceforth to be valued at a certain number to the pound, and that all payments to Government must be made at this rate. The man who had a payment to make to Government would find it increased by the difference between the real and the fictitious value thus attached to the rupee, if its value continued to fall as compared with English money. It would also be a premium on coining, as rupees in the form of coins would be worth more than their bullion value.

2. To introduce a double standard. If this was done, those who had payments to receive would always receive them in the metal which was, for the time, of less value.

3. To make gold the standard of value in India, and to retain silver as the currency with a fixed value rated in gold.

The Government of India in 1893, dreading a crushing fall in the value of silver, owing to the imminent repeal of the Sherman Act in the United States, attempted to fix the value of the rupee in gold at 1s. 4d. by closing the mints, and consenting (1) to receive gold coin and gold bullion at the mints in exchange for rupees at a ratio of 1s. 4d. per rupee; (2) to receive sovereigns and half-sovereigns in payment of Government dues at 15 rupees for a sovereign and 7½ rupees for a half-sovereign; (3) to issue currency notes in Calcutta or Bombay in exchange for gold coin or gold bullion at the rate of one rupee for 1s. 4d. It was intended to cut off the means of remittance of money to India in payment for its exports, by remitting silver to be coined into rupees, and to make Council Drafts the only means of payment. It is on this account that it was considered so important that the Secretary of State should insist on a minimum of 1s. 3¼d. for Council Drafts, instead of selling them for what they would fetch. It is doubtful whether the Secretary of State has the power to insist on a minimum. When the mints are closed, the rate of exchange is entirely governed by the demand for remittances between Europe and India, and this depends upon the amount of Indian exports offered for sale. If the Secretary of State fixed the minimum at a higher rate than the demand for bills warranted, none would be tendered for, and his action would be nugatory This policy has failed, because of the amount of silver bullion imported into India as a means of remittance, instead of Government bills. The Government looked to the rise in value of the rupee by natural shrinkage, when no more could be coined at the mints. They hoped to maintain the value of rupees by limiting their quantity. Bullion was imported into India in payment for commodities, and hoarded by the people, who then frustrated the policy of Government by producing large stocks of rupees from their hoards and replacing them by bullion. It was also imported for making ornaments, and, owing to the ignorance of the people, the importance of silver bullion was unprecedentedly profitable, as silver ornaments were sold at the price current before the fall in the value of silver, though the price of the material had fallen proportionally to the depreciation of silver. The value of the silver imported in 1893 was Rx.15,228,021, or, at the exchange of 15 Rs. to the £, £10,152,014. In the previous year it was Rx.10,603,733 or £7,069,155. The quantity of silver imported into India in the sixteen months previous to the closing of the Mints was 76 million ounces, and in the same period following the closing the importation was as much as 59 million ounces. The comparative failure of the Government policy is due to the fact that the importation of silver has not been more reduced by the closing of the Mints.

Time is needed to absorb these rupees which have been thrown on the circulation from the hoards of the people, and this process would have been much facilitated if the import duty on silver imposed in 1894 had been 20 instead of 5 per cent.

The Government policy has prevented the rupee from falling to 10¾d. (its bullion value with silver at 27d. an ounce), and kept it pretty constant about the level of 1s. 1d., though it produced a heavy fall in the sterling value of silver from 37d. to 30d. an ounce. It was supposed that a great premium would be placed upon illicit coining by the currency policy of the Indian Government, as rupees when coined are worth more than their bullion value, but this does not appear to have been as much the case as was feared. We may thus sum up the result of the closing of the Indian Mints.

1. Maintenance of the rupee at about 3½d. above its bullion value. This has resulted in a temporary dislocation of trade between India and silver-using countries such as China, where the coinage is still unlimited, and silver coins only exchange for their bullion value. It is argued that this artificial rise in the value of the rupee will handicap the Indian, as compared with the Chinese tea-grower, and the Indian mill industries, especially in the purchase of labour.

2. Indian exports have fallen off, and imports have been encouraged. The imports of 1893–4 exceeded those of the previous year by 16 per cent., and those of 1890–1 by 1½ per cent., in spite of the marked rise in the sterling exchange value of the rupee in that year.

The fluctuations in the value of both gold and silver show that no agreements should be made for fixed payments in perpetuity in either metal. Such payments, *e.g.*, land revenue in India, should be made to vary with the price of agricultural produce, as tithe does in England with the price of corn.

CHAPTER VI.

CREDIT.

MILL defines credit as the permission to use another's capital or the power to borrow wealth. It is not capital, for all capital, not his own, of which a person really has the use, must lessen proportionally the capital of some one else. He allows, however, that the amount of the capital of a country in productive employment is increased or diminished according as credit is given to productive or unproductive consumers. Credit to unproductive consumers is a detriment to the capital of the country. A. sells to B. £100 worth of goods, to be paid for at the end of five years. A. is compensated by the higher price he obtains, but £100 of his capital have been diverted from productive employment for five years, and the labourers are so much the worse off.

Credit increases the productive power of the resources of the community, for if it did not exist, persons who, from their occupations or from the want of the necessary skill, could not personally superintend the employment of their capital, would either waste it or foolishly risk it. By means of credit, these persons intrust their capital to those who possess the necessary skill and knowledge to turn it to a profitable account, and so allow the industrial talent of the country to be made full use of. Undertakings too large for individual resources are undertaken by joint-stock enterprises, which are only possible by means of credit.

Fawcett denies that credit is capital, for capital is a fund from which can be fed, credit is the power to borrow. Labourers cannot be fed on the power to borrow, therefore credit is not capital.

Macleod argues thus: Credit is a right to demand the price of goods at a future time, it is not the actual goods or capital that are lent, no capital being actually transferred.

Credit, according to him, is not a loan, it is a sale, goods being bought by promises to pay. "Credit is to money what money is to goods," *i.e.*, credit is an order for money and money is an order for goods. Everything which has purchasing power is wealth; credit has purchasing power, therefore credit is wealth. Capital is wealth applied to assist future production, so credit, when applied in the same way, is capital.

A bank note or a cheque for £20 paid to a man gives him purchasing power to that amount, based on credit, in addition to whatever credit he may have of his own. Money-lenders, by means of their promissory notes payable to bearer on demand, lend not only their capital but also their credit. Bank or promissory notes can both be used to assist future production, therefore it is difficult to resist the conclusion that credit, if employed productively, may be considered as capital. Credit being purchasing power, prices often depend more upon the state of credit than upon the actual quantity of money.

The forms of credit which create purchasing power are those in which no money passes from hand to hand at the time of their creation and often none at all passes. These are—

1. Book debts, which are set one against the other, and only the balance paid in money.

2. Assignment by B. to A. of a debt due from C. as a payment of B.'s debt to A. This is done by a bill of exchange, which is a transferable order by a creditor upon his debtor; this, when authenticated by the debtor's signature ("accepted") becomes an acknowledgment of the debt. Bills of exchange are often drawn by a creditor, who is to be paid in six months' time, upon his debtor; these bills are discounted, and the creditor receives the amount of his debt, less interest for the time it has yet to run (the discount). Credit is thus a means of bringing at once into action the present value of deferred payment. Accommodation bills or fictitious bills of exchange are drawn by A. upon B. and "accepted" by him upon the understanding that when the bill becomes due, A. will pay the amount or supply B. with the means to do so. The fictitious bill is discounted and ready money obtained upon it by the joint credit of the two persons who have signed it, just as in the case of a real bill of exchange, and it therefore exerts an equal effect in raising prices. The real bill of exchange is said to represent actual property, but this is certainly not so, for if A. sells to B. £100 worth of goods and takes a bill at six months, B. may sell the same goods at six months' credit to C. and so on, and within six months there may be six bills of exchange all discounted, only one of which represents actual goods. There is no power to prevent the property which the bill represents being turned to other purposes than that of paying the debt, and the holder of a real bill of exchange relies just as much on the general ability to pay of the person who has accepted it, as the holder of a fictitious bill. A fictitious bill is the same as a common promissory note with two signatures instead of one as securities for payment. It is called fictitious, as it imitates the form of a bill

of exchange based upon a sale of goods. It is one of the principal means whereby a private person can raise money, but is deemed disgraceful for a merchant. The amount of a man's actual sales forms some limit to the amount of his real wealth, and credit is given accordingly. This security is impossible in case of fictitious bills of exchange, which are therefore more likely to be unlimited in quantity than real bills. This is the principal objection to them.

3. Promissory Notes. These differ from bills of exchange in that they do not bear interest—bills of exchange do. Promissory notes are payable at sight—bills of exchange after an interval. Government also issues Exchequer Bills, which are a form of Promissory Notes, payable on demand, as by this means they can borrow money without interest.

4. Cheques. Money only passes in payment of cheques when the accounts are small, as in transactions between retail dealers and consumers and in payment of wages.

Most dealers keep an account with a bank, as then they have a claim to have their bills discounted.

In the city of London the banks exchange the cheques drawn on each other at the clearing house, settling the balance by cheques on the Bank of England. Credit acts on prices in whatever shape it is taken. No special form of credit has any particular influence on prices except so far as it facilitates transactions being carried on by credit. In a commercial crisis prices may rise from speculation and then fall back, but without credit this could not happen in connection with commodities generally. If certain articles are purchased in extravagant quantity, this must necessarily draw money away from the market for other articles, and so lower their prices in spite of the increased activity of trade and rapidity of the circulation of money usual in prosperous times.

The crisis of 1847 did not proceed from an unlimited extension of credit, but because the foreign payments, owing to the high price of cotton and an unprecedented importation of food, which was paid for by the proceeds of a Government loan, had withdrawn from the loan market much of the capital usually supplying it. The calls of railway companies and the payment for cotton and corn so much diminished the amount of money available for loans, that merchants could not command renewal of credit when they wanted it and became bankrupt. Exchequer bills and an issue of notes above the legal amount, representing smaller sums than those usually circulated, set free gold for home consumption, and filled up the drain of specie caused by the excess of imports over exports. So, too, in 1864, the loan market was drained by heavy payments for cotton, large investments in banking and other joint-stock enterprises, and the loan operations of foreign Governments, and the same result followed. The crisis of 1825, on the other hand, was caused by over-speculation on the recognition of the independence of Mexico and the South American republics. The Bank of England increased its issue of notes in the face of a falling market and a drain of gold, and then contracted it suddenly, and when notes were wanted to support the solvency of county banks, refused them. The panic was allayed by the issue of one-pound notes and five million pounds' paper money of higher denominations.

Bank notes have a greater influence on prices than bills of exchange or book credits, because they offer greater facilities to the multiplication of transactions on credit. They have not much influence in aiding the rise of prices in speculative times, as then purchases are chiefly conducted by means of book credits. If A. buys from B. by a book credit, B. cannot extend his credit by means of his debt from A. If A. has given a bill of exchange for the amount, B. can get it discounted and obtain money on the joint credit of himself and A., or he may pay away the bill for goods, which is equivalent to obtaining them on the same joint credit, and the bill may be again discounted or several times paid away for goods before being presented for payment. If A. obtains a loan of bank notes, and therewith pays B., B. is independent even of a discounter; A.'s bill is only taken by those convinced of his ability to pay, but the bank notes are taken by all the neighbourhood, and B.'s purchasing power, by means of his own credit, remains undrawn upon. If A. draws cheques against a loan he has received from a bank, these cheques, like bank notes, are purchasing power in the hands of the receiver, and if the receiver banks with the same bank as the drawer of the cheque, a transfer in the banker's books settles the account with one payment of money. If paid by the receiver into another bank, the cheque will not be presented for payment, but liquidated by being set off against other cheques. In the issue of bank notes, the usual reserve of one-third of the issue must be retained by the bank in money in order to preserve their convertibility; the remainder of the bank's deposits are available for productive employment. In the case of both bank notes and cheques, the purchasing power of the receiver by means of his own credit remains unimpaired.

Credit, like money, tells upon prices not simply in proportion to its amount, but to its amount multiplied by the number of times it changes hands. The influence of credit on prices depends upon whether it is a substitute for money, and causes a corresponding amount of metallic money to go out of circulation, or whether it is merely an addition to the metallic circulation. In the former case, no influence on prices will be exercised, in the latter they will rise. Bank notes promise immediate payment, bills of exchange a deferred one, and will not be accepted but by persons sure of the drawer and acceptor's ability to pay. Bank notes, therefore, are more easily circulated, and so exercise a greater effect on prices. Speculative purchases are, however, usually made on book credits, an increased capital being only required when, after the expiration of the period of credit, prices, owing to unforseen circumstances, fall; it is then that advances from bankers are applied for in order to hold out without selling when the high price calculated on has not arisen. The proportion of bank notes to bills of exchange is only 4 to 10, so it need not be feared that an unlimited resort to bank notes will heighten the speculative rise in prices, and, as cheques have an influence on prices equal to that of bank notes, the effect of a limitation of bank notes in lessening the fluctuations of prices cannot be of much importance. Bank of England notes are only legal tender from individuals, not from the bank, and the notes of private banks only with the consent of the receiver; they are therefore not money. Bank of England notes close transactions as regards the buyer; but, as regards the seller, since they depend for their value upon the solvency of a corporation, they cannot be considered money as opposed to credit. Bank notes are "coined credit," other credit is "credit in ingots." This means that bank notes are like coins in being universally received; other forms of credit are like uncoined masses of the precious metals, which are only received as money under certain special circumstances.

It is thought that as bills, cheques, and book credits are liquidated in money or notes, that notes are the basis on which all other forms of credit rest, and that they can be regulated by regulating the issue of bank notes. The willingness to give credit depends upon the lender's opinion of the solvency of the borrower, and of his own chance of obtaining the requisite accommodation in the loan market in the case of necessity. Credit will only be used when an alteration in the price of the commodity is expected, and when the borrower thinks that he will realise the profit he hopes before the time of payment comes. Whether this expectation will be realised or not, depends upon prices, not specially upon the amount of bank notes.

The most important influence of credit on prices depends upon the influence it exercises in increasing the purchasing power of a country. It allows commodities to be bought on speculation, and so causes great variations in their prices, owing to fluctuations in the demand for and supply of these commodities. Credit only increases the purchasing power of a country when it is added to the metallic currency, and does not cause a corresponding amount of it to cease to circulate. When it causes a corresponding amount of metallic money to go out of circulation, it acts merely as a cheap substitute for money, allowing the stock of metallic money to be devoted to productive employment. Its use in this case has been compared to the discovery of a way through the air, allowing the portion of the earth occupied by the roads to be brought under cultivation.

An inconvertible paper currency derives its value solely from convention; its value depends upon its quantity, and, like that, is arbitrary.

If a paper currency be issued to the amount of half an entirely metallic circulation, prices will rise, especially of things made of gold and silver, and an ounce of manufactured gold will become more valuable than an ounce of gold coin by more than the value of the workmanship. It will be thus profitable to melt down the gold currency for manufacturing purposes till as much has been taken from the currency as has been added to it by the paper issue. If this be repeated often enough, all the coin will be driven from circulation, leaving only enough for small coins, unless paper be issued of a denomination as low as that of the lowest coins. Gresham's law that bad money drives out good is only true, if the body of money composed of both heavy and light coins is in excess of the needs of the community and of the money work to be done.

The addition made to the gold and silver available for manufacture will reduce the value of articles made of the precious metals, and, though paper has been issued to the amount of the original metallic circulation, enough coin will remain in circulation with it as will keep down the value of the money to the reduced value of the metallic material. As the value of the precious metals will thus fall below the cost of production, a contraction of production will allow this surplus, added to the stock of the precious metals, to be consumed by natural shrinkage, and then the value of the precious metals and the currency will return to its former level, and prices will be as before, as the paper issue has not been added to but substituted for the metallic circulation. If the currency be convertible and more be issued than the amount of the original metallic circulation, general prices will rise, including that of gold and silver articles. Coin will be sought to be converted into bullion, because it is worth more in that form; there is no coin in circulation, but it may be had in exchange for notes; for this reason, enough paper will not be kept in circulation, over and above the amount equivalent to the original metallic circulation, to sink its value below that of the metal it represents.

If the paper currency be inconvertible and be made a legal tender, it will not affect prices, unless its amount be unduly increased beyond what can with certainty be redeemed. Any increase of the paper currency above this amount lowers its value and raises prices. It is only when paper is exchangeable at pleasure for its value in the precious metals that paper and metallic prices must correspond. The American issue of greenbacks at first only corresponded to the increased amount of money payments necessitated by the War of Secession, in 1869 they were depreciated 32 per cent. in value, and in 1876

12 per cent. When the mint price of an ounce of gold, coinable into £3, 17s. 10½d., is more than this in paper money, the difference is the measure of the depreciation of the currency, so the evils of an inconvertible paper currency might be avoided by contracting the issue, when this took place, till the market and mint prices of an ounce of gold corresponded.

Lord King thus states his law :—A rise of the paper or market price of bullion above the mint price, and a fall of the foreign exchanges below the limits of the real exchange, is the proof and measure of the depreciation of paper money.

In an inconvertible paper currency regulated by the price of bullion, no reserve of the precious metals is necessary, but Government, unless their honesty is doubted, need never keep so large a reserve as private issuers, and there is a danger of fraudulently tampering with the price of bullion for the purpose of acting upon the currency, as fictitious sales of corn were made during the Corn Laws for the sake of influencing the averages. The following fallacies are involved in an unlimited issue of inconvertible paper :—

1. That no paper currency can be issued in excess so long as every note represents property or has an actual foundation of property to rest on ; that the issuers of the notes must have property of their own or others intrusted to them, which, though it cannot be claimed in exchange for the notes, acts as a guarantee of the final reimbursement of the holders. If the notes are issued on the security of some valuable thing expressly pledged for their redemption, there is security that they will be redeemed in cash immediately or in the future. But they may be depreciated from excess of issue, as were the French assignats, issued on the security of the land of the crown nobles and Church ; this security failed from its slowness of negotiation. The value of the land in coin should have been fixed and assignats issued up to but not beyond this amount, and all holders of assignats should have been allowed to demand any piece of land on payment of assignats to the amount of its registered valuation. Assignats would thus have retained their purchasing power in land and would have been exchanged for it, before they were much depreciated with reference to other things. A paper currency convertible into land is disadvantageous compared with one

convertible into coin on account of the greater variability of land in value.

The scheme that Government should receive in pledge or mortgage any kind or amount of property, land, or stock, and should advance to the owners convertible paper money to the estimated value, would have none of the advantage of the assignats, since the receivers of this paper money could not demand from Government property which was only pledged. Law's Scotch Land Bank of 1705 failed for this reason.

2. That the increase of the currency quickens industry, for the consequent rise in prices stimulates every producer to his utmost exertions and brings all capital and labour into full employment. They are thus stimulated by the expectation of getting more real wealth in exchange for their labour, and if all prices rise equally this hope is disappointed.

Speculators in time of high prices hope to get rich because the high prices will not last, and whoever realises whilst the high prices last, after the recoil will find themselves in possession of more pounds sterling without their having become of less value. Hume thought that all prices would not rise simultaneously, and that some persons would obtain a real gain by obtaining a higher price for their own goods, whilst the price of what they want to buy has not risen. In this case one man's profit is another's loss, and the seller of the commodity the price of which rises most slowly can raise it.

If notes are added to the currency instead of being substituted for the metallic part of it, and thus saving the community the cost of the precious metals, the holders of the currency lose by depreciation of its value what the issuers gain, and those under pecuniary obligations profit, but the outrage to integrity and good faith outweighs the benefit to the productive classes by the increase of the circulating medium. On the resumption of cash payments after the period 1797–1819, in which the Bank of England was exempted from giving cash for its notes, which were thus inconvertible, it was contended that it was unjust to the tax-payers to pay interest on the same nominal sums in a currency of full value which were borrowed in a depreciated one. To the holders of the National Debt before 1797 an injustice was done in paying them interest for twenty-two years in a depreciated currency, and to the holders of the National Debt contracted in the earlier period an injustice was done in paying them interest in a currency more depreciated than that in which they had lent. If cash payments had been resumed at a lower rate than at par, an injury would have been done to the two former classes to avoid benefiting those who had lent at the time of the greatest depreciation. The Government had bound themselves to resume cash payments within six months after the peace, which they did not do; this was an additional argument against paying interest on the debt in cash at any less rate than at par.

CHAPTER VII.

LEGISLATION RESPECTING THE CURRENCY.

THE theory of Sir Robert Peel's Act of 1844, for limitation of the issue of bank notes by the Bank of England, is based upon the belief that an unlimited issue of notes raises prices and encourages speculation. Mr Tooke and Mr Fullarton consider that the bank issues, since they cannot be increased in amount without, and till after, an increase of business, cannot raise prices, and any increase of issues in a quiescent market comes back to the bank or remains unemployed in the purchase of commodities. The increase of the circulating medium is *not* the cause but the effect of the rise in prices. In times of speculation, purchases are chiefly made by cheques or bank credits, and if they were made by notes, these notes, after being so used, and not being wanted for current transactions, would be returned into deposit with the banks by the receivers.

The influence of bank notes in raising prices in times of speculation is greatly lessened by their issue being forbidden when less than £5 in value, as then they cannot be used in payment of wages.

After the market has begun to fall, advances are sought from the bank, in the form of notes, to save speculators from the necessity of realising, and to enable them to meet their existing engagements.

At this period in a commercial crisis, the issue of bank

notes is ordinarily increased, speculative prices are thus enabled to continue, and the drain of the precious metals, because the high price in England makes it too expensive to export goods to pay for the excess of imports over exports, is prolonged. This drain can only be stopped by fall of prices or the increase of the rate of interest and the consequent fall in the price of securities. The fall in the price of securities and rise in the rate of interest acts by persuading foreigners to leave the gold due to them in the country on account of the high rate of interest, and even to send more into the country. Whilst it continues, the banks become afraid of not being able to redeem their notes, and so contract their credit more suddenly and severely than they would otherwise have had to do had they not assisted speculators by notes to save them from having to realise. It is this assistance to speculation by means of bank notes which is limited by the Act.

The Act does not maintain the convertibility of the bank note; as the bank publishes its account weekly, it cannot force into circulation an undue amount of notes, for if there was any doubt of its solvency, these notes would be returned to the bank for conversion into gold.

The Act provides that the bank issues must not be more than fourteen million pounds (this limit has been subsequently extended to fifteen million pounds), except in exchange for gold laid up with the bank, or, unless superseding two-thirds of the issue of a country bank. The Act thus prevents the bank from making increased loans with its issues, though it leaves untouched its power of making these advances by opening a credit to a speculator from its deposits and allowing cheques to be drawn against this credit.

The object of the Act might have been attained by raising the rate of discount as rapidly as bullion flowed out of the country, and advances might have been allowed when the flow of bullion stopped.

The raising of the bank rate of discount—

1. Makes the taking of the bank's gold more difficult, by increasing price to the purchaser abroad, and so checks diminution of reserve.

2. Foreigners are induced to import gold to gain the higher rate of interest.

This replenishes the reserve, and, by acting on the exchanges, checks the demand for gold.

Objections :—

1. It prevents advances by the bank till after the arrival of the foreign gold. After the collapse, advances by the bank to solvent trade are not added to the ordinary floating credit, but only serve to replace a mass of credit which has been destroyed by failures. These notes do not circulate or affect the market for commodities, but are returned as deposits to the bank or kept in reserve.

Gold is drawn into the country by the contraction of credit and fall of prices, but the Act prevents the bank-note currency from enlarging itself till the gold has actually arrived.

2. In every case of an efflux of gold, the Act provides that it should be followed by a diminution in the issue of bank notes.

Such effluxes have occurred through—

A. Expenditure by Government for subsidies during the war with France and during the Russian war.

B. Exportation of capital for investment abroad.

C. Failure of crops of raw produce and consequent purchase of supplies at advanced prices.

D. Purchase of corn for importation on a bad harvest in England.

It is inferred that these payments must necessarily have been drawn from the circulation, whereas they are generally made from hoards kept in the form of bankers' reserves.

It is only fair to assume that gold is withdrawn from the currency when the drain is the last stage of a series of effects arising from an increase in the currency, or from an extension of credit tantamount in its effect on prices to such an increase.

In such a case the drain, being unlimited, will continue as long as currency and credit are undiminished. The hoards have to play a double part.

A. To supply the bullion demand for exportation.

B. To keep the home circulation up to its legitimate complement.

In England the hoards are represented by the Bank of England, and the currency doctrine requires that all those drains of metals which, if the currency were purely metallic, would be taken from hoards, should be allowed to operate on the bank, without diminution of currency or contraction of credit, with the only limit that they must not be so great as to exhaust the reserve of seven, ten, or twelve millions, and so threaten a stoppage of payments. The Act prevents the habitual reserve, never employed in being paid out in loans against deposits, but kept to be exchanged for bank notes or cheques, from sufficing for a crisis, by forcing a curtailment of the advances of the bank on the first appearance of a drain for exportation, whatever its cause, and whether, under a metallic currency, it involved a contraction of credit or not. The pressure on the market is rendered severer when the reserve is not sufficient to meet the foreign payments, and when measures are taken to meet them from the loanable capital of the country, because of the separation of the banking and issue departments. When three millions of notes are withdrawn from the banking and exchanged at the issue department against gold for exportation, the deposits in the banking department are three millions less, and the reserve of the issue department has also lost three millions.

The issue department has to protect itself by not re-issuing three millions of notes, and the banking department can safely reduce its reserve one million, as its liabilities have been lessened, but it has to allow two millions of its advances to run out and not renew them, in order to bring up its reserve to the required correspondence with its liabilities. Thus, whatever rise in the rate of interest and pressure on the money market was necessary on a drain of six millions is now necessary on a drain of three, for under the old system the bank would simply have transferred two millions in gold for notes from the issue to the banking department to protect it against unexpected demands by depositors. Unless the drain continued and seemed likely to exceed the reserve of gold in both departments, the bank would not have been obliged to refuse its customary advances to the public at a rate of interest corresponding to the increased demand.

It may be said that if a limitation of issues were not resorted to to check the drain at its commencement, it must take place afterwards, so that, by acting on prices to obtain gold, it may replenish the bank reserves. Gold may, however, be brought back by a rise in the rate of interest and fall of the price of securities. English securities might be bought by foreigners, or foreign securities, held in England, sent abroad for sale; thus the gold would be provided by contraction of loans. Or it may be provided by increased payments for English goods out of the increased gains of foreign dealers in England, or from the gold-producing countries, and the rest, without much rise of interest in England by the fall of it in foreign countries, owing to additions made to their loanable capital through the gains made in England.

Owing to the Act, the measures of the bank on a drain are governed entirely by the amount of gold in the banking department.

3. Depositors may withdraw all their deposits by cheques from the banking department without any contraction of the circulation, and therefore without any effect being produced on prices or the foreign exchanges by means of which the drain could be checked.

The question, whether the privilege of issuing bank notes should be confined to the Bank of England, depends upon whether the issue is to be a matter of fixed rule; if so, the valuable advantage should be secured for Government, and treasury notes, exchangeable for gold on demand, should be issued up to the minimum of a bank-note currency, the rest of the notes required being issued by one or more private banks. If the variation in the amount of issue be left to the discretion of issuers, it may be entrusted to the Bank of England on condition of lending fifteen to twenty millions of notes to Government without interest.

The objection to a plurality of issuers, that their mutual competition would lead to an injurious increase of notes, is not of importance, as the aggregate bank-note circulation has lately decreased. But whilst the bank is compelled to give gold in exchange for its notes, and is responsible for maintaining a sufficient reserve, the responsibility for the convertibility of bank-notes is preserved in full force by being concentrated on one establishment, and the other banks are relieved from the necessity of keeping part of their capital idle as reserve, by being allowed to pay in Bank of England notes. The present arrangement is therefore preferable.

In 1826 Parliament abolished all English and Irish notes below five pounds, as these were chiefly used in payment of wages, and therefore contributed to maintain speculation. The insecurity of banking was owing to the law forbidding all joint-stock banks with more than six partners. In 1826 this restriction was removed except within sixty-five miles of London, and in 1833 abolished altogether. Up to 1855 no joint-stock companies, including banks, could constitute themselves legally on the principle of limited liability without an act of Parliament or royal charter.

CHAPTER VIII.

ON THE RATE OF INTEREST.

THE permanent rate of interest depends upon the ratio between the loanable capital of the country and the demand for loans.

The loanable capital of a country consists of the deposits in the banks, the capital and credit of the bankers, and the funds of those who live upon the interest of their property.

The rate of interest for which people will invest money in a foreign country is always larger than the rate for which they will consent to invest in their own; this prevents a uniform rate of interest from prevailing in many countries. The rate of interest depends upon the profit to be made; in Australia the farmers obtain a rate of profit of 20 per cent. in agriculture, therefore they can afford to pay a much higher rate of interest than elsewhere.

Cheap food, whether imported or raised at home through agricultural improvements, diminishes cost of labour, and therefore raises profit and with it interest. Increased cheapness conduces to saving by affording consumers a surplus from which they can save consistently, and at the same time maintain, or while maintaining, their present standard of living. Whatever enables people to live equally well on smaller incomes induces them to lay by capital for a smaller rate of profit. The discoveries in the precious metals have increased the supply of loans by their additions to the stock of money seeking for investment, and so lowered the rate of interest. The mutual competition of banks, whose funds are constantly seeking for investment, is the chief cause of the tendency of the rate of interest in ordinary times to decline.

The following causes have influenced the supply of loans, increasing the means of investment, and so raising the rate of interest:—

1. Legalisation of joint-stock companies, the subscriptions to which are paid from funds formerly available as loans. A class, who were formerly lenders, have become traders on their own account to the extent of their shares in these companies.

2. Increased and increasing willingness to send capital abroad.

3. Government loans for war expenditure and new and attractive means of investment, &c., absorb capital which would otherwise have been thrown on the loan market, and have thus lowered interest.

4. The demand for a legal tender—money to pay debts, which always marks the commencement of a commercial crisis—causes an increase in the rate of interest.

5. Loanable capital is all of it in money; capital destined for production exists in many other forms. An inconvertible paper currency, by increasing the amount of money, depreciates the value of the real capital loanable, which exists only as money, and so raises interest. Estimated in capital, the amount offered is less, owing to the depreciation of its value, whilst the quantity required is the same as before. Estimated in currency, the amount offered is only the same as before, whilst the amount required, owing to the rise in prices, is greater. If a depreciated paper currency be called in or lessened in quantity, specie will rise in value, the amount of real capital seeking investment will be increased, and interest lowered.

A greater or smaller amount of money does not affect interest, but only a change from a greater to a smaller amount, and *vice versâ*.

6. The paper currency of England, being issued as loans by bankers, swells the aggregate loan market, and, considered as

an addition to loans, it tends to lower interest more than in its character of depreciation of the currency it tends to raise it. The lowering of interest depends upon the ratio of the paper money to the other money in the loan market, the depreciation on its ratio to all the money in existence.

7. A large payment for imports of food or for raw produce, by abstracting capital from a country, raises interest.

The public funds and shares in joint companies vary in price in inverse proportion to the rate of interest, being sold at a price which gives the market rate of interest of the purchase money in the income afforded. When the rate of interest is low, the price of the funds will be high and *vice versâ*. The rate of interest regulates the number of years' purchase for which land will exchange. Suppose land to return the same rate of interest as the funds (3 per cent.), an estate worth £3000 a year will sell for £100,000. If the rate of interest rose to 5 per cent., the estate, if still worth £3000, would only sell for £60,000 (the sum on which the annual income of £3000 is 5 per cent.). The temporary variations in the rate of interest are determined by alterations in the demand and supply of capital offered for loans in the form of money. A rise in the rate of discount is caused by an increased demand for ready money which usually follows a contraction of credit.

CHAPTER IX.

INTERNATIONAL TRADE.

INTERNATIONAL trade exerts an influence which cheapens the cost of production, and enables the productive forces of the world to be employed to the best effects. The greatest advantage consists in the division of labour, each nation applying itself to the production of that commodity for which it has the greatest natural advantage. The law of exchange depends upon relative difference in the cost of production. It does not, however, always hold good owing to the expense of removing capital to where it might be employed at a greater profit, and because countries are sometimes content to forego the advantage they possess, for the sake of exclusively producing that in which they have the greatest advantage.

If the cloth produced with 100 days' labour in Poland cost 150 days' labour in England, and the wheat produced with 150 days' labour in Poland cost 200 days' labour in England, England might advantageously import wheat and pay for it in cloth, as England would gain the difference between 200 and 150 days in buying wheat. If England abandoned some of this advantage in order to benefit Poland, the wheat produced by 100 days' labour in Poland must exchange for more cloth than Poland could produce by 150 days. England will be benefited if she obtain the corn, on which she would have to expend 200 days' labour, at any cost less than the value of 200 days' labour, but more than the value of 150 days.

It is a mistake to treat the export trade as more important than the import. The benefit of the former lies in giving the importing country commodities which it could not have produced at all, owing to physical condition, or, if it could, only at a much greater cost of production.

The export trade is an outlet for the surplus produce of the country, but the country produces this surplus as the cheapest means of paying for the imports. If the foreign trade were stopped, producers of exports would devote themselves to the production of some of the things imported to pay for them, and the consumers of imports would suffer in having to pay higher prices, caused by increased cost of production. Every country which produces for other countries besides itself can introduce more machinery, and carry division of labour further, and has more chance of making improvements in production than it otherwise could. It is helped in raising itself from barbarism by commercial intercourse with other nations. London is the banking centre of the world. Mr Goschen, in his *Theory of the Foreign Exchanges*, accounts for this by pointing to "the stupendous and never-ceasing exports of England, which have for effect that every country in the world, being in constant receipt of English manufactures, is under the necessity of making remittances to pay for them in bullion, produce, or in bills."

Besides this civilising tendency, the spread of trade is a guarantee of the peace of the world.

According to Mill, commodities produced at the same place, or at places sufficiently near for capital to move freely between them, exchange together at a value equivalent to the cost of production, but the value of an imported commodity depends upon the cost of production of the thing exported to pay for it and upon the demand for this export in the foreign country.

If England imports wine from Spain, giving for every pipe of wine a bale of cloth, the exchange value of the wine in England will depend upon the cost of production of the cloth in England. If the cloth cost twenty days' labour in England, the wine, even if it only cost the equivalent of ten days in Spain, it will exchange in England for the equivalent of twenty days' labour plus the cost of carriage to England. If a ton of iron be worth in England ten sacks of wheat and in France twenty sacks, and if England import wheat and export iron at the price of a ton of iron to fifteen sacks of wheat, she will make a profit of five sacks, and France will get a ton of iron at the price of five sacks of wheat less than before. A relative difference in the value of the commodities traded in is all that is required, it is not necessary that the first commodity should be dearer in the one country than in the other and the second cheaper. If the cost price of a ton of iron be £30 in France and of a sack of wheat 30s., a ton of iron will buy twenty sacks of wheat in France. The ton of iron in England is worth £10, the sack of wheat £1. Both iron and wheat are dearer in France than in England, but iron is three times as dear and wheat only one and a half times, so it will be profitable to France to export wheat. When two countries trade together in two commodities, the exchange value of these commodities relatively to each other will depend upon the supply of and demand for each commodity in the country which imports it, and will be such that the quantity required by each country of the commodity imported will exactly pay for the quantity of the commodity exported to pay for it.

The profit of the trade is shared in the inverse ratio of the demand which one country has for the commodity it exports from the other. If England is willing to send to France, upon the terms of fifteen sacks to a ton of iron, more iron than France requires, these terms will become less favourable, as iron must become cheaper to equalise the supply to the demand. The price of iron estimated in French wheat will decline, and a ton of it will only be worth fourteen sacks of wheat. The English iron merchant's profit will be diminished and he will export less, whilst the demand for iron in France will be greater, on account of its increased cheapness. If the supply be not equalised to the demand by these influences, the number of sacks of wheat to be given for the ton of iron will still further decrease, and the share of profit from the trade gained by France will proportionally increase.

The limits within which the variations in value are confined are the two extremes of the ratio of the respective costs of production in the two countries: a ton of iron cannot exchange in either country for more than twenty or less than ten sacks of wheat.

If an improvement took place in the production of iron in England, by which the same labour and capital produced $1\frac{1}{2}$ ton which formerly produced 1 ton, iron would fall 50 per cent. in the English market in relation to English commodities, including imported wheat. Fourteen sacks of wheat, which formerly exchanged for 1 ton of iron, would now exchange for $1\frac{1}{2}$ ton. If the French demand was increased in proportion to the cheapness, France would take 50 per cent. more iron than before, and if England would take an undiminished amount of wheat, which would cost her no more than before, as $1\frac{1}{2}$ ton of iron is now of the same value as 1 ton, France would obtain iron 50 per cent. cheaper, and would gain the same advantage as was obtained by England.

If the demand for iron in France were to increase in a greater ratio than the cheapness, then France must offer wheat on cheaper terms by being willing to take less than $1\frac{1}{2}$ ton of iron in exchange for fourteen sacks of wheat.

If the French demand increase in a less proportion than the cheapness, England will have to offer more than $1\frac{1}{2}$ ton in exchange for fourteen sacks of wheat, and iron will become actually cheaper in France than in England.

If the commodity be one generally desired, such as coffee, sugar, wine, and its fall in price allow people with much smaller incomes to buy it than before, it may happen that the demand may be increased in a greater ratio than the cheapness. Generally, if a commodity fall in price, a greater quantity will be consumed but a less value.

If cost of carriage did not exist, a country would produce for other markets just as much as for its own. On account of the cost of carriage, each produces bulky articles for itself. The cost of carriage swallows up the difference in the cost of production of the coarser kinds of food and manufacture. The proportion of the cost of carriage which will be borne by each country depends upon the amount to which the demand for imported commodities is diminished thereby.

If the cost of carriage of iron from England to France be £1 a ton, and that of a sack of wheat from France to England be 2s., then the price of iron in France will be £16 and of a sack of wheat in England 22s. If the rise in price of iron diminish the demand for iron by one-tenth, English iron merchants may have to submit to a reduction in price of 5s. a ton, and France will bear 75 per cent. of the cost of carriage. The price of iron in England will be £14. 15s., and in France it will be the same, plus £1 cost of carriage = £15. 15s. If the cost of carriage raise the price of French wheat in England to 22s., and so cause the demand to fall off one-fifth, French wheat merchants will have to allow a reduction of 1s. in the price. Thus England will pay 50 per cent. of the cost of carriage. The French wheat merchants will receive only 19s. per sack, that is 21s. the price in England less 2s. deducted for cost of carriage. The difference in the price of any commodity in two countries enjoying Free Trade together, cannot be more than the cost of carriage between them.

If two countries trade together in several commodities, it may often happen that one country will not take enough of one export of another country at a certain price to pay for the quantity of its own commodities that the other country desires to import, but will receive some other exports of the first country to make up the desired amount. The produce of fifty days' English labour in coal, cloth, and cotton, exchanges for the produce of same number of days of French labour in wheat, wine, and silk, according to the equation of the international demand, on the basis of all the English exports collectively paying for all her imports. That country can sell its exports at the dearest price, for the exports of which there is in foreign countries the greatest demand and one most susceptible of growth from increased cheapness, and which possesses the least amount of capital that can be set free from the production of commodities for home consumption, for the purpose of producing exports.

A country gets its own imports the cheaper, the greater the efficiency of its own labour (thus reducing the cost of producing exports), and the less the extent and intensity of its own demand for them. If England sends iron to France at the rate of 1 ton to fifteen sacks of wheat, and if Belgium enters the trade, it must give France a ton of iron for every fifteen sacks of wheat, as England does. If the ton of iron is produced with only half as much labour in England than in Belgium, the wheat of France will cost England only half as much labour as it costs Belgium.

The cost to England of the commodities it imports is a function of two variables :—

1. The quantity of her exports which she gives for them.
2. The cost of these exports to her.

If England trade with France in cotton, and Belgium trade with France in iron, the comparative demand in France for cotton and iron would determine the comparative cost in labour and capital with which England and Belgium would obtain French products. If iron were more in demand in France than cotton, Belgium would recover, through France, part of her disadvantage in iron as compared with England; if it were less in demand than cotton, her disadvantage would be increased.

If more than two countries trade together, the produce of each of them will exchange for the produce of the others at such values that the whole of her exports will pay for the whole of the imports from all the other countries. England and France trade together at the rate of 1 ton of iron to fourteen sacks of wheat. If Russia enter the trade and England could obtain from her wheat at fifteen sacks for the ton of iron, England would not continue to trade with France at fourteen sacks for the ton of iron, but France would be undersold and have to give fifteen sacks. If the trade with Russia were on less favourable terms, and even if England had to accept from it fourteen sacks of wheat to the ton of iron as she did from France, yet there would be two markets instead of one for English produce, and the two countries together would require more English produce than either of them singly, and so would have to force a market in England by offering their exports at a cheaper price. Even if Russia exported nothing to England in exchange for English produce, she might pay for what she imports from England by orders on French purchasers of Russian goods. French goods have thus to pay both for their own and for the Russian imports from England, and this can only be done after bringing about an increased demand for them in England by reducing their price.

An increase of demand for a country's exports in any foreign country enables that country to obtain more cheaply even those imports it procures from elsewhere. An increase of her own demand for any foreign commodity tends to compel her to buy all her imports at a dearer price. The price of the imported commodity is generally lowered in the importing country, and consumers of the imported commodity enjoy the benefit of the cheapening of the cost of production brought about by foreign commerce. Before the trade began, a ton of iron was worth twenty sacks of wheat in France and only ten in England. The price of the iron in France would be £20 and of wheat £1 a sack, and in England iron would be £15 a ton and wheat 30s. a sack. After the trade is started, a ton of iron in France will only be worth fifteen sacks of wheat, the price for which England will sell a ton of iron. Ten sacks of wheat in England will no longer be worth a ton of iron in England, as fifteen can be obtained in France. If wheat continue to be £1 a sack in France, a ton of iron will only sell for £15, a reduction of 25 per cent. in price. If the price of iron continue to be £10 a ton, fifteen sacks of wheat will only sell for £10; the price of wheat will thus be reduced to 13s. 4d. a sack, a reduction in price of 33 per cent. The price of the imported commodity is thus lowered in the importing country.

The price of iron in France will remain at £15 a ton and that of wheat in England at 13s. 4d. a sack, only if the price of iron in England and the price of wheat in France remain unaffected by the international trade; but this is not the case. England requires 500,000 tons of iron for her own use, and by diverting capital and labour from the production of wheat to that of iron she produces an additional amount of 100,000 tons for export to France. France, on the other hand, by diverting capital and labour from producing iron, can produce 1,500,000 additional sacks of wheat to be exported to England. If the iron exactly satisfied the French demand, it would naturally exchange for the 1,500,000 additional sacks of wheat which France could produce. If it more than satisfied the demand, less wheat would have to be taken in exchange up to the limit of 1,000,000, for England can produce wheat for herself at the price of ten sacks of wheat to the ton of iron. The additional 100,000 tons will have to be produced at a greater cost of production, as less productive veins of iron ore will have to be worked than were required before, and the rise of price which results from this will extend to the whole supply, therefore the price of iron in England may rise from £10 to £12 a ton. The effect of this is that, though England still obtains fifteen sacks of wheat for a ton of iron, yet, as this ton of iron is now worth £12, instead of £10, the fifteen sacks of wheat will also be worth £12, or 16s. instead of 13s. 4d. each.

It is an argument for Protection that the position of the home producer of the imported commodity is injuriously affected by the fall in its price brought about by international trade. Let us consider how the position of the English wheat-grower is affected by the importation of wheat from France.

Before the trade began, England required 6,000,000 sacks of wheat at the price of 30s. a ton, she now imports 1,500,000 sacks from France. The ratio of the price of the ton of iron to the sack of wheat in England is as 15 to 1, so, as its price is £12, the price of the wheat will be 16s. a sack.

We have now to consider how the price of the imported wheat is affected by the amount of wheat which can be grown in England. As England imports 1,500,000 sacks of wheat, she will now only require 4,500,000.

Owing to the falling off of the quantity required of English wheat, its price will fall, but it will not fall to the level of 16s., the import price of French wheat, but will be fixed at some figure midway, standing at the same proportion to the original cost as the quantity imported stands to the quantity now required at home: 1,500,000 sacks is a third of 4,500,000, therefore the original price of 30s. will be diminished by one-third to 20s. On these terms the English ironmaster will at first profit; he only gets £12 in England for the ton of iron, but by sending it to France he will get fifteen sacks of wheat, worth in England £15; he will thus gain an extra profit of £3 a ton. The competition of ironmasters to share in this profit will cause the French market to be over-supplied with iron, and iron will fall in price or exchange for a less quantity of wheat, it may be for only twelve sacks instead of fifteen. If this fall in the price of iron in France cause the quantity exported from England to increase, it might rise to 120,000 tons, but this extra demand in France would influence the price of English iron and it might rise to £13 a ton. If the ton of iron, price £13, be worth twelve sacks of wheat, the price of the wheat per sack would be 21s. 6d.

The effect of the international trade in England has therefore been to lower the price of the imported commodity, wheat, from 30s. to 21s. 6d., and to raise that of the exported commodity, iron, from £10 to £13.

The particular classes most injured by the trade would be the French consumers of wheat, as no amount of cheap iron will compensate for a rise in the price of bread. The English grower of wheat will be injured by the fall in the price of wheat from 30s. to 21s. 6d. a sack, but he will ultimately be compensated by the reduction of rent consequent on the widening of the margin of cultivation when the less fertile lands no longer require to be cultivated. The farmers bound by long leases will suffer till rents can be readjusted, but the interests of a class cannot be weighed against the benefit to the community of cheapening food.

The benefit of reducing the price of wheat may be understood when we consider that home-grown is to imported wheat only as 12 is to 26.

Protectionists see the injury to different classes from international Free Trade, but they do not see the benefit to the community of cheapening the cost of production of the commodities imported. Their policy champions the rights of certain classes as producers against the rights of the whole community as consumers.

The exports of some countries permanently exceed the imports, *e.g.*, in the decade 1876-86, the excess of value of the exports of India over the imports averaged nineteen million pounds; this is because of the home charges of the Indian Government in England, which is defrayed by India by means of a permanent excess of exports over imports. If a country is permanently indebted to another country, its exports to that country will permanently exceed its imports from that country by the amount of the debt. The exports from the United States to England permanently exceed the imports into the United States from England, by the amount due to England for performing the carrying trade of the United States in her ships.

The excess of English imports over her exports in value thus represents the payments due from India and the United States, and the interest of foreign loans raised in England.

The payment due from one country to another is first made in money; this raises prices in the country to which the remittance is made and lowers them in the remitting country. Hence the exports from the remitting to the receiving country are increased and the imports diminished. A payment would be due from the receiving to the remitting country, as the exports from it exceed the imports into it in value, and when this is equal to the tribute, all money payments cease and the payment is made in goods by means of a permanent excess of exports over imports in value. The remitting country, besides losing what it pays, loses something more in having to offer its exports more cheaply in order to bring about an excess of them over imports.

Taxation exercises a powerful influence over international trade. In the event of England taxing exported iron, the effect of the tax would depend upon how the demand in France was influenced by the rise in price.

If the demand fell off so little that, owing to the rise in price, even a greater money value was bought than before, iron will rise in value in France because it does in England, and wheat falls in value in France and also in England. England pays less for imports and has more money to pay, therefore she gains more than the duty. The Government monopoly of opium in India is equivalent to an export tax, and it is paid by foreigners, as it does not cause the demand to fall off.

If, after imposition of the duty, the demand for iron in France be reduced to such an extent that the total money value exported is the same as before, England will gain the duty, which will be paid at the expense of France. If France requires a less pecuniary value than before, English exports will no longer pay for her imports, a balance of payment will be due from England to France, and iron will fall in price and wheat rise, till France will take enough iron to pay for the increased value of exported wheat. The tax is partly paid by English consumers of wheat, who have to pay a higher price for it on account of the tax on our exported iron, and, from the efflux of money and the fall of prices, have smaller money incomes to pay for wheat at the higher price.

If the demand for iron in France falls off so much that she imports a smaller money value than before, and the value of the wheat exported to England is undiminished, a balance of payment is due from England to France, and the price of wheat rises in France and also in England. The higher the price of wheat, the greater will be the money value of the wheat exported to England, and the greater the balance of payment. The price of iron may fall more than the total amount of the duty, in order to induce France to take a sufficient amount of iron to pay for the increased value of the wheat.

If we tax imported wheat, it will diminish the quantity bought, a balance of payment will be due from France to England to pay for the excess of value of its imported iron over the exported wheat. This is paid by the foreign consumers of exported commodities, not by the persons from whom we buy our wheat.

Taxes on imports are open to retaliation, by means of taxes on our commodities which foreign countries import.

Taxes on imports only fall on the foreign producer—

1. In the case of a tax laid upon the subject of monopoly. The price cannot be raised higher in proportion to the tax, as it is already as high as it can be. The tax must therefore be paid out of the producer's profits.

2. If a duty on the produce of lands or mines be so high as to cause abandonment of some of the least productive, prices will fall to purchasers, both in the country itself and those who deal with it, and the profits of the producers would be reduced.

Underselling depends—

1. On the underselling country having a greater advantage than the undersold in the production of the article exported by both.

2. On the underselling country being able to give away to the customer more than the whole advantage in production possessed by the country undersold.

3. On the extent to which one country trades with borrowed capital more than another. The trader with his own capital requires the current rate of profit on the whole sum he invests; the trader with borrowed capital is content with the ordinary rate of interest on it, which is often less than the ordinary rate of profit, therefore he can sell his goods at a cheaper price.

The loss suffered by a country on being undersold and so deprived of a market, or compelled to carry on traffic at a reduced rate of profit, falls chiefly on the consumers of imports, who, with money incomes reduced in amount by the falling off of the market for exports, have to pay the same or even a higher price for all articles produced abroad.

The higher wages of English as compared with Continental workmen do not affect underselling, as the Continental workmen do less work. In America, though the wages are higher, the efficiency of labour is so great that the real cost of labour is less than in Europe, and commodities can be sold very cheaply at a high rate of profit.

In America, where the general rate of wages is so high, slave-grown produce can be sold cheaper than it would otherwise be, as there is nothing to pay as wages. So, too, the manufactures of Zurich, which are carried on only in the intervals of agriculture, and on which the workers do not depend entirely for their living, can be disposed of at an unusually low price.

General low wages do not produce low prices in a country, or allow its exports to be sold cheaper, they produce a high rate of profit and so allow a country to resist being undersold for a longer time than under other circumstances, as it can submit to its rate of profit being diminished without being driven out of the trade.

Those articles will be the staple of foreign trade in which the national industry is specially productive. If wages are high, this will indicate high productiveness in commodities with which gold and silver can be cheaply purchased. High wages are therefore not an hindrance to the extension of foreign trade.

CHAPTER X.

THE PRECIOUS METALS AS IMPORTED COMMODITIES.

THE precious metals are imported in bullion as commodities, or sent as money from one country to another for investment, or to pay for goods.

They differ from other commodities in that their total value is often less than their total cost of production.

Australia exports gold to England as one of her staple commodities; this raises prices in England, and the value of gold, estimated in the commodities imported from England, declines, till the increased amount is absorbed on account of its decline in value.

When gold and silver are considered as imported commodities their value is regulated by the cost of production of the commodity exported to pay for it.

Cheap importation of bullion and hence money of low value and high prices depend :—

1. On the exports of the country being much in demand abroad and on their containing high value in small bulk. England obtains bullion comparatively cheaply, because her exports are of a less bulky nature than the raw materials and food stuffs of other countries. The quantity of the exporting country's labour necessarily expended upon producing the exports will depend upon its efficiency.

2. On the importing country having a small demand for foreign imports.

3. On the importing country being near to the countries which produce the precious metals. The cost of carriage is thus saved.

Though England exported nothing to the bullion-producing countries, she can still obtain bullion from them cheaply in payment for her exports to other countries, which pay for these exports in bullion obtained from the countries which produce it. All the exports being exchanged against all the imports, gold and silver are sold at such a rate, and so combined with the other imports, that the sale of exports as a whole pays for them.

On the opening of a new branch of export trade from England, a demand is created for it abroad, and the imports into England, including bullion, no longer pay for the exports. To re-establish the equation of international demand, the commodities imported into England, including bullion, will have to be offered at a cheaper rate, and money will flow into England till prices rise. These high prices in England will cause English exports to fall off, owing to the demand abroad being checked.

If English producers use the greater abundance of money they possess, owing to the high prices prevalent in England, to buy more imports, these will be increased and exports diminished, and so equilibrium will be produced. An extension of the foreign demand for English exports from natural causes, such as the increase of population or the abolition of duties, or a check to the English demand for foreign imports by the imposition of import duties in England or export duties abroad, will also have the effect that English imports no longer pay for her exports. The countries which take English exports must offer their commodities, and among them bullion, at a cheaper rate. Cheap money and a high rate of prices in England will thus result from the above causes also. If a country requires more imports than the exports pay for (unless similar causes to those mentioned in the last chapter as accounting for this excess in the case of England apply), it is a sign that it has more of the precious metals or their substitutes than can permanently circulate, and must part with

K

some of them. The currency is contracted and prices fall, hence there is a greater demand for exports. The drain will last till the fall in the prices of English goods induces foreigners to take a larger pecuniary value, or the increased price of foreign goods, owing to the efflux of the precious metals abroad, makes England take a less pecuniary value.

The cause of bullion being imported is either when the price of goods is so low in England and so high in foreign markets as to tempt foreigners to send to England to buy goods, or when the price of goods is so low in the foreign market and so high in England that nothing but specie can be sent in payment of goods exported from England.

The causes of bullion being exported are:—

(1) That there is some great and pressing demand for some article in this country, and other commodities are so scarce and dear that they cannot be exported with profit to pay for it; or

(2) The article to be imported into England is required in such great quantities that foreigners cannot consume our goods, which we should prefer them to take in payment, fast enough; or

(3) The markets abroad are overstocked with English produce, which are thus depressed below their natural value; or

(4) When the exporting country has a depreciated paper currency; or

(5) In the case of a prohibitive tariff on imports. For this reason England cannot send goods to Russia in payment for her hemp, tallow, and flax.

The English system of bonded warehousing, which allows goods to be stored duty free till they are sold, reduces the necessity of exporting bullion to a minimum.

If the wealth and population of a country increase, prices will decline unless a greater amount of money is brought into circulation, or the substitutes for money are brought into greater use.

If a large increase is suddenly made to the currency, prices rise, exports are discouraged, and imports exceed exports, the exchanges become unfavourable and continue so till the increase in the precious metals has spread itself equally over all commercial countries. If twenty millions of bank notes were sent into circulation in addition to a metallic currency of that amount, and were employed as loans or in the purchase of securities, they would depress the rate of interest and cause the greater part of the twenty millions in gold to be sent abroad for investment. If the twenty millions of bank notes were carried into the market for commodities, prices would rise, exportation diminish, and importation be increased. A great balance of payments would cause the metallic money to spread itself over commercial countries, till only those differences existed in its value which corresponded to permanent differences in the cost of production. These twenty millions of metallic money would be gradually absorbed by diminution in production from the bullion-producing countries, and prices would return to their former level, and the world would gain the benefit of twenty millions being added to its productive capital and being replaced by the cheaper substitute of paper money.

Small disturbances of the equilibrium of imports and exports correct themselves by the premium on bills of exchange. Larger ones require the subtraction of actual money from the currency, or an annihilation of credit equivalent to it.

The rise of prices consequent on the over-issue of an inconvertible paper currency does not stimulate import or discourage export. Imports and exports are regulated by the metallic, not the paper price of commodities. The exchanges are affected. When the exports pay for the imports, the exchange is "at par," and a bill on France for the equivalent of five sovereigns is worth £5. If the currency in England is depreciated, a bill on France for the equivalent of five sovereigns will be worth £6. There is therefore a nominal exchange against the country, the currency of which is depreciated, of as much per cent. as the amount of the depreciation, whatever the amount of the real exchange, which is governed by the variations of international supply and demand, may be.

In times of commercial speculation, prices rise, exportation is checked, and importation stimulated: this necessitates a drain of gold to pay for the excess of imports over exports, and it can only be checked by a fall of prices or a rise in the rate of interest in the country in which the speculation is going on.

Ricardo states the law of the general distribution of the precious metals thus:—" Gold and silver having been chosen for the general medium of circulation, they are, by the competition of commerce, distributed in such proportions among the different countries as to accommodate themselves to the natural traffic which would take place if no such metals existed and the trade between countries were purely a trade of barter."

If the exports from England to France are less than the imports into England from France, the bills in France drawn on England will exceed in value those in England drawn on France. English merchants will compete for bills on France which are said to be at "a premium," and bills on England are at "a discount" in France as they have to be sent to England to be cashed. The exchange is then said to be "unfavourable" to England, or against England and in favour of France. The premium on bills on France cannot exceed the cost of sending bullion from England to France, but at a time of unfavourable exchange it is not always necessary to export bullion, because the fluctuations of commerce are constantly increasing exports or diminishing imports. In time of anticipated scarcity of the precious metals the premium on bills may amount to more than the cost of carriage, as when Napoleon returned from Elba, the premium on bills on foreign countries in England amounted to 10 per cent.

When the exchange is against one country and in favour of the other, the money of the former country will be depreciated when compared to the money of the other.

When the exchange is at par, £1 is equivalent to 25 francs, but if the exchange is against England, and it is desired to change English money for French in London, French money will have to be brought from France for the purpose, and to compensate for this it will exchange for more than its value in English money, and 25 francs will exchange for more than £1. If the exchange is in favour of England, there will be a surplus of French money in England, and it will be at a discount compared with English money.

An unfavourable exchange cannot be of long continuance, as specie cannot long be subtracted from the currency, to pay for an excess of imports over exports, without lowering prices.

This will increase exports, as it will be more profitable to sell commodities abroad than at home. Imports will fall off, as foreigners will not import goods if low prices prevail. When a country's exports exceed its imports, the exchange will again become favourable to it.

BOOK IV.

GENERAL FUNCTIONS OF GOVERNMENT.

CHAPTER I.

GENERAL FUNCTIONS OF GOVERNMENT.

THOSE who wish to restrict the functions of Government within the narrowest possible limits, think that it should confine itself to protecting person and property from force or fraud.

The upholders of the principle of *laissez faire* in politics consider that, within the above limits, the general wellbeing of society is best promoted by allowing free play to personal interests. The functions of Government cannot, however, be thus narrowly confined, as the establishment of laws of inheritance, of laws for the settlement of civil disputes, of registries of legal documents and of births, deaths, and marriages, and the exclusive right of coining, are all duties of Government, which cannot be classed under either of the two above-mentioned heads.

Mill is of opinion that the only general justification for Government interference is to be found in expediency. He points out that there are two kinds of Government interference, authoritative and permissive. The former forbids certain acts, or proscribes a certain way of doing them.

The whole theory of State Socialism is based upon the authoritative interference of the State. The State, or the collective strength of society, is to do for individuals what they are powerless to do for themselves: this is the basis of schemes like old age insurance at the partial cost of the State.

Mr Benjamin Kidd, in his *Social Evolution*, finds in the legislation of the present day, "a tendency to strengthen and equip, *at the general expense,* the lower and weaker against the higher and wealthier classes of the community." The lower classes have already been given equal political rights, it is the object of the new movement to give them *equal social opportunities* for self-elevation and improvement.

Permissive Government interference sets up an agency of its own, to work for objects of public interest, such as an Established Church or a Government medical service, but it does not interfere with the private agency of ministers of religion of other denominations or private doctors in the pursuit of the same objects.

Mill gives the following reasons against the extension of an authoritative Government interference :—

1. That any interference of the Government with the internal or external life of the individual checks the formation of private opinion, and makes individuals slavishly conform to the opinion of the majority. The arbitrary power of public opinion is thus increased, and every tendency to individuality of character checked.

2. Every addition to the functions of Government increases its power both in the direct form of authority and in the indirect form of influence. This power is not that of the nation over itself, but of a mere majority of the nation, and often merely that of the most noisy and obtrusive section of this majority.

3. Every fresh assumption of power by the Government causes it to be more overloaded with duties, which are in consequence badly performed. From neglect of division of labour, the attention of ministers is occupied with trivial details, and they have not sufficient time to attend to really important matters.

4. It is inexpedient that all the business skill and experience, and power of organised action existing in the community should be concentrated in the class of Government officials.

5. Even if the Government could unite in its service all the most eminent talent of the nation, the conduct of a large portion of the affairs of the nation should still be left in the hands of those most nearly interested in them, because the " business of life is an essential part of the practical education of a people."

The doctrine of non-interference on the part of Government, because people are the best judges of their own interests, does not hold good in the case of lunatics or young children. Mill thinks the law with reference to lunatics should be altered.

1. The property of lunatics should not be given over to their heirs during their lifetime, but managed by trustees till their death or recovery.

2. The costs of inquiry into the lunacy of an individual should be borne by the promoter, with the right of being indemnified his costs out of the estate if the lunacy be established.

The freedom of contract of young children insufficiently educated or too weak for long employment should be regulated by Government. Government should not, however, interfere with the employment of women in factories, on the plea that they should have time to devote themselves to their household duties, for, to improve their position, access should be given them to independent industrial employment.

The action of Government is justifiable in the following cases :—

1. The provision of education for the nation, as Government can reasonably claim to possess more mental cultivation than the average of the people. Another reason is the importance of intelligence and the other qualities fostered by education, and the actual injury the citizens of a State suffer from the ignorance of their fellow citizens.

2. In the case of contracts for perpetuity, *e.g.*, marriage, two individuals attempt to decide what will be best for their interests at some future time. Government, in compensation for not allowing the parties to the agreement to annul their contract, should grant them a release from it on due cause shown before a competent tribunal.

3. What can only be done by joint-stock agency, the managers being the delegates of the shareholders, is often as well done by the State. If the State does not take these enterprises under its direct control, as the Prussian State has done the railways, it may at least superintend their management. Railways and waterworks are practical monopolies created by the State, which should only issue the concession for a limited period, and reserve to itself a claim to a right of

property in public works, or else retain the right of regulating the tariff of tolls. It may even be proprietor of an industrial concern without working it, and allow others to rent and work it for limited periods.

4. The State can justifiably interfere to give the force of law to the agreement of workmen not to work for more than eight hours a day. It may also bring about by legislation the Wakefield system of colonisation, which establishes a fund for emigration by the sale of unoccupied lands, and which obliges emigrants to a new colony to serve for some time as hired labourers before they are allowed to settle upon land of their own.

In both these instances, however advantageous the course of action may be, no one will follow it, unless he is sure that everyone else will do so, and the passing of a law on the subject is the best means of certainty on this point.

Colonisation should be carried on at the expense of the colony to which the emigrants are sent. No individual can conduct emigration on a sufficiently large scale or can be sure of recovering the cost; Government alone can do so by taxation of those who are benefited by the imported labour.

5. In the case of the Poor Law, it is best that the State should conduct the business of providing subsistence for the indigent poor, as private charity is apt to do too much or too little. It may leave to private charity the task of discriminating between various cases for relief. The State must act by general rules in this case, and can give no more than subsistence to the deserving poor or less than subsistence to the undeserving.

6. Government should build lighthouses, lay down buoys, and bear the cost of public works and scientific or geographical exploration, in spite of there being no prospect of an immediate return for the money spent. It may also finance scientific research by establishing professorships with duties of instruction attached.

Mill estimates the value of a Government according to
- A. Its system of raising a revenue by taxation.
- B. Its laws on property and contract.
- C. The character of the judicial system it establishes to enforce the jurisdiction of its laws.

CHAPTER II.

GENERAL PRINCIPLES OF TAXATION.

Adam Smith's Canons of Taxation.

1. "The subjects of every State ought to contribute to the support of the Government, as nearly as possible in proportion to their respective abilities; that is, in proportion to the revenue which they respectively enjoy under the protection of the State. In the observation or neglect of this maxim consists what is called equality or inequality of taxation."

2. "The tax which each individual is bound to pay ought to be certain and not arbitrary. The time of payment, the manner of payment, the quantity to be paid ought all to be clear and plain to the contributor and to every other person. Where it is otherwise, every person subject to the tax is put more or less under the power of the tax-gatherer, who can either aggravate the tax upon any obnoxious contributor, or extort, by the terror of such aggravation, some present or perquisite for himself. The uncertainty of taxation encourages the insolence and favours the corruption of a body of men who are naturally unpopular, even when they are neither insolent nor corrupt. The uncertainty of what each individual ought to pay is in taxation a matter of so great importance, that a very considerable degree of inequality, as appears, I believe, from the experience of all nations, is not near so great an evil as a very small degree of uncertainty."

3. "Every tax ought to be levied at the time, or in the manner, in which it is most likely to be convenient for the contributor to pay it. A tax upon the rent of land or of houses, payable at the same term at which such rents are usually paid, is levied at the time when it is most likely to be convenient for the contributor to pay; or when he is most likely to have wherewithal to pay. Taxes upon such consumable goods as are articles of luxury are finally paid by the consumer, and generally in a manner that is very convenient to him. He

pays them little by little as he has occasion to buy the goods. As he is at liberty, too, either to buy or not to buy, as he pleases, it must be his own fault if he ever suffers any considerable inconvenience from such taxes."

4. "Every tax ought to be so contrived as both to take out and to keep out of the pockets of the people as little as possible over and above what it brings into the public treasury of the State. A tax may either take out or keep out of the pockets of the people a great deal more than it brings into the public treasury in four ways:—

(i.) "The levying of it may require a great number of officers, whose salaries may eat up the greater part of the produce, and whose perquisites may impose another additional tax upon the people.

(ii.) "It may divert a portion of the labour and capital of the community from a more to a less productive employment.

(iii.) "By the forfeitures and other penalties which those unfortunate individuals incur who attempt unsuccessfully to evade the tax, it may frequently ruin them, and therefore put an end to the benefit which the community might have derived from the employments of their capitals. An injudicious tax offers a great temptation to smuggling.

(iv.) "By subjecting the people to the frequent and odious examination of the tax-gatherers, it may expose them to much unnecessary trouble, vexation, and oppression."

The restrictions intended to prevent the evasion of a tax often impose insuperable obstacles in the way of making improvements in the process of manufacture.

We have now to consider what is meant by "equality of taxation." Adam Smith gives two equivalent expressions to explain this, but "contributing to a Government in proportion to a person's ability to pay" is not the same thing as "contributing in proportion to the revenue which he enjoys under the protection of the State." Two men may have the same money income, and yet one have much less ability to pay than the other on account of the claims of a large family on his purse. For the same reason, it cannot be maintained that the protection of life should be requited by a poll-tax paid by each person of the community, and that protection to property should be paid for in proportion to property. Large incomes do not always require proportionally more protection than small, and the above principle neglects the fact that an income of a certain amount may have claims upon it which reduce its "ability to pay" much below that of an income of equal nominal amount without incumbrances.

If the protection of Government had to be paid for by a tax in proportion to the benefit derived from it, in order to find out who profit most by this protection, it would have to be considered who would suffer most if it were withdrawn; we should find these to be children and lunatics. To such persons the protection of Government is most indispensable, and according to this theory they should bear the greater part of its cost. The untenability of this theory may thus be regarded as proved.

Equality of taxation Mill explains to mean the demand of equal sacrifices from all, and he inquires whether this is really done if all incomes are taxed at the same percentage. The smaller the income the more heavily any deduction from it by taxation presses upon its possessor, whilst the same proportion taken from a larger income would be hardly felt. This is an argument for a graduated income tax, which taxes incomes over a certain amount at an higher percentage than those below it. A graduated income tax lessens the inequalities of wealth; on this account, some politicians have supported it. Mill disapproves of such a tax, which he regards as a tax upon the industry and economy which have enabled these larger fortunes to be accumulated. All large fortunes, however, that are bequeathed by former possessors should be taxed to the full amount that would not encourage evasion, and inheritance, in the case of collaterals, should cease, the property of all persons dying without direct heirs escheating to the State. The graduated death duties introduced by Sir William Harcourt's Budget in 1894 are in accordance with Mill's views on this subject.

In order to avoid trenching upon a man's ability to provide himself with the necessities of life, the minimum income necessary for this purpose should be exempted from taxation. This is done by the English income tax, which exempts from taxation all incomes under £160, and only levies the tax on incomes up to £400 on the surplus over £160.

If the income tax be permanent, there is no reason, arithmetically speaking, why the holder of a temporary income, such as a salary or professional emoluments, should pay less to the income tax than the possessor of a permanent income from land or the funds. Liability to the tax ceases with the income, whereas the holder of a perpetual income remains liable in perpetuity.

Mill bases the claim of the possessor of the temporary income to a lower rate of assessment, not on his having smaller means, but on his having "greater necessities." He would allow the possessors of temporary incomes to be released from assessment to income tax as regards all their savings, as otherwise a man who saves pays income tax twice over, first on his income, and again on the interest he receives from his savings from his income. This principle is followed in allowing payments for premiums to insurances to be released from assessment to income tax. In the absence of any trustworthy information as to what a man really saves, the possessor of a temporary income should be entitled to deduct one-fourth of his income from the total before assessment to the tax, it being assumed that one-fourth is the amount on the average saved as a provision for heirs and for old age.

In the case of business incomes, part is interest on capital invested in the business and perpetual, and part is the remuneration for superintendence depending on the life of the individual. Therefore, if life incomes are assessed at only three-fourths of their total amounts, business incomes should likewise be so assessed, and should pay on that assessment a lower rate; or the possessors of business incomes may be allowed to deduct one-fourth of the entire amount, interest of capital included.

Fawcett is in favour of an uniform income tax. He points out that, if uniform, it can be easily and cheaply collected, but endless complications would result if it is attempted to adjust it on the plan of capitalising temporary incomes. The principle of equality of taxation can be best maintained by contemplating the revenue as a whole, and placing those, on whom a certain tax presses most heavily, in a more favourable position as regards other taxation, rather than by any attempt to adjust the tax by complicated arrangements

Thus the tea consumed by the working classes is taxed more heavily in proportion than the dearer kinds of tea. There are difficulties in the way of making the tea tax *ad valorem*, but instead of doing this, it is better to exempt the working classes from the income tax.

CHAPTER III.

DIRECT TAXATION.

A DIRECT tax is paid by the person on whom it is levied, an indirect tax is levied from the manufacturer or importer, with the intention that he should recoup himself the amount of the tax he has advanced to Government by raising the price of the commodity to the consumer. Direct taxes are either on income or in expenditure (only in the case of the house, horse, carriage, and servant taxes).

The incidence of the income tax differs according as the income is in the form of rent, profits, or wages. If an income tax be levied on rent, it is paid by the landlord. This is proved by the fact that if the rates on landed property, though nominally paid by the tenant, were not levied, the landlord could exact so much additional rent. The land tax is a rent charge reserved from the beginning by the State; the amount of the land tax has never belonged to the landlords, and its existence cannot be held to exempt the landlords from bearing their fair share of other taxation.

Mill is a champion of the unearned increment theory that the State can justly levy an additional tax upon that portion of the wealth of landlords which has accrued to them without any exertions of their own, by their chancing to possess land which has been built over, or on account of the growth of great towns near their estates. To do this fairly, the landlords should be offered the present market value of their lands, and then the State might declare that, after a certain period, all the addition to rent that had not been brought about by the exertion of the landlords should be specially taxed.

The principle of Betterment declares that if a man's property is improved by any local improvement, such as the opening of a new street, he ought to bear a larger proportional share of the cost than those whose property is unaffected. If this principle be admitted, it entails the necessity of compensation if a man's property suffers any special damage.

A tax on the profits of any particular trade increases the cost of production, and raises prices at the expense of the consumer. A general tax on profits does not admit of compensation in this way, and falls upon the capitalist. A tax on profits anticipates the effect of the accumulation of capital in reducing profits, so that a country will possess at any given period a smaller capital and aggregate production, and will attain the stationary state earlier and with a smaller sum of national wealth than it otherwise would. If the rate of profit were already at the practical minimum, when all the increase of capital which reduces profits is carried off by exportation or speculation, and if then profits were reduced still lower by a tax on profits, a portion of the existing capital would be carried off by these causes, and the labourers would suffer by the diminution of the funds spent in employing them.

A tax on wages is temporarily borne by the labourers themselves, but it will probably check the increase of the labouring population, and then wages will rise again and the expense of the tax will fall on the employer. In new colonies, or in countries like the United States, where wages are kept up by the increase of capital, and do not depend upon the ratio of the number of the labourers to the amount spent in wages, a tax upon wages would probably not check the multiplication of the labouring class, and then must be borne by the labourers themselves.

The objection to the income tax is, that it can be accurately assessed on all whose income is known, and is deducted before payment of the income is made in the case of fund-holders and government officials. Farmers are assessed to the income tax on an income reckoned at half their rent. The income of business men, on the other hand, cannot be accurately known, and there is reason to believe that they escape their fair share of the tax by returning their incomes under the real amount. To this extent, therefore, the tax is unjust to fund-holders and government officials.

The house tax is generally levied for the purposes for which the local taxation rates are provided. It consists of two portions, a ground rent and a building rent; the ground rent varies from an amount equal to the rent of the ground, if used for agricultural purposes, to the monopoly rents paid for advantageous situations in crowded streets. The building rent consists of the ordinary profit on the builder's capital, and an annual amount sufficient, at the ordinary rate of interest, to repair the house and to replace the original capital by the time the house has decayed or the building lease has expired.

A tax upon building rent must fall upon the occupier, as otherwise the builder will not get the ordinary rate of profit for his capital, and houses will not be built. For some time the tax will be borne by the houseowner, as people will not pay their former rent with the tax in addition, and houses will be in excess of the demand. The supply of houses will thus be diminished, and as population increases a greater supply will be required and rents will rise, till it again becomes profitable to build houses, but this will not be done till the tax becomes payable by the occupier.

In the case of ground rents, when the supply of land on which houses can be built is unlimited, a tax on ground rents will fall upon the occupier. The value of land for house building in this case is regulated by supply and demand, and the supply of land is unaffected by the tax. The ground landlord cannot raise the ground rent if the tax is remitted, as the supply of land for building purposes being unlimited, the occupier may remove elsewhere. The occupier alone would profit by the remission of the tax, therefore its incidence is on him.

We will now consider the effect of a tax being laid upon ground rents in exceptionally valuable sites possessing a monopoly value. The value of land for house building ranges from its mere value as agricultural land up to a monopoly value, due to the fact that the supply of valuable sites in crowded streets is limited. The demand for land valuable for its situation depends upon the amount of profit which it is anticipated may be realised from the site, and is not affected by the tax on ground rents. This tax will not increase the cost of erecting the house, but, if it is remitted, the owner of the ground will be able to ask a larger rent. As the supply of sites is limited, those who wish to gain the advantage of building houses on the ground will be obliged to pay the additional rent. As the owner of the ground would thus profit by the remission of the tax, it follows that he practically pays it when it is imposed.

A tax of a certain percentage of the gross rent falls upon ground rent and building rent alike, and will be paid partly by the ground landlord and partly by the occupier, as pointed out above.

Mill considers a tax on houses, if paid by the occupier, and if justly proportioned to the value of the house, the fairest of all taxes, as the character of the house a man lives in is the best criterion of his means, and bears a close proportion to them.

The incidence of the horse, carriage, and servant tax is upon the person who uses them.

CHAPTER IV.

INDIRECT TAXATION.

INDIRECT taxes are paid by the manufacturer, or importer, of the commodity to the Government, but he is repaid the sum he advances by raising the price to the consumer. The advantage of this sort of taxation is, that it is paid by the consumer, little by little, at the time most likely to be convenient to him when he buys the taxed goods; the disadvantage is, that it often raises the price of the commodity to the consumer more than in proportion to the tax imposed. The interference of Government revenue officers in the processes of production, to prevent evasion of the tax, often causes unnecessary expense to producers. Indirect taxation is expensive to collect unless confined to a few articles of general consumption.

Taxes on corn or other necessaries either lower the condition of the labourers, or, if the standard of comfort of the labourers is not lowered, and they diminish their rate of multiplication, wages will rise enough to compensate labourers for the tax at the expense of profits. If the tax is a fixed proportion of the produce, like a tithe, it lowers corn rents, as it takes more corn from the more fertile lands than from the more barren, and so diminishes the difference between the best land and land at the margin of cultivation.

Rent estimated in money will not be lowered, as the corn, with the tithe deducted, will sell for as much as the whole quantity sold for before the tithe was imposed.

If the tax is of long standing, it will check the accumulation of capital, but will produce a similar effect to it in increasing the value and price of food and lowering profits.

If the tithe reduces profit to the practical minimum, it will put a stop to further saving, or cause the capital saved to be invested abroad, and the consumer will have somewhat earlier to pay the higher price which would be naturally brought about by the increase of wealth and population. The minimum of profits will thus be reached with a smaller capital and population and a lower rental than if the tax had not been imposed. Mr Senior compares the effect of a tithe to that of natural barrenness of land. If this barrenness were to come suddenly on the land, it might produce the effect of a tithe, but if it had existed from the beginning, population would not have increased as rapidly, and therefore there would have been no necessity for the price of corn to have risen. If England never had any tax imposed upon agricultural produce, the price of corn would probably have been by this time as high, owing to the increase of wealth and population, and the rate of profits as low, owing to the accumulation of capital. Before the Commutation of Tithes Act, tithe had thus ceased to be a cause of high prices or low profits, but had become a mere deduction from rent, as it deprived the landlord of the rise of rent which he would otherwise have obtained from the increase of population. The effect of the Commutation Act is that tithe is only levied upon such land as pays rent, and does not touch such land as has been freshly brought under cultivation. Therefore the tithe is not included in the cost of production of the produce of the land at the margin of cultivation, which can send its produce to market one-tenth more cheaply than when the tithe was imposed. The Commutation Act has had, therefore, its share in bringing about a fall in the price of corn, the tithe has become a rent charge which is borne by the landlord, and the increased cheapness to the consumer is at his expense. The Act was in another way a direct benefit to the landlords, because the gross 10th of the annual produce of tithcable land was, on an average of the years from 1829 to 1835, £6,756,105. It was commuted for only £4,053,666, so the landholders gained about 40 per cent.

Discriminating taxes are imposed on some particular process of producing a commodity. Mill gives the instance of tax on beetroot sugar, which makes it dearer instead of cheaper than cane sugar. Beetroot sugar is therefore substituted for cane sugar, and Government gains no revenue from the tax, but the consumers have to pay a higher price for the beetroot, which goes to compensate the producers for the misapplication of so much labour.

Customs duties on the produce of land, unless balanced by excise duties of a similar amount on home produce, are unjustifiable.

If a country consumes twenty million quarters of home-grown wheat, and imports one million, and a tax be laid upon this imported one million quarters, it will raise the price not only of the imported wheat but of all the wheat consumed in the country. The tax on imported wheat will go to the Government, but the rise in price of the home-grown wheat is so much additional profit to the landlords in the shape of rent. If the tax stops the importation of wheat and causes all the wheat required in the country to be grown at home, the extra million quarters grown at home will require a rise in price to compensate for bringing inferior lands into cultivation. The rise in price on the extra million quarters goes to compensate the growers, but the rise in price on the rest of the wheat goes as rent to the landlords. In this case, the Government gets no revenue, but the consumers suffer in proportion to the rise in price of the whole supply. Corn laws anticipate the rise in price and of rent which would have been brought about naturally by the increase of population and production.

The difference between a country without corn laws and a country which has long had them, is not that the latter has a higher price or a larger rental, but that it has the same price and the same rental with a smaller aggregate capital and a smaller population. The repeal of the corn laws lowers rents, but it allows the natural increase of capital and population to have increased effect in restoring them to their former level.

CHAPTER V.

MISCELLANEOUS TAXES.

A TAX on all purchases and sales is a tax on commodities, and, if general, does not affect prices; if levied from the sellers, it is a tax on profits, if from the buyers, it is a tax on consumption. A tax on one particular method of sale, such as on sale by auction, checks sale by this method, and it will only be resorted to in case of necessity. If the seller is obliged to sell, but the buyer not obliged to buy, in the case of a tax on sales by auction, the seller will have to be content with what price he can get, and he will therefore pay the tax.

Taxes on contracts are generally imposed by means of stamps, and the Government refuse to enforce the contracts unless they are executed on stamped paper. Taxes on contracts for the sale and purchase of landed property are especially to be deprecated, as they are obstacles to the free transfer of land. Stamp duties on leases and on insurances are economically indefensible, as putting obstacles in the way of transactions which should be encouraged.

A tax on newspapers obstructs the diffusion of knowledge, and a tax upon advertisements prevents business men from having recourse to this method of selling their goods. They are therefore both objectionable. Law taxes, or the exaction of fees to the revenue for the various operations required in a resort to the law-courts, are a tax on redress, and therefore an incitement to injury. Fees of court to pay the expenses of the law-courts cannot be defended by saying that those who profit by the administration of justice should bear the expenses of it. The law does not properly defend people if they have to resort to the law-courts for justice.

Mill suggests the following rules for the taxation of commodities:—

1. Those luxuries should be taxed highest which are used from motives of vanity, such as the most expensive dresses and ornaments.

2. The tax should be levied as far as possible on the consumer and not on the producer, to avoid raising the price more than in proportion to the tax if it is levied on the latter.

3. Taxes on luxuries of general consumption, such as tea, coffee, sugar, tobacco, beer, and spirits, should be arranged so that the poor may not bear more than their proper share. They should be therefore *ad valorem*, that is, the tax on the more expensive kinds of these commodities used by the rich should be increased in proportion to the value.

4. To diminish expense of collection, taxation should be concentrated on a few articles.

5. Stimulants should pay the heaviest tax of all luxuries of general consumption, since there is most danger of their being used in excess, and therefore it is most desirable to put a check to their consumption.

6. Taxation should be as far as possible levied on imported articles, but it must be levied on articles which will not be produced in the country itself. If not, a corresponding excise duty must be levied on the commodity when produced at home, or if an excise duty is not levied, the production of the article at home must be forbidden, as the production of tobacco is forbidden in England.

7. Taxation must never be so high as to encourage evasion or smuggling.

8. Fawcett adds that taxation should be levied on the finished article rather than the raw material. The reason of this is that the manufacturer advances the tax to Government, and therefore requires more capital; he will expect to be recouped this additional capital with the ordinary trade profit on it, and so the price must rise more than it would otherwise have done if no advance of the tax was necessary, and the tax was levied on the finished article.

CHAPTER VI.

GOVERNMENT INTERFERENCE FROM MISTAKEN THEORIES.

Usury laws were passed for two motives:—
1. The protection of the borrower against the lender.
2. A general opinion that it is for the public good that interest should be low.

The effect of usury laws is to make the rate of interest higher to the borrower, as the man who lends him money requires an insurance against the risk of penalties for breach of the law, and the danger of not being repaid his debt, and so demands an exorbitant rate of interest. The other alternative is that the lender will refuse to lend at all, and so necessitous persons are deprived of the accommodation they require.

If Government attempt to fix the price of food it must impose penalties on the producer to make him sell food at the required price, or grant him a bounty, at the expense of the general revenue, to enable him to do so. Government attempted to do this by the Act of 5 and 6 E. vi., cap. 12, against forestallers, engrossers, and regraters. Forestallers were those who bought grain on its way to market, with a view of selling it again at a higher price. Engrossers were those who attempted to control the market by purchasing all that was offered for sale with a similar view. Regraters were those who resold at a higher price goods previously purchased in the same market. This Act was repealed by 12 G. iii., cap. 71. In the time of scarcity, the effect of a rise in price is to reduce consumption; if Government will not allow this, all it can do is to counsel the rich to moderate their consumption. If the rich consume as much as in times of plenty, it is no good giving money to the poor to buy food, as their expenditure will only force up the price the more, to the benefit of the corn dealers.

When Government lays a tax on an imported commodity, and so gives the home producer a monopoly, the dearness which results is a tax levied on the consumer in the interests of the home producer. Thus French silks and ribbons are more liked in England than those of Coventry and Macclesfield, owing to the better taste of their colours and designs; if they were kept out of the English market by a protective duty, the English consumer would have to put up with the inferior article produced at home.

This monopoly produces inefficiency in business; producers follow the accustomed routine instead of introducing improvements in business. This inefficiency prevents anything being done to lower the price of the commodity, and so is an additional burden on the consumer.

The condemnation of monopolies does not extend to patents or the gift to inventors of the exclusive right of using their improvements as a reward for their invention.

Laws against combinations of workmen for raising wages are unjustifiable. These combinations enable workmen to sell their labour to the best advantage, and to inform each other of the state of the trade; they thus prevent strikes when trade is bad, and when it is therefore impossible to raise wages by this means. These combinations must be voluntary, and any compulsion put upon workmen to join them should be severely punished. They are, however, harmful if they try to do away with piecework or to prevent a workman from earning more than a certain sum per week, or to prevent workmen being paid a higher rate of wages in proportion to their skill.

It is prejudicial to industrial development if the Government attempt to enforce conformity to the established religion, or to ensure that no views in politics, morals, or law should be professed by the people except what it approves. This is proved by the industrial decadence of Spain and Portugal for two hundred years after the Reformation.

Protection is an attempt to make industrial correspond to political entities, that nations may be self-supporting, not dependent on outside sources for any portion of their supplies.

In Protectionist countries, such as Victoria, Canada, and the United States, the rights of consumers are neglected, as the general wellbeing of the community is believed to be promoted by a protective tariff.

Fawcett believes Protection to have sprung up in Victoria because the workmen who had emigrated to the gold-fields gave them up when they became less productive than formerly, and wished that the trades at which they had worked in England should be fostered by Protection in the colony.

The Corn Laws, in their extreme form, date from 1815, when all importation of corn was forbidden until home-grown corn was at eighty shillings a quarter.

In 1828 the sliding scale method was introduced, by which the duty on imported corn became heavier in proportion to the cheapness of the home-grown article.

In 1845 the Corn Laws were repealed, and Sir Robert Peel extended the Free Trade fiscal policy of Huskisson in various directions. In 1848 the Navigation Laws imposing a higher rate of duties upon goods imported in England in foreign ships were repealed, and a policy of Free Trade is regarded as thoroughly established at this date; its success is shown by the growth of English exports from 51 million pounds in value in 1840 to 291 million pounds in 1892.

It is sometimes argued that Free Trade should only be extended to those countries which admit our commodities duty free; in other words, that Free Trade should give way to Fair Trade or Reciprocity. If England wished to impose a duty on the goods imported from America, the commodities most affected would be raw cotton and food stuffs. A duty on raw cotton would raise its price, and hamper the Lancashire manufactory in competition with other countries. An import duty on American corn would raise the price of English home-grown wheat and go into the pocket of the landlords. If England taxed American food stuffs to punish America for not allowing her to import the products of her manufactories, it would be a case in which the words of Sir Louis Mallet would be applicable:—" If one tariff is bad, two are worse."

Protection in America dates from the Morrill Tariff of 1861.

The supporters of Free Trade believe that the industrial prosperity of America is in spite of and not owing to Protection. It is to be remarked:—

1. That the internal resources of America are so large, that the value of her imports is only two shillings per head of the population, as against eleven shillings in England.

2. Food stuffs, cotton, and raw materials make up 80 per cent. of American exports, and these are unaffected by Protec-

tion. Only one-tenth of the exports of the United States are articles manufactured in the country. This is because the American manufacturer expects the American profit; this expectation prevents him from competing with the producers of other countries in neutral markets.

3. The high tariff is an obstacle to the success of those manufactories which would naturally flourish without its aid, and upholds those which are a dead loss to the nation. Only one-tenth of the population is connected with manufactures, and in 1886 there were 17½ million labourers in the unprotected trades against 2½ millions in the protected.

4. The high tariff has diminished the customs revenue by nearly one-third during the decade 1872–82, from thirty-seven million pounds in 1869 to twenty-seven million pounds in 1879, though the population increased one-third during the same period. The United States, 1882, obtained a customs revenue of twenty-seven million pounds from a population of fifty millions, but the United Kingdom obtained a revenue of twenty million pounds from a population of thirty-five millions. The subsequent increase of the United States customs revenue has not been in proportion to the increase of population.

5. The high prices of American goods, which are brought about by Protection, destroy the effect of the tariff, and pay the entrance fees for goods into the country. Sheffield cutlery and English steel and iron compete with American in the Western States, in spite of the cost of carriage, and a 40 per cent. protective duty. These high prices act as a bounty which enables English goods to penetrate into the American market.

6. Protection is maintained in America by the power of the vested interests, which profit by it, and the ignorance of their true interests which actuates the masses of the people, who monopolise all political power in a country of manhood suffrage. It would be more economically prejudicial than it actually is in the United States, were it not for:—

    1. The wealth of the country's natural resources.
    2. The large amount of capital seeking investment in America.
    3. The complete freedom of the internal trade of the empire from protective duties. The comparative

smallness of the value of American imports, per head of the population, as compared with that of the English imports, shows that the country can supply its wants to a very considerable extent from home production.

7. A duty on exports is forbidden by the American constitution, and the taxing of imports diminishes the return which the country receives for its exports. The object of Protection is to secure an excess of exports over imports, but, when this is secured, a balance of payment will be due to the protecting country in money. This will increase the amount of money in the protecting country and so raise prices; this rise of prices will diminish exports and increase imports, for the purpose of sharing the high prices in the protecting country. It is probable, therefore, that Protection will defeat its own object of securing an excess of exports over imports.

Professor Fawcett, in his *Free Trade and Protection*, thus states the arguments mostly relied on by Protectionists, and the answers of Free Traders thereto:—

A. That it is advantageous for a country that as large a number of industries as possible should be practised in it, as its dependence on foreign countries is lessened. This argument is especially applicable to the United States, where the abundance of fertile land makes no industry so profitable as agriculture. Protection diverts a certain amount of capital into the protected trades, which are, as it were, galvanised into existence by the Government ensuring that they should continue profitable by artificially raising their price. In these trades two losses are incurred for one gain. If a tax be imposed on imported boots, raising their price to the lowest profitable selling price of the home produced article, the consumer pays a higher price than he need for the boots, and his power of buying other things is proportionally diminished by the necessity of having to pay this higher price, which is a loss to other producers.

Nations will only trade together if they can procure what they want at a less sacrifice than home protection requires. Protection nullifies this advantage, and makes the consumer pay an unnecessary high price for the commodity produced at home.

B. The Protectionists argue that the cost of carriage is paid by the exporting country, and raw produce, being more bulky than manufactured goods, is more expensive to transport than manufactured goods, therefore America is at a disadvantage as compared with England, and the balance should be redressed by means of a protective tax levied on English imports. The part of the cost of carriage which is borne by the importing country, depends upon whether the demand for the imported commodity is decreased more than in proportion to the cost, or in proportion to it, or less than in proportion to it. In the former case, the importing country will bear less of the cost of carriage, and in the third case more; in the second case the cost will be equally shared. The cost of carriage is never entirely paid by the exporting country.

Another reason against imposing Protection to save the cost of carriage of imports is, that the increase of price necessitated by home production under unfavourable circumstances is often more than in proportion to the benefit of saving the cost of carriage.

C. The home producer has to pay various taxes not levied from the foreigner, and so is placed at a disadvantage if not aided by Protection. The foreigner has to pay taxes in his own country, and if the Protectionists argue that the burden of taxation is heavier in a country with protective duties than in one without, the system of Protection stands condemned. If the home trader is to be protected in proportion to the taxation he has to bear, each addition to protective duties will be doubly burdensome to the general community, as it will create a demand for fresh protection. No protecting State can share in any improvement in production or decrease in the cost of carriage of the imported commodity, as the home producer, in dread of being undersold, at once demands fresh protective duties on imports.

D. It is considered an advantage of Protection that it encourages home trade and discourages imports. This ignores the fact that the importation of foreign imports is favourable to home production, as it must be paid for by the exports, and so home production is stimulated. If there was Free Trade between the two countries, the capital expended in American iron would be invested in English produce; and if America bought goods more largely from England, England would buy more American goods in return.

Injuries to foreign countries by protective tariffs decrease their power of buying the exports of the protecting country.

E. Protectionists assert that protective import duties fall upon the foreign producer. They assert that if America imported forty million pounds worth of goods when the import duty was 10 per cent., and only twenty million pounds worth when it was 35 per cent., the Government would not only obtain a larger revenue from a smaller importation of English goods, but England, owing to the lessened demand for them, would have to offer her goods at a cheaper rate.

The tax on imports raises their price in America, and also the price of any portion of the supply of the same commodities that are produced in America itself. The rise in price of American imports lessens the demand for them, and so they fall off in value, and English export merchants suffer. American exports exceed the imports, so a balance of payment is due to her from the countries which buy her exports; this will increase prices and so discourage exports and encourage imports. This rise in price will compensate the English export merchants for the tax.

F. As profits and wages are not higher in protected industries than in those not protected, it cannot be fairly said that Protection benefits a special trade at the expense of the community. If profits and wages are not higher in protected than in non-protected trades, it shows that the extra price paid by the consumer does not go to the capitalist and the labourer, but is merely the equivalent for the increased cost of production.

G. Protection benefits the working classes if the wages of protected trades in America are higher than those of the same trades in England. The general rate of wages is also higher in the former than in the latter country. The true cause of this general high rate of wages is to be found in the abundance of fertile land in America, which produces food for the people, and in the fact that the entire amount of agricultural produce goes to the farmer and the labourer, none being kept for rent. Agriculture is, therefore, unusually profitable, and the workmen in other trades require unusually high wages to keep them from engaging in agriculture, so that the rate of wages in agriculture regulates the rate in all other trades.

The difference in wages in America and in Europe is greatest in agriculture, and in this America can compete with Europe without protection. The rate of wages and the character of the external trade of a country are connected as joint effects of the same cause—the direction in which the national industry happens to be most productive. Foreign trade deals with the articles in which the national industry happens to be most productive, and measured in these, wages will be high. When wages are high, measured in money, they indicate abundance of the precious metals in the country, or special productiveness in those articles in exchange for which gold and silver can be procured from the bullion-producing countries. If wages are high, measured in food or clothing, they indicate high productiveness in these industries.

II. Protection would be unjust if only one industry were protected, because the general public could in that case obtain no compensation for the increased price they would have to pay for the protected commodity. If Protection were uniform, the injustice would be removed. Universal Protection, that everybody as producer should receive high prices to compensate for the high prices they had to pay as consumer, is impossible and useless, as only those trades which labour under any inferiority require protection. It would cause a general rise of prices, and would be equivalent to a depreciation of money.

All industries cannot be protected, *e.g.*, no wheat is imported into America or wine into France, and these trades have to pay the high prices caused by protection without any compensation. Professional men are another class who cannot be protected, and yet they suffer under the high prices caused by Protection.

The State is not qualified to decide upon the amount of protection to be assigned to various trades, and there is a tendency on the part of traders to exert political pressure upon the Government to obtain it.

I. Protection is temporarily advantageous, as various industries cannot be started without it, especially in new colonies, though they may ultimately prosper independently of its aid.

Workmen in a protected industry, who are learning their trade, cannot produce commodities except on a most limited scale, and therefore they cannot be much benefited by the price being raised. Protection, when once granted, is never willingly surrendered.

The object of the Bounty System was to aid native industry by enabling it to undersell the foreign producers in their own markets. In the case of bounties on the export of corn, consumers were taxed to raise the price of the food they consumed.

A drawback on refined sugar exported is given in France, amounting to 10 per cent. more than the duty on raw sugar imported. So much sugar is exported as to raise the price in France, and French producers, having the bounty of 10 per cent., can sell it to foreigners at below cost price. Thus the result of the bounty, given at the expense of the general revenue, is to raise the price of sugar to the French consumer. It is one of the chief objects of the English commercial policy, as regards foreign countries, to procure the abolition of bounties.

The Treaties of Commerce binding the contracting parties to differential duties are inadvisable; they should merely contain an obligation upon the contracting parties to extend to each other the "most favoured nation" treatment, that is, the most complete freedom of trade that the domestic policy of each will allow to be extended to the other.

The Treaty of Commerce with France, 1860, restricted English trade with other nations. England profited by admitting French goods at a low rate of duty, and by inducing France to do the same to English goods, but Spain and Portugal raised their tariffs against us on account of the new system of taxation of their wines brought in by the treaty. The treaty with France imposed a duty of 1s. a gallon on wine of 26 degrees of alcoholic strength, and of 2s. 6d. on wine of from 26 to 42 degrees of strength. Spanish wines just came within this limit, and they considered that there ought to have been an intermediate rate of duty.

CHAPTER VII.

LOCAL TAXATION.

LOCAL taxation differs from imperial in that, if more money is wanted, it can only be obtained by increasing the rates on real property. There is only one way of raising local, though there are various ways of raising imperial, taxation. Another contrast is that throughout the country local expenditure is in excess of local revenue, the difference being made up by loans. The amount of local taxation raised from land, as compared with that raised from other kinds of real property, has of late years decreased; this is because the quantity of land is limited, and its value, therefore, cannot increase indefinitely like that of buildings, which may be multiplied to any extent. The occupiers of houses bear most of the burden of local taxation, which has been shifted from the shoulders of the landlords.

The present state of local taxation is in a state of great confusion:—

1. Because of the number of different bodies which have the power of levying rates. In boroughs, the Board of Guardians, the Town Council, and the Local Board and the School Board can do so, and also the County Council for county purposes In rural districts, the County Council levies rates, but the areas of rating—petty sessional districts, highway districts, and poor-law unions—often run into each other.

2. The different areas of rating are not coincident. Part of the income of local bodies, such as market or harbour dues, are merely the price of services rendered, and cannot be justly classed as local taxation.

The tenant nominally pays the rates on land, but the incidence of these rates is really upon the landlord, who, but for them, could demand higher rent. Rates on land have of late much diminished with urban rates.

The incidence of the rates upon house property has been already considered. We have now to consider the incidence of rates upon manufactories and business premises. If the rate is uniform, it will fall upon the consumer, prices being raised in proportion to it; otherwise, the profits of trade would be reduced below their natural level. If the rate be higher in some localities than in others, the competition of localities with low rates will prevent the price being raised proportionally to the rate, and it will be paid from profits.

The rise of prices owing to rates can only partially be brought about if foreign producers compete with English in the English markets. The increase of supply prevents the rise in price necessary to compensate for the rate, so the burden is shared between the trader and consumer.

Rates upon railways, water-works, and gas-works fall upon the holders of shares in these undertakings. Fares and payments for gas and water are fixed at the amount which gives the maximum rate of profit; if the rates are then increased, railway fares and payments for gas and water cannot be raised without causing a reduction in the rate of profit, and therefore falling upon the shareholders. If the maximum dividend on gas and water-works has been fixed by Act of Parliament at 10 per cent., and all profits above this amount must be applied to reduce the price of the commodity, then rates most distinctly fall upon consumers, as, without them, there would be more to appropriate to reducing the price of the commodity.

The incidence of the rates upon house property is, as we have seen, upon the occupiers, but there is great injustice in forcing them to pay for improvements which will enable their landlords to raise the rent upon them at the termination of their leases. The consideration of this injustice, and of the means for remedying it, is called the Leasehold Question.

The problem of the Poor Law is to provide subsistence for the indigent poor, without putting a premium on idleness and improvidence by ensuring the means of living to those who will not work. If the maintenance of the poor is left to private charity, the poor are often induced to counterfeit suffering, by seeing that those who excite the most sympathy obtain the most generous relief.

The suppression of the monasteries at the Reformation, and the consequent extinction of the great source of relief to the poor during the Middle Ages, made the question of the maintenance of the poor a burning one at the commencement of the sixteenth century. With the exception of the monasteries, the corporations of the towns were the only relieving agencies. Under Henry VIII. acts were passed which made each locality responsible for the maintenance of its poor. Those who could not work were to be sent to the place where they were born and there maintained with kindness, but heavy penalties were imposed upon the poor who could work and refused the work which was to be offered to them (22 Hen. VIII., c. 12). All who wished to give alms to the poor were to place their offerings in a common fund to be administered by the bishop and his clergy; they were not to give indiscriminate relief under penalty of forfeiting ten times the amount given away (27 Hen. VIII., c. 25).

Independently of the cessation of monastic charity, the condition of the labourers had greatly deteriorated owing to the rise in prices brought about by the silver imported from the New World, and the debasement of the coinage by Henry VIII. and the Protector Somerset. Various acts were passed which attempted to palliate the distress, such as that of 1589, by which four acres of land were to be attached to every new labourer's cottage, and overcrowding was forbidden by severe penalties imposed on the proprietors.

The first real Poor Law was passed in the forty-third year of the reign of Queen Elizabeth (47 Eliz., c. 2). By it every deserving person obtained a legal right to relief, and a rate was to be raised for the purpose on real property, to be collected and administered by overseers, who were to be appointed annually in each parish. Paupers able to work were to be maintained at the expense of any of their relations able to support them, and were not to obtain relief without working for it.

In 1723 an Act (9 Geo. I., c. 7) was passed by which a parish or union of parishes was to build a workhouse for the maintenance of the poor, and those who would not consent to reside in it were not to obtain relief. In this year the pernicious system was introduced of hiring out able-bodied paupers to the farmers, to the great detriment of the self-supporting poor.

In 1782, by Gilbert's Act (22 Geo. III., c. 83), Guardians

of the Poor were established to protect them against the overseers, and the workhouse test was abolished, with most pernicious results in increasing the number of paupers. In 1795, by 36 Geo. III., c. 83, no one was called upon to enter the workhouse, and the magistrates were allowed to give outdoor relief to the people in their own homes. This policy was first initiated by the Berkshire Justices in the meeting at Speenhamland, 1795. Allowances were given to people in proportion to the number of children they had, thus rewarding them for being self-indulgent and improvident, and stimulating the increase of population. Wages were made up to the average amount by grants from the rates, so there was no reason for the poor to migrate to where they might obtain better wages. This last change was introduced by the Berkshire Justices in their meeting at Speenhamland in 1795.

The Law of Settlement (13 & 14, c. 11, 1662), which prevented labourers from leaving the place where they were born, was another reason which retained labour in places where it was not wanted.

The result of all this administration was such that almost all the profit from the land was eaten up by the rates. The growth of the Poor Law charges, proportionally to the population, will be understood from these figures—

Year.	Amount on Poor Rate.	Population.
1760	£1,250,000	£ 7,000,000
1818	7,870,000	11,876,000
1830	6,829,000	13,924,000

The system called loudly for reform, which was brought about by the New Poor Law, 1834, based upon the report of a Commission of Enquiry. This Act revived the workhouse test, and abolished allowances in aid of wages, and provided for the appointment of paid overseers and an official audit of accounts. The fathers of illegitimate children had to support them, instead of the old system of rewarding the mother and freeing the father from responsibility. The Law of Settlement was altered, by making it more difficult to obtain a settlement in a parish by occupation or labour; it was therefore no longer so important to prevent new labourers settling in a parish. The administration of the Poor

Law was placed under three Commissioners, and England and Wales were divided into twenty-one districts, each under an assistant Commissioner. Unions of parishes were formed, to distribute the expense of maintaining the poor over larger areas than single parishes, and to save expense by centralising the administration. The Poor Law Commission was, in 1847, replaced by the Local Government Board, formed to administer the laws relating to the Local Government, the Public Health, and the Relief of the Poor. The saving of expense under the new system is shown by the fact that, in the twelve years before the Poor Law Amendment Act, 1834, the relief of the poor cost £76,096,000, in the twelve years after it cost £57,247,000.

A Poor-Law Act was passed for Ireland in 1838, and one for Scotland soon after. In 1865, by the Union Chargeability Act, the Union became the area of rating for the poor rate and not the parish. In 1870 the Metropolitan Poor Act made the maintenance of the outdoor poor a charge upon the Union, but the maintenance of the indoor poor was to be paid for by London as a whole.

The effect of this is to discourage a resort to outdoor relief, and to diminish the number of those in receipt of outdoor relief in London. Outdoor relief is more economical than indoor relief, but this very advantage encourages its being given in excess, and Fawcett says that the London system should be extended to all England, the indoor poor being maintained out of the county rate and the outdoor poor by the Union.

The strict maintenance of the restrictions on outdoor relief has caused the number of paupers in Great Britain to decrease in spite of the increase of population, and a contrary policy in Ireland has produced a contrary effect. This is proved by the following statistics:—

Year.	Number of Paupers.	Number of Paupers per 1000 of Population.
1850	1,308,000	48
1860	973,000	34
1870	1,279,000	41
1880	1,016,000	29
1885	982,000	27

The pressure of the rates caused Parliament in 1872 to vote that the cost of the maintenance of lunatics and of the police should be defrayed out of the Consolidated Fund to the extent of four million pounds a year.

It has been proposed to throw the cost of the maintenance of the poor upon the general revenue, but, if this were done, the security for the economical management of the funds devoted to this purpose would be weakened. The effect of the Local Government Act of 1894 upon the administration of the Poor Law is not likely to be so good as it has been upon other departments of local self-government. The power of plural voting, the privilege of county magistrates being *ex-officio* guardians of the poor, and the qualification for elective guardians of an assessment on a rateable value of £40 have all been abolished. The powers of the guardians have been transferred to the rural District Council, but to be a member of the District Council it is only necessary to have resided for twelve months in the district; it is not even necessary to be a ratepayer.

Fawcett considers that the existence of a Poor Law, as a protection against extreme destitution, is a reason why Socialism has not gained any considerable hold on the masses of the English people.

The principal security against the extension of pauperism in England must be found in the extension of habits of saving among the people by means of Post-Office Savings Banks.

The number of women paupers exceeds that of men; on this account no obstacles should be put in the way of employment of adult women by means of Factory Acts. Reduction of hours, and intervals for rest and meals, can be secured for women without the aid of the State, and it is a mistake to throw any obstacles in the way of women freeing themselves from their present dependent position by securing separate industrial employment.

CHAPTER VIII.

ECONOMIC EFFECT OF THE LAWS OF PROPERTY AND CONTRACT IN ENGLAND.

MILL proposes that the Laws of Inheritance should be altered by : (1) Allowing Freedom of Bequest, with the reservation from the estate of enough to enable all descendants of the testator to support themselves. (2) No one should inherit more than a moderate competence. (3) In the case of intestacy, the property should escheat to the State, which should be bound to provide to a reasonable extent for the descendants of the owner of the property.

As an intermediate alternative to this, he recommends that the law of inheritance of personal property (freedom of bequest, and, in case of intestacy, equal division) should be extended to landed property. No right of inheritance should be allowed in collaterals, and the property of those without direct heirs should escheat to the State.

Primogeniture is intended to prevent the land being divided into portions too small for cultivation; this result would not necessarily follow the division of the estate equally among all the children, as their shares might be charged upon the estate by way of mortgage, or the property might be sold and the proceeds equally divided.

Primogeniture makes the landlords an impoverished class, as the income of the estate is charged for the benefit of the younger sons, and the owner has nothing to spare for improvements.

To prevent these charges being imposed on the property, the system of Entail has been devised, by which each owner in the course of the entail, being only a life-tenant of the property, has no power to impose a charge on it beyond his lifetime. No owner in the course of the entail could sell the property, or even grant a long lease, unless the strictness of the law of entail were relaxed. This is now no longer the case, owing to Lord Cairns' Settled Estates Act, 1881, which allows a life tenant to sell his estate, with the exception of the dwelling-house and the land immediately round it, for selling which the consent of the Court of Chancery or of the trustee of settlement is required.

The system of primogeniture and entail is economically prejudicial, as preventing the free transfer of land. The French system, which only allows the owner to leave by will a portion equal to the share of one of his children, and forces all the remainder to be equally divided, prevents the father from redressing any inequality among his children, as, for instance, when one is incapable of providing for himself owing to some natural infirmity, or has been already provided for by his own exertions.

Under English Contract Law, Mill discusses the Laws of Partnership and Bankruptcy. English Partnership Law is defective compared to that of France, in forbidding partnerships in *commandite*. In this kind of partnerships, the managers are responsible with their whole fortunes, but they have associated with them others who are only responsible up to the amount of the contributions, though they share in the profits according to the conditions agreed on. These persons, whose liability is limited, are termed *commanditaires*, and have no voice in the management of the concern. This system is particularly advantageous to an inventor wanting capital to carry his invention into practice. Commercial cases in France are decided by a tribunal of merchants, not by the expensive and tedious machinery of the ordinary law-courts.

In these respects the French law of partnership is superior to the English. It is inferior in not allowing joint-stock companies to be constituted without the consent of the Council of State, a body of officials mostly ignorant of matters of trade. Joint-stock companies with unlimited liability cannot exist in France, as the capital of such companies cannot be divided into transferable shares. The best laws of partnership are those of the New England states in the United States, where even lines of steamers and fishing vessels are owned in shares, some of which are in the hands of the crews.

Laws of Insolvency are economically important: (1) Because production is hampered by people not being able to trust each other; (2) because any cause which diminishes the necessity for insurance against bad debts, diminishes also the cost of production of commodities.

The law has abolished imprisonment for debt, and in doing so, has been unduly tender to debtors. It is not enough to place the creditors in possession of the debtor's property, it should punish improvident speculation or neglect of the ordinary business precautions, such as the maintenance of accurately kept books, and, as the French law does, should treat bankruptcy from these causes as an offence not as a misfortune.

CHAPTER IX.

CRITICISM OF THE ENGLISH LEGAL SYSTEM.

MILL adversely criticises: (1) The difficulty of understanding the English law, the quality which Bentham termed its "incognoscibility," and its uncertainty. Even when the facts are not disputed, a recourse to the law courts is necessary to obtain justice on this account.

(2) The procedure of the law courts is burdened by such expense and delay, that suitors often endure great injustice rather than seek redress from the courts. Thus the wrong side often gains the victory in the law courts, because the other party abandons litigation from want of funds or submits to a compromise, or the case is decided on some legal quibble, not on its merits. The only part of our legal system which he commends as free from the above faults is our Mercantile Law.

Mercantile law has grown up from giving the force of law to the customs of the merchants, so it has had the advantage of being made by those most interested in its goodness. The importance of credit, which depends upon the man who wants to borrow possessing a good character, makes the force of public opinion a considerable protection against mercantile dishonesty.

The faults of the Land Law are its uncertainty and technicality, which prevents an owner from acquiring an incontrovertible title to land, its failure to provide proper evidence of legal transactions by registration of legal documents, the prolixity and extravagant cost of the legal documents and formalities necessary for the purchase, sale, lease, or mortgage of real property, and the delay and expense of all legal proceedings relating to land.

Uncertainty of title diminishes the saleable value of land and discourages the investment of the landlord's capital in its improvement.

Land ought to be easily transferable, as in most countries it is either too much or too little subdivided. Large estates require to be subdivided, or small estates bought up.

The influence of the law, when it allows the rich to take advantage of their riches to institute unjust or resist just litigation, or permits the evasion of just obligation, is prejudicial to the economical prosperity of the country and to the morality of the people.

BOOK V.

SKETCH OF THE SUCCESSION OF THEORETIC IDEAS ABOUT ECONOMIC FACTS AND OF THE PRINCIPAL FACTS IN THE HISTORY OF ENGLISH TRADE.

Economic ideas in ancient times. ECONOMY is the art of managing a household so that the income of its inmates may be well administered, and they may live in the greatest possible comfort compatible with their outlay. Political economy is the application of these principles to the State, so that its revenues may be raised in such a manner as to be least burdensome to its citizens, and may be spent to the best advantage, and that the resources of the State may receive the greatest possible development.

We know little of political economy among the ancients, as ancient authors give only scanty details relating to the wealth and civilisation of the States they write about.

This is the more to be regretted, as it has limited the data upon which modern writers have been able to base their generalisations. Only the first rudiments of economic truths are to be found in Greek and Roman writers. The ancient Jews lived under a theocracy, and they paid exclusive attention to the moral side of economics. A proposal, from which important economic results might be expected, was estimated, not according to these results, but according to its effect upon the character of the people.

Economic ideas among the Greeks. The Greeks and Romans considered trade degrading. Lycurgus prohibited the Spartans from engaging in any form of commercial industry, from the fear that their warlike efficiency would be thereby injured. At Athens those trades which were considered unworthy of freemen were carried on by slaves.

Professor Mahaffy, in his *Social Life in Greece*, says: "One of the leading features of Athenian civilisation was the contempt of trade, or indeed of any occupation, which so absorbed a man as to deprive him of ample leisure."

The chief differences between ancient and modern industrial life are, that ancient industry is stereotyped by the unwritten law of custom confining the son to the occupation of the father; the ceaseless variety of the modern industrial system did not exist. Commerce was checked by the want of knowledge of geography, and the insufficiency of the means of communication. The contempt for industrial occupations was kept alive by their being mostly in the hands of slaves. Deficient knowledge of physical science prevented any use being made of natural powers for the purpose of production, and proved an insuperable obstacle to the use of machinery to any considerable extent. The sense of insecurity from constant war and misgovernment prevented the accumulation of large aggregates of capital.

<small>Differences between ancient and modern industrial life.</small>

Throughout Greek writers on economic subjects, we find the cardinal principle of the subordination of individuals to the State, the primary object of all government was the formation of good citizens, and every subject was studied from an ethical and educational point of view. Ancient philosophers dreaded the attainment of wealth, as tending to bring about luxury, and so to sap the foundation of warlike virtue. Plato, in the second book of the *Republic*, banishes artizans and merchants from his model State. In the twelfth book of the *Laws*, he says: "Nature has made neither bootmakers nor blacksmiths, such occupations degrade the people engaged in them, miserable mercenaries excluded by the very position from political rights." The *Republic* advocates community of property and of wives, to do away with every dictate of private interest. His ideal is a self-sufficing State, with no unnecessary contact with foreign nations, and its population restricted by exposure of infants and the prohibition of early marriages. The precious metals were to be interdicted as far as possible in internal commerce, and the loan of money at interest was forbidden, the debtor not being obliged to repay the principal of the loan unless he chose.

Plato's Republic is the pattern of the descriptions of the

ideal State, such as More's Utopia, Bacon's New Atlantis, and Harrington's Oceana. It was formerly the fashion to convey ideas on sociology disguised in this form of a sketch of what was, in the author's opinion, the most perfect form of society.

Xenophon's *Œconomicus* bears only indirectly upon political economy, as it deals with the best method of management of a man's household and property. His treatise on the revenues of Athens has some interesting remarks on increasing the wealth of the city by promoting the settlement of aliens in it, by better management of the silver mines at Laurium, and the purchase of slaves out of the revenues of the State, which was to make a profit by letting out their labour to hire.

Aristotle's *Politics* commences with a sketch of the origin of society; a description of the various forms of government extant at the time follows; the author then gives a historico-critical account of the various forms of political constitutions prevalent in Greece, and concludes with a consideration of the ideal State.

Aristotle's views on sociology deal mostly with the statics of the subject; on the development of society he is silent. He considers that society (a crowd made up of persons unlike each other, $\pi\lambda\hat{\eta}\theta os\ \epsilon\xi\ \dot{a}\nu o\mu o\iota\omega\nu$) originates from natural impulses, as man is naturally inclined to live with others, apart from all consideration of personal wants and mutual benefits, being $\pi o\lambda\iota\tau\iota\kappa o\nu\ \zeta\hat{\omega}o\nu$, a social animal; and our author therefore does not approve of Plato's suppression of private freedom and initiative by doing away monogamy and private property. Community of wives will do away with family affections, and so weaken the State; community of property will be the fruitful parent of discord. The household of the family is the source of the State. The object of the State is $\dot{a}\rho\epsilon\tau\eta$, happy life, as it is attained by virtue. The politics and the ethics are therefore closely connected, as the State cannot attain its first object, unless morality prevails among its citizens. He despises trade quite as much as Plato. "In the State which is best governed, the citizens must not lead the life of mechanics or tradesmen, for such a life is ignoble and inimical to virtue."[1] "For the life of mechanics, tradesmen, and

[1] Pliny, *Nat. Hist.*, xviii. 73.

labourers is a low one; nor have any of the occupations in which such people engage any necessary connection with virtue."[1]

ἡ χρηματιστική, or the art of money-making, is (1) Natural, and arises from the appropriation of natural products and their application to household uses. The means of natural acquisition are hunting, fishing, cattle-rearing, and agriculture.

(2) By means of exchange (μεταβλητική). The means of acquisition by exchange are commerce, usury, hiring, contracting.

Aristotle's freedom from the mercantile fallacy is not a little remarkable; he tells the story of Midas to show that the possession of gold is not always equivalent to the possession of wealth.

At Rome all the processes of industry were carried on by slaves, and the productive powers of the land were ruined by the pernicious system of Latifundia, the large estates of the nobles which crowded out the free cultivator, and were cultivated by slave labour. "Latifundia perdidere Italiam jam rus et provincias."[2] There were a few opponents of this state of things. Varro and Columella, writers on agriculture, boldly expressed their preference for free labour in the cultivation of the soil. Pliny says, "Coli rura ab ergastulis pessimum est." The Romans shared Plato's objection to interest; the rate of interest was fixed by the Twelve Tables, and it was forbidden to exact interest at all by the Genucian Law. Cicero compares the exactions of interest to murder, "Quid fenerari, quid hominem occidere." Cicero shared to the full the contempt for commercial pursuits prevalent in Rome. He considers that there is nothing honourable in a workshop; that traders never prosper unless they lie. Commerce on a small scale is, according to him, mean and despicable, and if it is on a large scale the most he will say of it is that "it is not much to be found fault with" (non admodum vituperanda).[3] The Romans forbade the exportation of gold, because they believed that the wealth of a State consisted only in the amount of the precious metals it possessed. Cicero observes:

Economic ideas among the Romans.

[1] *Politics*, vii. cap. ix.   [2] *Politics*, vii. cap. iv.
[3] *De Officiis*, i. cap. 42.

"The Senate many times before, and most deliberately in my consulship, came to the decision that gold ought not to be exported."[1]

Economic ideas in the Middle Ages. Influence of Feudalism. In the Middle Ages, Feudalism was based upon territorial property, and looked down upon all handicrafts, except those which were useful for war and the chase.

Ascetic exaggeration of the Canon Law was also prejudicial to economic progress. It was a maxim of Canon **Influence of Canon Law.** Law, " Dulcissima rerum possessio communis est." Agriculture meets with qualified praise, " Deo non displicet "; trade, on the other hand, on account of the tendency to fraud, " Deo placere non potest." Usury was forbidden.

.The enlargement of men's knowledge of distant lands by **Approximations to the modern order of things.** the Crusades, the growth of the power of the Burgher class in the towns, the regulation of production by means of Guilds, and the replacement of villenage by a system of leases, were all influences favourable to the growth of trade, and an approximation to the modern order of things.

The growing importance of commerce may be seen by a **Growing importance of Commerce.** glance at English customary law, at the Statute-book, and the history of the revenue. The principal exports in Anglo-Saxon times were wool, lead, and tin. As early as 796 Karl the Great, or Charlemagne, granted protection, by a Treaty of Commerce, to traders from Mercia. As early as Athelstan, every London merchant who made three long voyages on his own account was ranked as a thane, and the Ceapmmnanne or Merchant Gilds are met within very early times. The laws of Oleron, which were originally made to be observed by the fleet of Richard the First on its voyage to the Holy Land, were accepted as a code of Commercial Law during a great part of the Middle Ages. Clause 41 of Magna Charta allows foreign merchants to come and go in England, and in case of war to be treated as English merchants were in the hostile country. This was distinctly in advance of France, where the Droit d'Aubaine, or Right of Escheat, existed down to

[1] *Pro L. Flacco*, sect. 48.

the time of Colbert. The Statute of Merchants, or Acton Burnell, 1283, allowed the registration of debts due to merchants, and their recovery by the distraint of the debtors' goods or the imprisonment of their persons. This statute fostered trade at home, and the Carta Mercatoria, 1303, granted privileges to foreign merchants in England.

As the wealth of the merchants grew, their wealth became more and more the object of royal exactions, and maletotes, or tolls levied on wool by the royal prerogative, are constantly complained of. In 1362 and 1371 it is enacted by statute that neither the merchants nor any other body should henceforth set any subsidy or charge on wool without consent of Parliament.

The customs originating in prisage (the king's right to take at a fixed minimum price one-tenth of the wine imported into England in English ships), the custuma antiqua et magna (export duty on wool, skins, and leather), and poundage (10 per cent. on all goods sold by the pound of less value than £100, and 5 per cent. on goods above that value) first come into notice under Edward I. The right of prisage was commuted for a fixed money payment (tonnage), which was first regularly granted to the king in Parliament from 1373.

Thorold Rogers derives the guilds from the Sodalitia or Collegia of the Roman Republic and Empire. However this may be, the guilds provided the most important machinery for the organisation of labour during the Middle Ages. The guild of weavers is mentioned as early as 1130, when Robert, son of Lefstan, paid on its behalf £16 into the Exchequer. Henry II. tried to suppress the Goldsmiths' Guild, so it must have been powerful before his day.

The merchant guilds controlled all matters relating to their own trades, and admission to them was gained only by a strictly regulated system of apprenticeship. They are important in the history of the development of towns, as the chief guild often agreed to pay the Firma Burgi or sum at which the town was assessed to the royal revenue, and in return were allowed to assume the municipal government by royal charter. They also provided a machinery of enfranchisement, for if a villein entered a guild and remained unclaimed by his lord for a year and a day he became free.

There were also craft guilds of inferior workmen, under Henry II. We hear of eighteen being fined as adulterine, *i.e.*, as not having bought charters of association from the king. There were carpenters' and masons' guilds under Edward III.; and, according to Thorold Rogers, even the peasant labourers possessed organisations for the regulation of labour. Foreign settlers first arrived in England under William the Conqueror; and the Flemish weavers who had come over then were transferred by Henry I. to Pembrokeshire in 1111.

Henry of Huntingdon, 1155, is the first chronicler who notices anything relating to trade. He says that in his time English trade with Germany consisted of lead, tin, fish, meat, fat cattle, and fine wool for the looms of Ghent and Bruges. Thorold Rogers supposes that the principal source of the silver used in the Middle Ages, before the discovery of the mines of Peru, was England. The lead, which was exported in the form of the sulphuret, was almost always largely combined with silver. The chief imports into England were fine woven cloths, furs, and iron, from the shores of the Baltic. It is noteworthy that salt seems to have been imported, and that the art of manufacturing it from the brine deposits of Worcestershire and Cheshire was temporarily lost, though we know that the Romans made use of locally manufactured salt in Worcestershire.

In the time of Edward III., the wool trade was almost a monopoly of England, as is proved by the fact that Parliament could levy a tax upon it of from 100 to 150 per cent. of its value, without bringing out stores from any other country or materially depressing the price which continental manufacturers were willing to pay for English wool. England was much more peaceable than the Continent, and the English wool production reached such a pitch of excellence that even Spanish wool, its only other rival, could not be used unless largely mixed with English. Missenden's *Circle of Commerce* gives the annual export of wool about 1350 as 11,648,000 lbs., valued then at £100,683. A further colony of Flemings settled in England under Edward III., and established the chief textile centres for the manufacture of cloth in Norfolk and Suffolk. They took up their residence at York and Norwich about 1330, and about the same time

John Kemp established the manufactury of "Kendal Green" cloths at Kendal in Westmoreland. Worsted goods were also then first manufactured: they were so called from the village of Worstead, near Norwich. From the end of the fourteenth century the export of wool as raw material declines in proportion as the growth of the home manufacture increases. Fine cloth was imported from Flanders, linen from Liege, velvet and silk from Genoa and Venice. It was the period of the great fairs, such as Winchester and Stourbridge near Cambridge, which were supplied with Eastern goods by the Venetian fleet which touched annually on the southern shores of England.

It was the peculiarity of English trade that it was localised at certain places for easier superintendence and the readier collection of the king's dues.

By the Statute of the Staple 27 Ed. III., 1354, the trade in wool, sheepskins, leather, and lead was to be localised at Newcastle-on-Tyne, York, Lincoln, Norwich, Westminster, Canterbury, Chichester, Winchester, Exeter, Bristol, Carnarvon, Dublin, Drogheda, Waterford, and Cork. Some of these towns had their special ports from which alone the commodities of the Staple could be exported,—*e.g.*, Lincoln had for its special port St Botolph, Norwich, Yarmouth, Canterbury Sandwich, Winchester Southampton. The seat of the Staple abroad was at Calais, and after the capture of that place by the French, Bruges. It was at these places alone that the wool, sheepskins, leather, and lead exported by England were bought and sold. These restrictions upon commerce were imposed by royal authority for convenience of taxation. When wool was no longer imported as raw material from England, but cloth was manufactured at home, the wealth of the Merchants of the Staple declined, and their place as the leading trade corporation was taken by the Merchant Adventurers, who were incorporated by Queen Elizabeth. It was in the interests of this latter body that the commercial treaty of 1490 between England and Florence, and that entitled the "Magnus Intercursus," between England and Burgundy in 1496, were negotiated.

Towards the end of the fifteenth, and the beginning of the sixteenth centuries, the industrial privileges possessed by the guilds cramped the development of manufacturing towns, and led to their decay. No one could carry on a trade or mystery in a town where this trade or mystery had been authorised by charter who was not a freeman of the town or had not been apprenticed to the trade. Industrial villages grew, and form the germ of modern manufacturing towns and of the factory system. The guild lands, the proceeds of which were used by the guilds for the relief of their poorer members, were confiscated by Protector Somerset without much outcry.

The principal English exports at this time were tin from Cornwall, lead from Derbyshire, wool, friezes from Manchester, coverlets from York, and broadcloth from the West of England.

The imports were iron and war horses from Portugal and Spain; wine from Gascony; velvet, linen, and fine cloths from Ghent, Liege, and Bruges; herrings, pitch, timber, furs, and amber imported into England by the merchants of the Hanse Towns from the Baltic. These merchants were for a long time incorporated in London as the Merchants of the Steelyard, the corporation lasting down to 1597, when it was abolished. Satins, silks, velvet, glass, spices, precious stones, camphor, saffron, fine damasks and cottons were imported by the Venetian fleet, which paid its last visit to England in 1532. The carrying trade of Venice was ruined by the conquest of Egypt by Selim I., Sultan of Turkey. Antwerp succeeded Venice as the universal *entrepot* of trade, and its sack by Farnese in 1584 gave a remarkable impulse to the commercial prosperity of England.

In 1554 was founded the Russia Company for trade with Russia, *via* Archangel; and the East India Company dates from the commencement of the next century. The Flemings, driven out by the religious persecutions, settled in Sandwich and Rye: in 1570 there were 4000 of them in Norwich alone. They introduced cutlery, the finer sorts of cloth manufacture, dyeing, hat making, and pottery. Improvements in weaving and lace making were also transplanted by French refugees from Alençon and Valenciennes to Cranfield in Bedfordshire, the Midland counties of Buckinghamshire, Oxford, and Northamptonshire, and to Honiton in Devon.

The exiles who made their way to England after the revocation of the Edict of Nantes in 1585 proved equally useful to the industrial development of their adopted country. They introduced the manufacture of silk, paper, and glass. The agriculture of the Middle Ages was on the three-field system, the first year a crop of wheat or rye being sown, the second year one of oats or barley, and the third year was left fallow. The arable land was only held in individual ownership till the crops were gathered, and then it was used as common pasturage for the cattle of all the tenants of the Manor. The landlord had his socage tenants who paid him a fixed rent of money or produce, and his villeins, who were bound by their tenure to give their labour to assist in cultivating the lord's demesne, which he kept in his own hands.

After the Black Death, 1348, the lords insisted severely on the performance of such labour dues as had not been commuted for money, and tried to treat as villeins all who had no legal documentary evidence to prove that they held their lands in a free tenancy. The diminution in the number of the labourers produced an inevitable rise in wages, which was not prevented by the Statutes of Labourers, which were passed ordering them to work for the same wages as they received before the Black Death. The consequent rise in the expenses of cultivation made the landlords give up cultivating their demesne, and they began to let them on lease to tenants, commuting the labour due from their villein tenants into a money payment. The same cause, coupled with a rise in the price of wool, caused a preference for pasture over arable land. The Act 17 Rich. II., 1394, fruitlessly attempted to arrest this tendency by forbidding the export of corn.

In 1450 the art of brickmaking was re-discovered, and the labourers gained the advantage of an improved material for building their cottages, which were formerly mere hovels of wattle and mud.

The Monasteries followed the "stock and lease" system, by which a certain quantity of stock was let with the land, for which the tenant had to account at the end of the lease either in money or kind. This was particularly favourable to the tenants; but, after the dissolution of the Monasteries, the new grantees sold off the stock, and raised the rents. The condition of the labourers throughout the sixteenth century was bad, as, owing to the debasement of the coinage, and the rise of prices owing to the influx of American silver, their wages no longer purchased the same amount of necessaries. They had lost their right of pasturing their cattle on commons, as, owing to the increased price of wool, many of these had been inclosed.

The Fleming and Dutch refugees improved our agriculture by teaching us the use of manure, and introducing new vegetables, such as carrots, celery, and cabbage. Hops, which owed their origin to the same source, were first grown in Kent in 1524.

Perhaps the measure the most prejudicial to the interests of the labourers which was ever passed, and which has affected them down to the beginning of the present century, was the act of 5 Elizabeth c. 4, 1563, by which the justices, an interested body of employers of labour, were empowered to fix the rate of wages for agricultural labourers and handicraftsmen.

The main discoveries of agriculture have been, in the sixteenth century, the use of winter roots to keep cattle alive during the winter instead of salting; in the seventeenth century, the use of artificial pasture, such as clover, sainfoin, and rye grass; in the eighteenth century, the use of the Norfolk or fourfold rotation of crops, by which roots, especially turnips, were substituted for bare fallows, and the ground was fertilised by the practice of feeding off the root crop with sheep. In the present century the use of dissolved bones and Peruvian guano in growing turnips, of mineral phosphates such as phosphate of ammonia, and chemical manures such as nitrate of soda, has become widely spread, so much so that £10 an acre is reckoned as the smallest amount of capital which the farmer can expend upon the soil consistently with proper cultivation.

Debasement of Money.
The kings of the Middle Ages were accustomed arbitrarily to debase the standard of money, considering that they could make a coin pass for whatever value they chose by their mere fiat.

Nicolas Oresme, first writer on Economic Subjects.
The first treatise extant on any subject akin to Political Economy is on the subject of money, by Nicolas Oresme, Bishop of Lisieux and counsellor of Charles V. of France, who died in 1382. It is entitled *Tractatus de Origine Natura Jure et Mercationibus Monetarum*, and is wonderfully correct in the views it enunciates. Nicolas Oresme was far in advance of his time, for in England in 1511 we find the mercantile fallacy receiving legislative sanction by the Statute 3 Henry VIII. cap. i., which ordered all persons carrying over sea coin, plate, or jewels to forfeit, on detection, double the value.

Economic effect of the Reformation, and Discovery of America.
The Reformation was an impulse to production, as the freedom of opinion which resulted from it had an important influence on invention and the trial of new methods in industry. The chief economic effect of the discovery of America was the alteration it produced in the ratio of silver to gold, after the discovery of the silver mines of Potosi in 1542. The stock of silver in circulation was greatly increased, and a rise in prices followed. Spain tried to keep the benefit to herself by taxation of imports, even of raw produce, and prohibiting the exportation of the precious metals; no one in Spain could even practise a trade without a license. The object of these regulations was to sell as much as possible to, and to buy as little as possible from, the foreigner, and to prevent the precious metals from becoming articles of exchange, and thereby to increase, or, at all events, keep undiminished, the stock of precious metals in the country. The regulations are known under the name of the Spanish Prohibitive System.

Royal interference with English Trade.
Under Elizabeth and James the First, royal interference with trade took the form of granting monopolies, or the exclusive right of producing and dealing in certain commodities. The merchant adventurers were given, by charter 1604 and 1617, the exclusive right of exporting woollen cloths to the Netherlands and Germany. In 1637 Sir Thomas Tempest and his partners were given the monopoly of the sale of Newcastle coal for twenty-one years. These rights of monopoly were described at the time "as the restraint

of anything public in a city to a private use," and persons who enjoyed them were denounced "as the whirlpool of the prince's profit." Elizabeth cancelled all monopolies after parliamentary remonstrance in 1601, but they were revived by James the First and Charles the First, and Colepepper thus spoke of the monopolists in the Long Parliament: "They sip in our cup, they dip in our dish, they sit by our fire; we find them in the dye vat, wash bowl, and powdering tub; they share with the butler in his box; they have marked and sealed us from head to foot. Mr Speaker, they will bate us a pin; we may not buy our own clothes without their brokage." These monopolies and exclusive patents were finally forbidden by the Declaration of Right.

James the First and Charles the First imposed prohibitions on various branches of the export trade by proclamation, mainly for the object of making the merchants buy licenses of exemption. We find the exportation of wool and the materials of cloth-making forbidden in 1622. The Long Parliament continued the restriction on the export of wool in 1648.

Rate of Customs arbitrarily increased by James I. James the First claimed the right to arbitrarily increase the rates at which customs duties were levied, and this claim received judicial sanction in Bates' case, the judges deciding that the right claimed formed part of the king's prerogative of managing the foreign relations of the country.

Navigation Law and the corresponding Law in France. Under the Commonwealth was passed the famous Navigation Law for the purpose of fostering the British navy, which forbade goods to be imported into England except in English ships, or in the ships of the countries whence the imports originated. The law was aimed at the carrying trade of the Dutch.

Fouquet, under Louis XIV., levied a corresponding duty of fifty sous per ton on every ship entering or leaving a French port. This tax failed in its object of destroying the carrying trade, which still remained in the hands of the Dutch; its only effect was to raise the rate of freight for goods imported into France by sea.

William Stafford. William Stafford's *Brief Conceipt of English Policy*, 1581, is the first treatise of any importance in the history of economics. Stafford traces very correctly the effect of inclosures in increasing the number of paupers. He is especially in advance of his age in advocating free trade in corn.

Early Italian writers on Economic Subjects. About this time were written *The Tuscan Cultivation*, by Bernardo Davanzati Bostichi, 1529–1606, which is an important authority on the economic condition of that part of Italy at the time; Gaspar Scaruffi's *Discourse on Money and the true Proportion of Gold and Silver*, 1582; and Antonio Serra's *Brief Treatise on the Causes which make Gold and Silver abundant in Kingdoms*, 1613. These last two works were written to show the loss arising from arbitrary debasement of the coinage by governments.

Discussion about the Mercantile Fallacy in England. Restrictions on the Exportation of the precious metals relaxed in favour of the East India Company. At the beginning of the seventeenth century, the Mercantile Fallacy also began to be called in question in England, and the discussion was started by the East India Company. They imported goods from India, but could find no market there for English goods, so they had to buy with silver or not at all. The Levant Company, the rival of the East India Company, on the other hand, bought the goods it imported in Mediterranean ports, and found a ready market there for English goods to pay for them. The first concession allowed to the East India Company was a permission to export £30,000, if they re-imported within six months of the termination of each voyage the same amount of gold and silver.

Sir Dudley Digges. Sir Dudley Digges' *Defence of Trade*, 1613, defended the trade with India, in spite of the export of the precious metals, on account of the cheapening of Indian goods it brought about.

Sir Thomas Mun. Sir Thomas Mun's *Discourse of Trade from England unto the East Indies*, 1621, and his petition, entitled *England's Treasure by Foreign Trade*, presented to Parliament 1628, and published posthumously in 1664, showed that the Company's imports from India were re-exported to other countries, and so more bullion was brought into England in return for them than was paid for them in India.

He also shows that the imports of a country are the true measure of the benefit it receives from foreign trade, and that they should not be considered of comparatively little importance as compared with the exports.

In 1663, all restrictions in England on the export of bullion were removed, the only obligation being to enter the amount exported at the Customs House.

The importance of the East Indian trade to England is shown by the number of early treatises on political economy connected with it.

The end of the sixteenth and the beginning of the seventeenth centuries was the period of power of Maximilian de Bethune, Duke of Sully, prime minister of Henry IV. of France. He was the first minister who set himself to further the trade of his country on a consistent plan. He regarded tillage and pasturage as "les deux mamelles," or paps, which nourished the State, and devoted himself to patronising agriculture by—

Sully the first minister who paid much attention to Finance.

1. Relaxation of the prohibitions against the export of corn and raw produce, and diminution of the taxes pressing directly upon the cultivators of the soil. He caused five million livres to be remitted from the Taille. The law on the exportation of corn in England at this time was settled by 15 C. II. c. 7; corn might be exported if the price was below 48s. a quarter, and imported, on payment of a duty of 5s. a quarter, if the price was above this minimum.

Sully's measures.

2. He reduced by half the taxes on the internal transport of corn imposed by the Provincial Estates.

3. He discouraged manufactures, that there might be a race of agricultural labourers possessed of the necessary strength for the cultivation of the soil.

4. He projected the canal of Briare, to afford facilities for internal transport of goods, which was not finished till 1740, under Louis XV. With the same object he started a posting system for travellers, and placed boats which plied for public passenger traffic on all the navigable rivers.

5. He committed a great error in allowing the heavy transit duties on goods sent from the Levant to Northern Europe, which used to pass through Marseilles and Lyons, to remain unreduced and without any distinction in favour of goods intended for consumption in France. This heavy taxation eventually diverted the trade to other routes.

Theory of the Balance of Trade. The Mercantile Theory is connected with the theory of the Balance of Trade, which led statesmen to concentrate their efforts on bringing about an excess of exports over imports by means of bounties and such like expedients, so that a balance of payment in money might always be due to their own country, and so increase the amount of specie it possessed.

Colbert's financial measures. Colbert, the famous finance minister of Louis XIV., is the next great name to that of Sully in the economic history of France, but he differed from him in favouring manufactures at the expense of agriculture.

1. He prohibited the exportation of agricultural produce. The result of this was that a large amount of land went out of cultivation, and a dearth followed, bringing about the rise of price which he wished to prevent.

2. The customs, which were hitherto farmed out in five branches, were combined in one system, and the tariff was arranged in 1664 so as to promote the export of French raw materials and manufactured goods, and the import of foreign raw materials needed for French industries, but to check the importation of foreign manufactured goods. The Dutch imposed retaliatory duties on French spirits and manufactures till the French gave way, and free trade between France and Holland was sanctioned by the treaty of Nimeguen, 1678.

3. Colbert offered bounties to those who carried on commerce by sea, or formed new companies, or introduced new manufactures. He allowed the free export of gold and silver. He abolished the Droit d'Aubaine at Marseilles, by which the goods of merchants dying in the town unnaturalised escheated to the crown, in order to induce Levant merchants to settle there. He established free ports for the deposit of

foreign merchandise which might be exported thence duty free. He lessened the transit duties on foreign produce passing through France, and projected the canal of Languedoc to unite the Atlantic and Mediterranean seas.

4. It was thought that the value saved by France becoming a manufacturer of all sorts of goods, and not depending on foreign imports, would compensate the agriculturist for the loss of his market abroad.

5. Colbert gave France its first code of commercial law in the Ordonnance de la Marine, 1572.

Harrington's Oceana. Harrington's *Oceana*, 1656, is remarkable for the way in which it traces the connection between the distribution of power and the distribution of wealth.

Sir William Petty. Sir William Petty is the first English writer on political economy of any real note; he wrote a *Treatise on Taxes and Contributions*, 1667, in which he enunciated the principle that "labour is the father and active principle of wealth, as lands are the mother." His other works were *Quantulumcunque*, 1682, written to combat the idea that an unfavourable balance of trade drained England of her wealth, and an *Essay on Political Arithmetic*, 1699. This essay was the first attempt to use statistics for eonomic purposes. Statistics are collections of facts capable of expression in a numerical or tabular form.

Sir Josiah Child. Sir Josiah Child's *Brief Observations concerning Trade and the Interest of Money*, 1668, contains the curious error that the low rate of interest prevalent in Holland is the *causa causans* of the commercial prosperity of the Dutch, and that the rate of interest should be fixed by the Government of the country.

Closing of the Exchequer. The year 1672 was the year of the closing of the Exchequer by Charles II. at the advice of his minister, Clifford. By this measure Charles stopped the payment of principal or interest on the loans advanced by the London goldsmiths to Government. These loans had been made by the goldsmiths out of the sums placed on deposit with them; in this custom of receiving money on deposit, the goldsmiths were the direct predecessors of modern banks. This debt of £1,328,526 was taken over by the South Sea Company, and subsequently became part of the National Debt.

Sir William Temple, in 1673, wrote an *Essay on the Trade of Ireland*, which shows that the author was still infected with the fallacious doctrine of the balance of trade.

Sir William Temple.

Locke's two Treatises on Civil Government, 1690, contains the first attempt at a theory of value: "Of the products of the earth useful to the life of man, nine-tenths are the effects of labour; nay, if we will rightly consider things as they come to our use, and cast up the several expenses about them, what in them is purely owing to nature, and what to labour, we shall find that, in most of them, ninety-nine hundredths are to be put on the account of labour." They are also important "as the expression of the rights of the individual, both political and social, to be governed according to his own ideas, and to be secured in the control of his own property."

John Locke.

Locke's Tracts on money prevented the debasement of the coinage, which was in contemplation before Sir Isaac Newton restored it to its former value in 1695. Their full title is, *Considerations on the lowering of Interest and raising the value of Money*, 1691, and *Further Considerations*. They plainly maintain the mercantile fallacy. "Gold and silver, though they serve for few, yet command all the necessaries of life, and in plenty of them consists riches." "Riches consist in a plenty of gold and silver, that is in having more in proportion of these metals than the rest of the world or our neighbours." Locke is in error, on the question of the value of money, that it depends upon "that estimate which common consent has placed upon it."

He seems to have anticipated the physiocrats in the following opinion: "Taxes, however contrived, and out of whose hands soever immediately taken, do in a country where the great fund is in land for the most part terminate upon land." This reminds us of the impot unique.

That versatile author, Daniel Defoe, offered his contribution to economics in his *Giving alms no charity*, in which he shows the prejudicial effect of indiscriminate almsgiving. His *Tour through Great*

Daniel Defoe.

Britain, 1724-25, gives a valuable account of the manufacturers on a small scale who followed the domestic system of production. He wrote before the north of England had attracted to itself the largest share of the population, and says of England south of the Trent that it is "by far the largest as well as the richest and most populous" portion of the country.

About this time originated one of the great financial institutions of the world—the Bank of England. In 1694, Montague, Chancellor of the Exchequer, borrowed £1,200,000 for the purposes of the Government, and caused the creditors of Government, who had lent the money, to be incorporated as the Bank of England. The loan to Government was treated as part of the bank's capital, and the interest at 8 per cent. secured on the taxes. The Bank of England was formed on the plan of William Paterson; it traded in bullion and bills of exchange, and received money on deposit, and lent it out at interest. The stability of the Bank of England has been in a great measure owing to "the Rest," a guarantee fund formed out of surplus profits in the first quarter of the last century. In 1742, it was given the profitable monopoly of the right of issuing bank notes. The Bank of England was a Whig institution; the Tories supported its rival, the Land Bank. The object of this bank was to lend money on landed security, the theory being that every one who had real property should have besides the use of paper money up to the full value of his property. Its originators, John Briscoe and Hugh Chamberlayne, considered that, if an estate worth £1000 was pledged to the bank for 100 years, paper money up to £100,000 might be issued on security of it, regardless of the fact that the fee simple of land does not sell for more than twenty years' purchase. Chamberlayne undertook to raise £8000 on every freehold estate of £150 a year "brought into the bank," without dispossessing the freeholder, though the fee simple of such an estate would only sell for £3000. The bank was to advance two and a half million pounds to Government at $7\frac{1}{2}$ per cent., but the subscriptions never amounted to more than £7500, and the enterprise failed.

The Bank of England.

Chamberlayne's Land Bank.

The fallacies of John Law of Lauriston, 1671–1729, in connection with the issue of paper money, merit some consideration. Law's theories are given in his *Money and Trade, considered with a Proposal for Supplying the Nation with Money*, 1705. He considered money not the result, but the cause of wealth. To increase the stock of money by a properly regulated paper currency must be beneficial. He proposed to concentrate the management of foreign trade and internal finance in the hands of a huge monopolist corporation carrying on business with paper money. This scheme he eventually realised in his Royal Bank and Trading Company of the Indies in France. He conceived the idea that it was possible for a nation to make two uses of the same capital, as the banker lends the capital deposited with him to be used productively, and the depositor often makes use unproductively of the credit of the banker, with whom he has deposited his money, by means of cheques or notes. Law wished to establish an inconvertible paper currency, and he maintained that it would be beneficial on the following grounds:—

Law's Theories of Paper Money.

1. Paper money maintained at par with specie would not fluctuate in value so much as the precious metals, and would be an equally good common measure of value.

2. Paper money is more easy to count and transport than metallic money.

3. The material of paper money costs nothing, thereby saving the community the cost of production of the precious metals.

4. Paper money is not exported, and its quantity can be easily regulated to suit changes in the demand.

Law revived the project of a Land Bank in Scotland, 1705. He proposed to issue paper money on the security of land assigned to the forty commissioners appointed by the Parliament of Scotland. The land was to be valued at twenty years' purchase, according to what would be given for it in silver money, and was to be redeemable in a term of years. It was contended that other goods, if made the security for paper money, might lose their value on a change of fashion, but that land might always be turned to account. This theory neglects the fact that the

Law's Land Bank.

security of silver is that of so much past labour, that of land is the security of an instrument of production, requiring the combined employment of actual produce, such as seed and tools and human labour.

If land is enclosed and cleared, it is realised capital, but liable to deteriorate in value from natural causes, unless fresh labour and capital are employed on it. If money be issued on the security of land, it is only the mortgage of eventual capital. The issue of notes on the security of land also failed in the case of the French Revolutionary Assignats.

Law retired to France when his schemes failed in Scotland, and in 1716 founded the General Bank, which issued notes payable on demand in livres of a fixed fineness of metal and weight. The capital of this bank was 1200 shares of 5000 livres, and as three-fourths of its share capital might be paid for in billets d'Etat or State paper, it absorbed a considerable portion of the paper money in circulation, and so raised the credit of Government. In 1717, these notes were ordered to be received by all revenue officers in payment of State dues, and to be cashed on demand. Notes were to be issued to those who required circulating, and bank stock to those who wished for a means of investment. Notes were to be exchanged for stock when they became redundant.

Law wished that his bank should manage the public revenues, make all State payments, and negotiate all State loans.

In 1717 the Company of the West was set on foot; it possessed the sovereignty of Louisiana and Illinois, the exclusive right of trade between these countries and France for twenty-five years, and the monopoly of the beaver trade. This was called the Mississippi Scheme. The capital of this Company was 100 million livres, in 200,000 shares of 500 livres each, payable in State notes; but as these were at a discount of 75 per cent., the capital really amounted to only about 250 million livres in sterling.

In 1719 the bank became a royal bank, issuing notes payable on demand in current coin; but as the State had just issued a coinage debased $\frac{1}{3}$ in value, these notes were $\frac{1}{3}$ less in value than those of Law's banks.

The Company of the West acquired the rights of the merchants of St Malo trading to the West Indies, and of the Company of Senegal trading to Africa, and was reconstituted as the Company of the Indies, with an additional capital of 50,000 shares of 500 livres each. The bank took a lease of the Mint for nine years, and of the Customs, and lent 1500 million livres to the State at 3 per cent.

<small>Trading Company of the Indies.</small>

In 1720 the Bank and Company of the Indies were amalgamated, and Law was made Counsellor of State and Controller of the Finances.

All these additions to its business required new issues of State notes, which were at a huge discount as compared with their nominal value. Nevertheless, in November 1719, the whole of the shares of the Company of the Indies, a nominal value of 300 million livres, had a market price of 12,000 million livres. To pay 5 per cent. on this required an annual income of 500 million livres, but the whole income of the Company could only pay 5 per cent. on the original capital of 1677 million livres. In spite of this, Law promised an annual income of 200 livres from each share of 500 livres; and as these had been paid for in depreciated State money, such an income would have been equivalent to a profit of 120 per cent.

The scheme failed on account of the inconvertibility of the notes into cash, except at an enormous loss, on account of their being issued out of all proportion to the security. Shareholders converted their shares into notes, to exchange them for money, and a run on the bank took place. It was attempted to keep the notes in circulation by forbidding gold to circulate at all, and silver was only allowed to pass current in small quantities. The crash was accelerated by the order of the Regent Orleans, March 1720, reducing the value of the original shares of 500 livres to 9000 livres, instead of 20,000, which was the extreme limit of price they touched in December 1719. The final blow was given by the order of the same authority (May 1720), which reduced the notes, and, consequently, the shares, to half their nominal value. The Bank was not necessarily bound to the Trading Company of the Indies; and had the connection been severed, and its note issue been limited, it might have survived. The edict of March 1720, which made the shares of the Company convertible into notes of the Bank, ruined the Bank without saving the Company.

The success of the East India Company made the Scotch anxious to found a trading company of their own, and a site was fixed on for its operations by Robert Paterson, founder of the Bank of England, on the Isthmus of Darien. In 1695 this trading company was constituted by an Act of the Scotch Parliament as the African Company, and given power to make settlements, build fortifications, and contract alliances in Asia, Africa, or America. The enterprise failed, owing to the jealousy of the Spaniards, ignorance of the countries to be traded with, and consequent ill assortment of the goods taken out from England for purposes of trade to the needs of tropical countries, and the deadly nature of the climate of Central America.

In 1711 the South Sea Company was formed to trade with the Spanish American colonies, a privilege granted to England by the subsequent Peace of Utrecht, along with the asiento or right of supplying the Spanish colonies with negro slaves. The Company lent ten million pounds, and allowed the debt to be funded at 6 per cent. in return for a monopoly of the trade to South America and the Pacific Coast of North America. In 1717 they lent another five million pounds to Government, and in 1720 they agreed to take over thirty-five million pounds of Government annuities, and to persuade the holders to take in exchange South Sea stock. This company failed, because its capital was sunk in procuring concessions and in lending money to Government; there was none left to trade with.

The eighteenth century is the era of wars for trading purposes. War was no longer made for the spreading of particular systems of religion, or for the aggrandisement of dynasties, but to reap commercial advantages. "It cannot be denied that mistaken views of commerce, like those so frequently entertained of religion, have been the cause of many wars and much bloodshed."[1]

Eighteenth century period of commercial wars.

"Mistaken views of commerce have made each nation regard the welfare of its neighbours as incompatible with its

[1] M'Culloch's *Principles of Political Economy*, p. 140.

own; hence the reciprocal desire of injuring and impoverishing each other; and hence that spirit of commercial rivalry which has been the immediate or remote cause of the great number of modern wars."[1]

It is the work of political economy to dissipate these erroneous ideas, and so to contribute to the security of peace.

To resume the account of the literature of political economy in England. Sir Dudley North's *Discourses on Trade*, 1697, argue against the theory of the balance of trade. "Money is a merchandise whereof there may be a glut as well as a scarcity, and that even to an inconvenience." "People cannot want money to serve the ordinary dealing, and more than enough they will not have."

Sir Dudley North.

"The whole world as to trade is but one nation or people, and therein nations are as persons. The loss of a trade with one nation is not that only separately considered, but so much of the trade of the world rescinded and lost, for all are bound together. There can be no trade unprofitable to the public, for if any prove so, men leave it off, and wherever traders thrive, the public, of which they are a part, thrive also. To force men to deal in any prescribed manner may profit such as happen to serve them, but the public gains not, because it is taking from one subject to give to another."

An anonymous tract, *Considerations on the East India Trade*, 1701, is devoted to proving that if the imported Indian silk ruined the English silk manufacture, the English labour devoted to the production of silk could be profitably diverted to other employment.

Considerations on East Indian Trade.

Sir William Davenant, Inspector-General of Exports and Imports, wrote an Essay on the East India Trade, 1696, and an Essay on the probable ways of making the people gainers in the balance of trade. He approaches the correct view of wealth. "Gold and silver are indeed the measure of trade, but the spring and original of all wealth in all nations is the natural or artificial products of the country, *i.e.*, what its land or labour produces."

Sir William Davenant.

He thus defines the object of political economy: "The principal object of this science is to secure a certain fund of

---

[1] M'Culloch's *Principles of Political Economy*, pp. 37, 38.

subsistence for all the inhabitants, to obviate every circumstance which may render it precarious, to provide everything necessary for supplying the wants of the society, and to employ the inhabitants in such a manner as to naturally create reciprocal relations and dependencies between them, so as to make their several interests lead them to supply one another with their reciprocal wants."

Sir Robert Walpole was the first Prime Minister to devote himself systematically to the improvement of commerce. In 1720 the king announced, in a speech from the throne, that nothing would be more advantageous to the improvement of trade " than to make the exportation of our own manufactures, and the importation of the commodities used in the manufacturing of them, as practicable and easy as may be." In pursuance of this policy, he took off the duties from more than 100 British exports and from nearly 40 articles of importation. In 1730 he allowed Georgia and North and South Carolina to export rice direct to Europe, and abolished the restriction that it must necessarily pass through an English port.

<small>Walpole as a Finance Minister.</small>

In 1733 Walpole brought forward his proposal for creating bonded warehouses, in which merchants might deposit goods till required for consumption without paying any tax, and for collecting the taxes on spirits, tea, coffee, wine, and tobacco, in the form of excise throughout the kingdom, instead of in the form of customs at the ports of import. He wished to keep the necessaries of life and the raw materials of industry absolutely untaxed. The proposal for bonded warehouses would have made London a free port, and doubled English trade, and the excise proposal would have greatly increased the revenue, but both proposals were thrown out, mainly on account of the jealousy of the army of officials they would have necessitated.

Josiah Tucker, Dean of Gloucester, was the author of the following writings having reference to economics: *Essay on French and English Trade* (1750), *Questions on Commerce* (1755), and the *Elements of Commerce and the Theory of Taxes*, written for the education of the Prince of Wales (afterwards George IV.). Tucker was an advocate of Free Trade, and recommended that America

<small>Josiah Tucker.</small>

should be allowed to be independent. "What will be gained by conquering America?" he asks. "Not an increase of trade, that is impossible, for a shopkeeper will never get more custom by beating his customers, and what is true of a shopkeeper is also true of a shopkeeping nation." America will only trade with England as long as she can get the best market for her commodities there. A war for commercial purposes between two parts of the same empire is therefore an absurdity.

Sir James Steuart wrote an *Enquiry concerning the Principles of Political Economy*, 1766; but his book does not occupy an important place in the history of the gradual development of the science.

Sir James Steuart.

In our survey of political economy, two names in France deserve passing mention—they are those of Pierre le Pesant, Seigneur de Bois-Guilbert, and of Marshal Vauban.

De Bois-Guilbert published in 1697 his *Detail de France*, a sort of economic handbook descriptive of the country and upholding mercantilist principles. Other works of the same author are a *Treatise on the Nature of Grains, and on the Trade Therein; Dissertations on the Nature of Riches, of Money, and of Tributes; Essay on the Scarcity of Silver.*

In 1707, Marshal Vauban published *Project d'un dixme Royale*, or plan for making all kinds of income contribute equally to the necessities of the State, by means of a tax called the Royal Tenth. He puts forward the famous principle that, if the peasants are poor, the kingdom is poor; if the kingdom is poor, the king is poor.

The Physiocratic School of political economists in France derived their name from Dupont de Nemours' book, published 1768, *Physiocracy, or the Natural Constitution of Government the most advantageous to the Human Race.* Physiocracy means government according to nature, and the physiocrats held that, if their maxims were followed, there would be in economic matters a return to the pristine state of nature for which Rousseau yearned, and a desire for which is expressed in the Stoic conception of duty—to live conformably to nature. The members of this school were sometimes called the economists. Amongst them the best known are Francis Quesnay, physician

The Physiocratic School, also called the Economists.

of Louis XV., 1694–1774, author of a Treatise on Natural Law; *The Economic Picture*, with its explanation or analysis of the *Royal Economics* of Sully, to which is attached the motto from Vauban's writings, "Pauvre paysans, pauvre royaume, pauvre royaume, pauvre roi"; *The General Maxims for the Economical Government of an Agricultural Kingdom*, 1758, and the article on "Farms and Grains" in the *Encyclopædia* of Diderot and D'Alembert, 1755.

Quesnay was more a believer in the projects of Sully than in those of Colbert, whom he considered Italian in his sympathies. In his *Maxims* he denies that the nation suffers any loss by trading with foreigners, and exposes the fallacy of the balance of trade. His advice is—"Let entire freedom of commerce be maintained; for the regulation of commerce, both internal and external, the most sure, the most exact, the most profitable to the nation and to the state, consists in entire freedom of competition."

Robert James Turgot, 1727–81, finance minister of Louis XVI., 1775–76. He wrote *Reflections on the Formation and Distribution of Riches*.

Dupont de Nemours, 1739–1817, besides the book mentioned above, wrote a treatise *On the Exportation and Importation of Grains*.

Lemercier de la Riviere, author of *The Natural and Essential Order of all Political Societies*, 1767. "Property, security, liberty, these comprise the whole social order; the right of property is a tree, of which the institutions of society are the branches."

John Claud Marie Vincent, Sieur de Gournay, 1712–59. He considers the objection against commerce, that it is unproductive, untenable.

Victor Mirabeau, 1715–89, father of the famous orator. His works on this subject were *The Friend of Men, or a Treatise on Population*, 1756, *Theory of Taxation*, 1760, *The Economists*, 1760, and *Rural Philosophy, or the General and Political Economy of Agriculture*.

Other names sometimes mentioned in connection with the school are those of the Abbe Baudeau, author of the *Introduction to Economic Philosophy*, and Le Trosne.

Voltaire was in sympathy with the opinions of the economists, especially in the matter of Free Trade, which he held should be universal. According to Buckle, Voltaire has anticipated Malthus in the relation that he draws between the increase of population and the increase of food.

The physiocratic doctrines are first found in an essay *On the Nature of Commerce in General*, written by an author of the name of Cantillon, in 1755. According to them, the earth was the only source of riches. Agriculture alone produces a surplus of wealth over and above what is necessary to maintain its labourers, so that wealth from agriculture increases without its being necessary for the labourers to deprive themselves of any part of their subsistence.

Merchants and manufacturers merely reproduce funds equal in value to the supplies provided for their support by agriculture; hence in trade or manufacture there is no net produce. It follows that the wealth of a trading or manufacturing community cannot increase, unless the labourers go without a portion of the funds necessary for their maintenance, so as to provide a means for saving. This view was also shared by Montesquieu, who has a chapter in his *Spirit of the Laws*, headed "To some nations it is disadvantageous to trade."

The surplus realised by agriculture, after repaying the capital invested in it, is the disposable capital of the country. On this account all existing taxes were to be repealed, and the impot unique, or single tax, levied direct upon the produce of land. In all other things the physiocrats wished for complete freedom of industry. Their maxim was "laisser faire, laisser passer,"—let every one make what he liked, and take his labour and his goods to whatever market he liked. They considered it of especial importance that industry should be free from the vexatious interference of internal tolls that was so common in France at the time. Government should not interfere with industry. Dictation, like that to the clothmakers, of what size and pattern they were to make their cloths, was particularly prejudicial to the development of trade.

There is a certain law of nature, distinguished by simplicity and harmony, which consists of the sentiments naturally innate in every mind, being implanted there by God for the guidance of human life; hence it is said to be that "which natural reason appoints for all mankind." The laws of the country were to be first brought into accordance with this law of nature, and then Quesnay advised the Dauphin "to do nothing but let the laws rule."

It has been pointed out that the year 1776 is the year of the publication of the *Wealth of Nations*, and of the refutation of the previous English colonial policy by the Declaration of the Independence of America. Our colonial trade was jealously confined to England, till Walpole, in 1723, allowed Georgia and the Carolinas to export rice direct to Europe. The colonials could raise the raw materials of silk and linen, and manufacture them for their own use, but not for other markets. The trade in iron and furs, including hats, in which the colonies possessed special natural advantages, were discouraged.

The first two books of the *Wealth of Nations* deal with economic theory, and with the circumstances of production and distribution. The wealth of a country is the annual produce of its land and labour, and each nation supplies itself with necessaries and conveniences by means of this; labour is "the real measure of the exchangeable value of all commodities." An explanation of the division of labour and of its advantages follows. Wages are the reward of labour, and their inequality in various trades is accounted for. He next describes profit. The book ends with a description of rent, but his statement that all land which grows food must yield rent is erroneous.

Adam Smith, 1723-90.

Contents of the "Wealth of Nations."

The second book deals with "the nature, accumulation, and improvement of stock." Capital is divided into (1) Fixed; (2) Circulating. Under the former head are classed machines, buildings, agricultural improvement, and personal capital (the abilities of the members of society). Under the latter head are classed money, provisions, materials, and completed work.

Labour is (1) Productive; (2) Unproductive; and the distinction between these two kinds of labour is explained.

There are four methods for the employment of capital.

1. Procuring the food of society.
2. Preparing raw produce for the use of society, *e.g.*, in the manufactory of goods.

3. Transport of the raw or manufactured produce from the place where it is abundant to the place where it is wanted, *i.e.*, the carrying trade.

4. Keeping small portions of manufactured or raw produce on sale to suit the occasional needs of those requiring them, *i.e.*, the retail trade.

Smith considers that agriculture possesses this special advantage, among the employments to which man can devote himself, that "nature labours along with man," and reproduces the capital of the farmer with profit and rent.

Cliffe Leslie shows that the third and fourth books, in logical order, come before the first and second, as they contain the induction on which is based the conclusion that the State has only to protect individual liberty, and labour (or the natural effort of every individual to better his own condition) will supply all the necessaries and conveniences of life, will divide its functions spontaneously in the best manner, and will distribute its produce in a natural order, and with equality.

In the third book the author studies the development of the various forms of industry among the various nations of Europe, the natural order being—(1) Agriculture; (2) Manufacture; (3) Wholesale Trade: (A) Home Trade; (B) Carrying Trade. In some nations the industry of the country receives the greater encouragement, in others the industry of the towns.

The fourth book deals with systems of political economy, and contains the attack on the mercantile system, the description of the effect of bounties, and the development of the true characteristics of wealth. It also contains remarks on the treatment of their colonies by various nations, and upon the commercial policy of England to her colonies. The doctrine of the physiocrats, that agriculture is the only productive form of industry, is refuted.

The fifth book deals with the raising of a revenue to meet the expenses of the sovereign or the commonwealth, and lays down certain canons of taxation. The author of the *History of Civilisation* thus describes Smith's method:—

"The *Wealth of Nations* is entirely deductive, since in it Smith generalises the laws of wealth, not from the phenomena of wealth, not from statistical statements, but from the phenomena of selfishness; thus making a deductive application of one set of mental principles to the whole set of economical facts."[1]

Adam Smith is not essentially deductive, as Buckle states, seeing that he combines deduction with the historical inductive system of Montesquieu, which investigates, in history and the phenomena of actual life, the different states of society, and tries to discover their causes. Cliffe Leslie has pointed out that deduction is legitimate when based upon the universal facts of human nature and the external world, but vicious when not from facts verified by observation, but from an *a priori* assumption, half theological half metaphysical, regarding a supposed harmonious and beneficent natural order of the world. It is on this theory of nature, that there is "a beneficent and harmonious order, which appears when nature is left to itself," that Smith's philosophy is based. "His reasoning is faulty in arguing *a priori* from assumptions obtained not by interrogation but by anticipation of nature; what is assumed as nature is at bottom a mere conjecture respecting its constitution and arrangements." Smith uses the word "natural" as meaning that which the existing forces tend to produce, sometimes as meaning that which his conception of the law of nature makes him consider that they ought to produce.

Method of the "Wealth of Nations."

Dugald Stewart says, in the preface to his edition of the *Wealth of Nations*, "the great and leading object of his speculations is to illustrate the provisions made by nature, in the principles of the human mind, and in the circumstances of man's external situation, for a gradual and progressive augmentation in the means of human wealth, and to demonstrate that the most effectual means of advancing a people to greatness is to maintain that order of things which nature has pointed out." The good of the community is therefore best attained by allowing free play to individual cupidities, provided that the law restrains any one from interfering with the selfishness of another. "The natural effort of every individual to better his own condition, when suffered to exert itself with freedom and security, is, alone and without any assistance, not only capable

Interest of the Community best maintained by allowing free play to Individual Cupidities.

[1] *History of Civilisation*, i. 259.

of carrying on the society to wealth and prosperity, but of surmounting an hundred impertinent obstructions, with which the folly of human laws too often encumbers its operations."[1]

"Every individual necessarily labours to render the annual revenue of the society as great as he can. He generally indeed neither intends to promote the public interest, or knows how much he is promoting it. He intends only his own gain, and he is in this, as in many other cases, led by an invisible hand to promote an end which was no part of his intentions."

This is the foundation of the tenets of the Manchester school, and of that set of opinions which the Germans call "Smithianismus," that individual interests work together so as to produce the greatest amount of national wealth.

"As long as men do not come into collision by maintaining their individual rights of self-interest, the interference of government is unjust and impolitic, as hindering the natural development of agencies by which men's wants are supplied."

"All systems either of preference or restraint being completely taken, the simple and obvious system of natural liberty establishes itself of its own accord."[2]

The interference of government should be limited to—

Limitation of the Interference of Government. 1. The protection of the nation from foreign aggression. 2. The administration of justice. 3. The maintenance of certain institutions beyond the reach of individual enterprise.

"The statesman who should attempt to direct private people in what manner they ought to employ their capitals, would not only load himself with a most unnecessary attention, but assume an authority which could be safely trusted not only to no single person, but to no senate or council whatever, and which would nowhere be so dangerous as in the hands of a man who had folly and presumption enough as to deem himself fit to exercise it."[3]

[1] *Wealth of Nations*, iv. 5, 423, edition Dugald Stewart.
[2] *Ibid.*, iv. 5, 509, ,, ,,
[3] *Ibid.*, iv. 2, ,, ,,

Adam Smith's view, that all land which grows food must
Erroneous views yield rent, is erroneous. He is also wrong in
of the "Wealth supposing that foreign trade is merely beneficial
of Nations." as a vent for the surplus of a country, and that
the gain from commerce lies in its maintaining a high rate of
mercantile profit. His account of the causes regulating the
distribution of the precious metals in the world is insufficient.

Smith's approval of a maximum legal rate of interest was adversely criticised by Jeremy Bentham in *Letters on Usury*, 1787. These shortcomings are in a great measure to be accounted for by the state of industry in his time. The time of the vast extension of British commerce by means of Free Trade was not yet: the importation of corn was only 23,000 quarters; hence Smith delivers it as his opinion that the freest system of importation would not affect the price of corn in England.

Boulton and Watts had not yet perfected the steam engine, which was only in the preliminary stage of Newcomen. Hargreaves's spinning jenny, Arkwright's water frame, carding machine, and discovery how to spin by rollers, Crompton's spinning mule (a combination of the spinning jenny and the water frame), all which facilitated the spinning of the yarn, and Cartwright's power-loom for weaving it, had not revolutionised the textile industry. Cart had not discovered the method of rolling and riddling iron, or Roebuck that of smelting iron with coal instead of charcoal. The beds of iron and coal in close proximity in the North of England, which rendered possible the collective or factory system of production, had not yet been revealed. The machines and the system of division of labour made use of in the cloth manufacture were as they were a hundred years ago, and only three important improvements in production had been introduced since the time of Edward IV. Speaking generally, production was on the domestic system, and in the hands of small capitalists who were also labourers. The capitalist was distinct from the labourer only in agriculture.

Inland trade was comparatively free, but hampered by the rights of trade corporations, the obligations of apprenticeship, and the restrictions on the movement of labourers, from the fear of their obtaining a settlement in a parish, or the right of having their relief made chargeable to its rates.

His philosophy was too materialistic: he seems to have paid too much attention to the accumulation of wealth, and too little to the way in which a state should employ its wealth. He neglects "the moral factor" in economics. This may be explained by his having intended his *Wealth of Nations* to be read along with his *Theory of the Moral Sentiments*. In the latter work he neglects all those qualities which conflict with a man's sympathy for his fellow-creatures, quite as much as, in the *Wealth of Nations*, he neglects those qualities which conflict with a man's desire for wealth.

His political economy is too universal: he does not realise that there may be types of society to which the account he gives of economic phenomena will not apply. The great work of Adam Smith was to prove that the labour of merchants and manufacturers was not unproductive, as the physiocrats thought, and to give an impulse to Free Trade.

Hume said of the *Wealth of Nations* that "it is so much illustrated with curious facts that it must take the public attention."

Influence of the "Wealth of Nations."

Sir James Mackintosh thus describes its influence: "It is perhaps the only book which produced an immediate general and irrevocable change in some of the most important parts of the legislation of all civilised states."[1]

Bagehot has an equally high opinion of its importance. "No other form of political philosophy has ever had one-thousandth part of the influence upon us; its teachings have settled down into the common sense of the nation, and become irreversible."[2]

The influence of the *Wealth of Nations* can be traced on Pitt in his offer of Free Trade to Ireland, with a relaxation of the prohibition of the import of Irish cattle into England, and in his treaty of commerce with France, 1787. By this treaty the subjects of either country might reside or travel in the other without license or passport, all prohibitions on trade were abolished, and every import duty reduced. The Methuen treaty, 1707, admitting Portuguese wines into England at one-third less duty than French wines, was abrogated. Pitt's policy of freeing the poorer members of

[1] *Ethical Philosophy*, p. 232.   [2] *Economical Studies*.

society, as far as possible, from taxation, which led him to repeal the taxes on women servants, on carts and waggons, and on windows in small houses, and to lower the taxes on tea and spirits, may also be traced to Smith's teaching.

Hume's essays on *Commerce* and on *Jealousy in Trade* were published in 1752. The former asserts that "everything in the world is purchased by labour, and our passions are the only causes of labour."

Hume.

The essay on *Jealousy in Trade* contradicted the doctrine that the commercial progress of one state must be prejudicial to the profit of others. "Not only as a man, but as a British subject, I pray for the flourishing commerce of Germany, Spain, Italy, even France itself." Hume proves Smith to be in error in asserting that rent is part of the price of agricultural produce. The essay on *Money* refutes the confusion of money with wealth. "In the national stock of labour consists all real power and riches."

The essay on *Interest* combats the idea that it depends on the quantity of money in a country; a reduction in the rate of interest can only be brought about by industry, frugality, and an improvement of the arts and commerce; a low rate of interest is therefore a barometer of the prosperity of a country.

Jeremy Bentham, whose *Letters on Usury*, 1787, adversely criticises Smith's approval of a legal maximum rate of interest, always resolutely opposed government interference for which a clear justification could not be given. Bentham published a *Manual of Political Economy* in 1843.

Bentham.

Malthus's *Essay on Population*, 1798, was the first thorough application of the inductive method to economic topics. Its full title was *An Essay on the Principle of Population as it affects the Future Improvement of Society, with Remarks on the Speculations of Mr Goodwin, M. Condorcet, and other Writers*. This Goodwin here referred to was William Goodwin, 1756–1836, who wrote *Political Justice*, 1793, in which he advocated an arrangement of society in which marriage and property were unknown, and *The Enquirer*, 1797, a series of essays on social subjects, in which, especially in the essay on "Avarice and Profusion," he carried on a controversy with Malthus. Malthus adversely

Malthus.

criticised his writings by pointing out that it would be difficult for moral restraint as a check on population, unless the principle is admitted that the father of a family is responsible for the maintenance of his children.

Condorcet's work here alluded to was a *Sketch of an Historical Picture of the Human Mind*, which is important as putting forward, for the first time, the theory of social dynamics founded on history.

In the second edition of the essay, published in 1803, Malthus admitted the operation of moral checks in limiting the increase of the population, as well as the influence of vice and misery. He disapproved of the Poor Laws, and advocated their gradual abolition, that the checks on the increase of population might freely operate. The title of the second edition of the essay was altered. It runs thus:—*An Essay on the Principle of Population, and a View of its Present Effects on Human Happiness, with an Enquiry into our Prospects respecting the Future Removal or Mitigation of the Evils which it Occasions*. Malthus was also the author of the *Enquiry into the Nature and Progress of Rent*, 1815, in which he enunciates the true theory of rent, showing especially that it is not an element in the cost of production of corn. The occasion of this work was the passing of a law in 1815, raising the limit at which foreign corn might be imported for consumption to 80s. a quarter. Malthus advocated the further restriction on the importation of foreign corn, but Ricardo, in his *Essay on the Influence of a Low Price of Corn on the Profits of Stock*, came to an opposite conclusion, and by showing the effect of an increase in the price of raw produce on wages and profits, extracted from it a strong argument in favour of Free Trade in corn.

Almost simultaneously with the works of Malthus and Ricardo, "A Fellow of University College, Oxford" (Sir Edward West), wrote his *Essay on the Application of Capital to Land*.

Both Malthus and West state the theory of rent correctly, but it was left for Ricardo to apply the theory of rent to the question of the Corn Laws, and to condemn them by showing their effect in lowering profits, and in raising the price of the labourers' food.

<small>True Theory of Rent.</small>

Dr Anderson, in his *Enquiry into the Nature of the Corn Laws*, published at Edinburgh, 1777, and in his *Agricultural Recreations* (vol. v. p. 401), published 1801, has anticipated all three authors in his remarks on rent.

David Ricardo, 1772–1823. His first work was *The High Price of Bullion a Proof of the Depreciation of Bank Notes*. This led the Bullion Committee of the House of Commons, over which Horner presided, to decide that the inconvertible paper currency of the Bank of England had been depreciated; the House of Commons, under the dictation of Vansittart, Chancellor of the Exchequer, subsequently negatived this resolution. A merchant of the name of Bosanquet controverted the resolution of the Bullion Committee, and Ricardo attacked his arguments in his *Reply to Mr Bosanquet's Practical Observations on the Report of the Bullion Committee*.

Ricardo and his Works. In 1815 Ricardo published his *Essay on the Influence of a Low Price of Corn on the Profits of Stock*, which has been before alluded to.

In 1816 his *Proposals for an Economical and Secure Currency, with Observations on the Profits of the Bank of England*, appeared. He proposed to exchange bank notes for bars of gold bullion of the standard and purity. This plan would check the issue of bank notes quite as effectually as making them convertible into gold coin; while, as bars could not be used as the circulating medium, no gold could get into circulation, and so the expenses of coinage, and the wear and tear and loss of coins, would be saved.

In 1817 Ricardo published his *Principles of Political Economy and Taxation*. Of this work, M'Culloch says that "It is not even a systematic treatise, but it is principally an inquiry concerning fundamental principles. And although it be often exceedingly difficult, or, it may be, all but impossible, to estimate the extent to which these principles may in certain cases be modified by other principles and combinations of circumstances, it is obviously of the greatest importance to have ascertained their existence."

In 1820 Ricardo contributed an article on the funding system to the supplement to the *Encyclopædia Britannica*.

In 1822 he wrote his tract *On Protection to Agriculture*, zealously advocating Free Trade in corn.

His *Political Economy and Taxation* is a series of loosely connected essays on the various economic subjects with which he deals; as a Jew he was particularly fitted to deal with abstractions, and he is at his best in dealing with abstract questions like that of money, into which the moral element enters little.

Ricardo is the chief of the abstract school of political economicians, whose method Mill has thus described in his *Essay on the Definition and Method of Political Economy*: "Political economy is concerned with man solely as a being who desires to possess wealth. It makes entire abstraction of every other human passion or motive, except those which may be regarded as perpetually antagonising principles to the desire of wealth, namely, aversion to labour, and desire of the present enjoyment of costly indulgences. These it takes, to a certain extent, into its calculation, because these do not merely, like other desires, occasionally conflict with the pursuit of wealth, but accompany it always as a drag or impediment, and are therefore inseparably mixed up in the consideration of it."

Senior says, "That every man desires to obtain wealth with as little sacrifice as possible, is in political economy what gravitation is in physics, or the *dictum de omni et nullo* in logic, the ultimate fact beyond which reasoning cannot go, and of which almost every other proposition is merely an illustration." Cliffe Leslie has pointed out that "The desire of wealth is a general name for a great variety of wants, desires, and sentiments differing widely in their economic character and effects." In its first form, the desire of wealth has its origin in the desire of satisfying hunger and thirst; in the next stage of society, in the desire of acquiring property in cattle; and, when society has reached the agricultural stage, in the desire of acquiring property in land. It is precisely, however, because such a variety of ideas are comprehended under the general name of the desire for wealth, that the general statement that all men are actuated by this motive is broadly true.

The Abstract Method of Political Economy.

Buckle defends "the abstraction of every other human passion or motive," by saying that, as the geometrician, by an intellectual artifice, reasons of a line as having length but not breadth although it has some breadth, so political economy reasons of the abstract man as being actuated only by the desire of wealth and aversion from labour; by pure selfishness, in fact, because the subject would be too large if all the qualities on the sympathetic side of human nature were considered.

Buckle's Defence of the "Abstract" Method.

Ricardo sets out from arbitrary assumptions, reasons deductively from them, and then announces his conclusions as true, without making any allowance for the unreality of his assumptions or comparing his results with experience. He imagines two savages bartering things together, and then tries to guess how they would act.

Ricardo's Deductive Method.

He assumes that, "in the early stage of society, the exchangeable value of commodities depends almost exclusively on the comparative quantity of labour expended on each." Even if it be true that, in a savage society, things exchange together in proportion of the labour required to produce them, it does not follow, as he assumes, that they will do so in a complicated capitalistic society. In his remark that exchange value is regulated by the labour necessary for the production of the commodity, Ricardo has confused the cause or determinant with the measure of value.

Ricardo's Doctrine, that the Exchange Value of a commodity is regulated by the labour necessary for its production, examined.

The labour with which a thing was or can be made is not the cause of its value, but the quantity of labour it will exchange for is the measure of its value; that is, it shows what its value is, and how much it has varied from time or from place to place.

The political economy of the school of Ricardo labours under the following drawbacks from its usefulness:—

1. It is essentially limited in its application. Bagehot has pointed out that it is only applicable to large trading communities like England, that it is an analysis of the "great commerce" which has enriched England; "it will not explain

the economic life of earlier times, or even that of other communities in our time."

2. It is too abstract, deduction is too preponderant in its processes of reasoning, and its conclusions are stated in too absolute a manner, as though, being true of our capitalistic society, they must necessarily be true of all sorts of society in all times. It seems to neglect the tendency to change in the habits and institutions of industry. It proceeds on the assumption that competition is all powerful, but that custom has no influence in economic matters.

3. The conclusions it comes to are too little compared with and verified by experience.

4. In modern political economy the "ethical factor," the question of man's duty to his neighbour, is more prominent than in the school of Ricardo.

5. The theory of rent has been denied by the American economist, Henry Carey, who contradicts the law of decreased return from land.

Sidgwick considers that this theory "combines in a somewhat confusing manner three distinct theories": 1. The historical theory as to the origin of rent. 2. A statical theory of the economic forces tending to determine rent at the present time. 3. A dynamical theory of the causes continually tending to increase rent, as wealth and population increases.[1]

6. In his theory of wages, that they ultimately depend upon the price of food, and that "there is no way of keeping profits up but by keeping wages down," he neglects the fact that an improvement in the efficiency of labour may leave wages at their former level, and yet, by increasing the total produce, allow the rate of profit to rise. He also makes no allowance for emigration altering the ratio of population to capital.

Besides the theories of wages and rent, Ricardo is chiefly important in the history of economics as having established the following principles:—

1. That foreign commerce is not only a vent for surplus produce, but that its benefit consists "simply and solely in this, that it enables each nation to obtain, with a given

[1] *Principles of Political Economy*, 2, vi. sc. 1.

amount of labour and capital, a greater quantity of all commodities taken together."

2. Net income, excess of produce of land and labour over the cost of production (rent and profits), is what is important for a nation.

Soon after the death of Ricardo occurred the commencement of the change in England's commercial policy which converted it from an agricultural into a manufacturing nation. The old policy was that England should be commercially self-sufficing; foreign trade was merely a vent for surplus products, so there was no occasion to strive much for the extension of the export trade. The new policy was that manufacturers no longer worked up native products, but imported raw produce; the food supply of England thus became insufficient, and she had to become dependent on importation from abroad. The first step in the change of policy was the formation of a Committee of the House of Commons, to consider the commercial position of the country, in 1820, which was originated by a petition to Parliament of the merchants of London.

Change in English Commercial Policy.

The restrictions originating in the Navigation Act, that all goods imported from America into England must be carried in English ships, were relaxed in 1796; this concession was extended to Spanish America and the Spanish West Indies in 1822. In 1822 Huskisson, as President of the Board of Trade, carried a measure which allowed direct trade between the colonies and foreign countries in foreign or British ships, but reserved the trade between England and the colonies. In 1823 the king, in Council, was empowered to place the shipping of any country, as regards duties, on an equal footing with our own, provided that England gained the same concessions in the country thus privileged. The last remaining restrictions on Free Trade imposed by the Navigation Act were repealed by Lord John Russell's Ministry in 1849. The same policy of Free Trade was followed in our commercial intercourse with India and the East. In 1813 the East India Company's monopoly of the trade was abolished, but the Company maintained that of the trade to China. In 1833 the Company ceased entirely to be a trading corporation.

Repeal of the Navigation Laws.

P

Huskisson commenced the policy of relieving the English fiscal system of various vexatious imposts which brought in little to the revenue, and of concentrating taxation on certain important articles of consumption. The duties on raw silk, coal, glass, soap, were repealed in the period 1821–30. This policy was continued by Sir Robert Peel in his Ministry, 1841–46, when the Income Tax was imposed to make up the deficit; and by Mr Gladstone, the great finance minister of modern times, when Chancellor of the Exchequer, 1852.

As regards the protective duties on corn, for nearly four centuries after the Conquest its exportation was totally forbidden. Its average price 1401–50 was 6s. per quarter, from 1603–1702 41s., in 1800 113s., in 1812 137s., in 1817 126s. Under Henry VI. it was allowed to be exported when the average price was less than 6s. 8d. a quarter; but its importation was forbidden till the price exceeded this limit. In 1670, wheat was allowed to be exported when the price was below 53s. 4d., and it could be imported, if above this price, on paying a duty of 8s. a quarter. In 1698, when the price of corn was below 48s., a bounty of 5s. a quarter was given on its exportation.

History of the Protective Duties on Corn.

This bounty was supposed to render wheat scarcer and dearer in England by encouraging exportation. It failed in this object, as it served as a premium on which wheat-growers could speculate. They grew more corn in consequence, and the increase of production caused prices to fall. In 1773 Lord North caused the bounty on the export of corn to cease when the price reached 44s. a quarter; no corn was to be exported when the price was above this limit. When the price of corn was above 48s. per quarter, it might be imported on paying a duty of 6d. a quarter.

In 1791 a bounty was allowed on the exportation of corn when its price was below 44s.; its exportation was allowed without a bounty up to 46s. When the price of corn was below 50s., imported corn paid a duty of 4s. 3d. a quarter, 2s. 6d. when the price was from 50s. to 54s., and 6d. when the price was above 54s. In 1801 the duty of 4s. 3d. a quarter was imposed when corn was below 63s., 2s. 6d. when its price was from 63s. to 66s., and 6d. when its price was above 66s. In 1815 no importation of foreign corn was allowed till wheat reached the price of 80s. a quarter; this limit was reduced to 70s. in 1822. In 1827 a great change was introduced in the Corn Laws. Foreign wheat might be imported independently of the price of English wheat, but the sliding scale was introduced, by which the duty, which was 20s. with the price of wheat at 60s. a quarter, was to increase when the price of wheat in England fell, and fall when it rose. It was hoped thus to secure to the home producer the protection of a heavy import duty, when corn was cheap, and to give the consumer the benefit of large supplies when it was dear.

Repeal of the Protective Duties on Corn. The Corn Laws were finally repealed in 1846 by Sir Robert Peel, mainly owing to the vigorous propagandist efforts of the Anti-Corn Law League, headed by Messrs Bright and Villiers.

James Mill. James Mill, the father of John, published his *Elements of Political Economy*, 1821, and is known chiefly as a thoroughgoing follower of Ricardo.

M'Culloch. J. R. M'Culloch, 1779–1864, published editions of Adam Smith and Ricardo; to the former he added an introductory survey of political economy before the time of Smith, to the latter some notes on the life and writings of Ricardo.

Richard Jones. Richard Jones, 1790–1855, Professor of Political Economy at the East India Company's College at Haileybury. In his *Essay on the Distribution of Wealth*, 1831, he acknowledges that farmers' rent conforms to Ricardo's law, but points out that the rents paid by peasants obey the influence of custom rather than that of competition. The rents paid by serfs, metayers, rayats, and cottiers are all examples of peasant rent.

John Stuart Mill. His Works. John Stuart Mill, 1806–73, wrote, 1844–45, *Essays on some unsettled questions of Political Economy*, including:—

1. The law of international exchange.
2. The influence of consumption on production.
3. The terms productive and unproductive as applied to labour, production, and expenditure.
4. Profits and interest.
5. The definitions and method of political economy.

In 1848 his *Principles of Political Economy, with some of*

their Applications to Social Philosophy, was published. Mill is a champion of the *a priori* method of reasoning; he thinks the *a posteriori* method "is altogether inefficacious in these sciences as a means of arriving at any considerable body of valuable truth." The *a priori* method considers the effects of one particular set of causes by themselves, by imagining hypotheses and deducing their results, and comparing these results with actual experience.

Sidgwick, in his *Elements of Political Economy*, 1883, considers Mill only refers to the statics of distribution and exchange, and points out that, even when thus limited, the deductive method only applies to a fully-developed industrial community, and requires that its conclusions should be modified by a rough conjectural allowance for the elements omitted in the premises. He shows too that, in considering production, Mill follows the "specialised form of induction" known as comparison, and obtains his results by "merely analysing and systematising our common empirical knowledge of the facts of industry."

Mill's Method.

Comte taught Mill that the *a posteriori* was the only true method in sociology, hence Mill appears to have been in doubt as to the true relation of political economy to sociology. Sometimes he considers it a subordinate department of sociology, sometimes an independent study preparatory and auxiliary to it.

Mill's view of the relation of Political Economy to Sociology.

Mill was a pupil of the school of Jeremy Bentham, of the straitest sect of philosophical radicalism, whose organ was the *Westminster Review*. The tenets of this school were, that all morality is enlightened selfishness, that the interests of the individual necessarily coincided with those of the community, that our minds were "bundles of sensations," and our characters the mouldings of circumstances. All ethics were to them explainable by the doctrine of the greatest happiness of the greatest number, and all economics by that of laisser faire and the population question. Bagehot points out that "Euclid was to this school the one type of scientific thought."[1]

Mill's training.

Mill, in his later days, altered very materially the views he

[1] *Economic Studies*, 156.

held in his youth. In his youth "he had seen little further than the old school of political economy into the possibilities of fundamental improvement in social arrangements. Private property, as now understood, and inheritance appeared the *dernier mot* of legislation." In his *Principles of Political Economy* he advocates very considerable limitation of the right of bequest, and shows great modification of his views regarding the sacredness of property. "If, therefore, the choice were made between Communism with all its chances, and the present state of society with all its sufferings; if the institutions of private property necessarily carried with it as a consequence, that the produce of labour should be apportioned as we now see it, almost in an inverse ratio to labour,—the largest portions to those who have not worked at all, the next largest to those whose work is almost nominal, and so in a descending scale, the remuneration dwindling as the work grows harder and more disagreeable, until the most fatiguing and exhausting bodily labour cannot count with certainty on being able to earn even the necessaries of life; if this or Communism were the alternative, all the difficulties, great or small, of Communism would be as dust in the balance."[1]

Alteration in Mill's views.

In the same way, in his review of Mr Thornton's book on labour (1869), he recanted the extreme form of the wages fund theory which he put forward in his *Principles of Political Economy*.

Auguste Comte published his six volumes on Positive Philosophy from 1830 to 1842. He may be regarded as the founder of the historical or realistic (as opposed to the abstract) school of political economy. He comes to the following conclusions on sociology, that (1) It is the science which studies all the elements of the social state in their mutual relations. (2) Its theory must be dynamical as well as statical, *i.e.*, it must give an account of society in a state of stable equilibrium as well as in a state of change. Comte acknowledges his obligations to Condorcet's *Sketch of an Historical Picture of the Human Mind*, as the first work in which the necessity of a dynamical theory of sociology founded on history is put prominently forward. (3) It should eliminate

[1] *Elements of Political Economy*, II. 1, sc. 3.

the absolute substituting for an imaginary fixity the element of ordered change. (4) Its method is that of historical comparison. The successive stages of society have to be systematically compared to discover their laws of sequence, and the connection between their characteristic features. Whatever useful indications may be derived from our general knowledge of human nature, the economic structure of society and its mode of development cannot be deductively foreseen, but must be ascertained by historical investigation. Social facts should be dealt with in the "ensemble," parallel investigations being carried on contemporaneously into all the co-existing portions of the complex whole. There must be no specialisation or study in detail, as society is too complex, and its elements too "solidaires," to be broken up. This is possible in the physical but not in the natural or organic sciences. We must proceed from the known to the unknown by means of inductive logic.

(5) Comte's philosophy is pervaded by moral ideas; he considers social duties of more importance than individual rights.

(6) Comte proposes to try the political economy of his day by the tests of fecundity and continuity, by both of which he finds it fail. There have been no important improvements in the science since Adam Smith, and it is only a few of its doctrines, such as Free Trade, that can be shown to depend on a "rational filiation" of events, being a train of consequences depending on an original cause.

Mill thus replies to Comte's view: "This shows, according to Comte, that a man is not likely to be a good economist who is nothing else. Social phenomena, acting and reacting on one another, they cannot be rightly understood apart. This by no means proves that the material and industrial phenomena of society are not themselves susceptible of useful generalisations, but only that these generalisations must be necessarily relative to a given form of civilisation and a given stage of social development."[1]

The most thoroughgoing opponents of the physiocratic school were of Italian birth.

The Abbé Ferdinando Galiani, 1728–87, when Secretary of

[1] *Mill on Comte*, p. 83.

the Neapolitan Embassy in Paris, wrote a French treatise *On Commerce in Grains*, 1770, which drew Mercier de la Rivière into controversy. He also wrote in Italian a *Treatise on Money*.

Political Economy in Italy.

Cæsar Beccaria, 1738-94, lectured before the University of Milan against the physiocratic school in 1768-9, on which occasion he delivered as lectures his *Elements of Political Economy*, which were not published till 1804.

Other works of his were, *On the Abuses of Coinage and their Remedies*, 1762, and a treatise on the advantage of uniformity in measures, in which he advocated the decimal division which has since become the metrical system.

Pietro Verri, 1728-97, wrote *Meditations on Political Economy*, 1771. He argues that the reproduction of value is shown by that amount of price which the wares or manufactured goods bear above the original value of the raw materials, and the cost of the commodities consumed during the process of fabrication.

Sallust Bandini, 1677-1760, in his *Economic Discourse*, published 1775, set before himself the duty of proving to the Archduke of Tuscany, Peter Leopold, that the Siennese Maremma had fallen out of cultivation because the heavy indirect duties and restrictions on the traffic in grain deprived the cultivators of all profit. He advocated that a direct tax on rent should be substituted for all taxes on the consumption and transport of corn.

John Baptiste Say, 1767-1832. His *Treatise on Political Economy, or Simple Explanation of the Manner in which Riches are Formed, Distributed, and Consumed*, disproved the economic possibility of a glut of commodities from over-production, but attributes them rightly to a faulty application of productive power. It passed through four subsequent editions in 1814, '17, '19, '26.

Political Economy in France.

He published his *Complete Course of Practical Political Economy* in 1828.

With reference to international trade, he proves that the interests of nations are reciprocal, that they can only pay for produce with produce, and that prohibitions against buying are also obstacles to selling.

Ricardo says of Say, that "he was the first, or among the

first, of continental writers who justly appreciated and applied the principles of Smith, and who has done more than all continental writers taken together to recommend the principles of that enlightened and beneficial system to the nations of Europe, and has succeeded in placing the science in a more logical and more instructive order."

John Charles Sismondi, 1773–1842, wrote a treatise *On Commercial Riches*, 1803, and *New Principles of Political Economy, or of Riches, in its Relation with Population.*

He found fault with political economy that it paid too much attention to the increase of wealth, and not enough to its use for the promotion of the general happiness of mankind. He brings into especial prominence the evils of a purely industrial state of society.

Charles Dunoyer, 1786–1862, author of *Liberty of Work*. His motto was "Experimental Research," and he professed to build on the groundwork of observation and experience.

All productive effort is divisible according as its action is on men or things; it is unfortunate that it is upon the latter that effort has hitherto been principally concentrated.

The industries that act upon man can be divided according as they deal with—
1. The amelioration of physical nature.
2. The culture of the imagination and sentiments.
3. The education of intelligence.
4. The improvement of moral habits.

He approves of the doctrine of laisser faire, because the spontaneous desire of an individual for improvement, by developing foresight, energy, and perseverance, is the most efficient means of social culture.

Frederic Bastiat, 1801–50, wrote, 1845, *Cobden and the League* (Anti-Corn Law League); 1845–48, *Economic Sophisms, Economic Harmonies.*

He wishes to see political economy treated more in connection with final causes. He points out that the effect of economic progress is to transfer more and more of the elements of utility from the domain of property into that of community, or of universal and unpurchased enjoyment.

He conceives it to be the part of political economy " to explain and justify the laws of wealth, that which is, is that which ought to be, according to the aspirations of the universal conscience"; he wishes to prove that, left to themselves, human interests are harmonious, but he does not care to enquire what the consequence of a certain set of social arrangements would be, which alone can be properly considered a scientific object of enquiry."

He fuses together the two distinct aspects of fact and right, and thus defends Free Trade: "Exchange is a natural right. Every citizen who has created or acquired a product ought to have the option of either applying it immediately to his own use, or of ceding it to whosoever on the surface of the globe consents to give him the object of his desires. To deprive him of this faculty, whilst he makes no use of it contrary to public order or good morals, is to legalise spoliation, to do violence to the law of justice." His theory of sociology is founded upon the groundwork of abstract rights, which he wishes to be rigidly respected.

He maintains that a gift, once obtained gratuitously from nature, such as a spring of water or a pearl picked up upon the shore, can never acquire value except from labour bestowed on it. He denies that a gratuitous gift of nature, such as water, if limited in supply, can acquire value. Value depends upon "service" or human effort, and varies with its magnitude. The diamond picked up by chance has value, because the person on whom I bestow it thinks that I do him a service. Land has value, because, after the native powers of the soil have been appropriated, it cannot be acquired without giving in exchange the equivalent of the labour spent on it, which is the true cause of its value. Rent, wages, and interest are analogous to each other, and depend upon the measure of utility of land, labour, and capital in production. He denies that "value can depend upon the degree of satisfaction an object will give, the degree of limitation set to the supply of natural objects or of acts depending upon natural endowments, or the natural superiority of some objects furnished by nature over others." Cairnes remarks on this: "Having been at infinite pains to exclude gratuitous gifts of nature from the possible elements of value, and pointedly identified the phenomenon with human effort as its sole source, he designates human effort by the term 'service,' and then employs this term to admit as sources of value those very gratuitous natural gifts, the exclusion of which in this capacity constituted the very essence of his doctrine."

Augustine Cournot, 1801–77, was the author of *Researches on the Mathematical Principles of the Theory of Riches*. This was the first application of mathematical principles to the treatment of economic questions. The principal advantage of stating economic problems mathematically is the exact acquaintance it gives with the problem, and with the conditions under which it is intended to be solved. Cournot wrote another book, *Principles of the Theory of Riches*, 1863, in which he abandoned the attempt to make use of mathematics.

Michael Chevalier, 1806–79, in his youth was an ardent supporter of Saint Simonism, and edited *The New Book*, the Gospel of the Sect, along with Enfantin. He was also the author of the *Material Interests in France*, 1838; of the *Letters on the Organisation of Work, and on the question of the Workers*, written to combat Louis Blanc and the Socialists, 1838, and of *The Fall in the Value of Gold*, 1858, which was translated by Cobden; and of the *Course of Political Economy*, 1842–50.

J. J. Courcelle-Seneuil translated J. S. Mill's works on Political Economy into French, and wrote the following works: *A Theoretical and Practical Treatise on Banking Operations*, 1856; *The Theory of Industrial Enterprises*, 1856; *Treatise on Political Economy*, 1858–59.

Antoine Elise Cherbuliez, died 1869. He wrote the *Analysis of Economic Science*, 1862.

Leonce de Lavergne, author of *Rural Economy of England, Scotland, and Ireland*, 1854; *Rural Economy of France since 1789*, published in 1857. The authority for the period immediately before 1789 is Arthur Young, Secretary to the Board of Agriculture, who wrote *Travels in France*. M. de Lavergne is also the author of *The French Economists in the Eighteenth Century*, 1870.

Adam Muller, 1779–1829, wrote *Elements of Statesmanship*, in which he led a reaction against "Smithianismus" as too material.

Political Economy in Germany.
Most of the writers on economics in Germany before his day had confined themselves to interpreting Smith's views to his countrymen.

Frederic Nebenius, 1784-1857, was the author of the German *Zollverein*, or *Customs' Union*, and wrote besides a treatise on *Public Credit*.

Charles Henry Raw, 1792-1870, wrote a *Lehrbuch* or *Manual of Political Economy*, which was intended to be an encyclopædia of all the ideas which were current on the subject up to the time in which he wrote.

Frederic List, 1798-1846. His great work is the *National System of Political Economy*, in which he denies Smith's doctrine that the following of immediate private interests will eventually further the good of the community.

The true wealth of a nation consists not in the quantity of exchange values it possesses, but in the full and many-sided development of its productive powers. Agriculture, manufactures, and commerce must alike be cared for.

Every nation passes through the following stages in its economic history: (1) Pastoral life; (2) Agricultural; (3) Agriculture in combination with manufactures; (4) Agriculture, manufactures, and commerce, all practised together.

Every nation should commence with Free Trade, it should then adopt Protection to allow its manufactures to be fully developed, and finally, should again adopt Free Trade to allow itself to be incorporated with "the universal industrial union." He considers Spain and Portugal to be purely in the agricultural stage, the United States and Germany to be in the stage of developing their manufactures, whilst France has almost attained to the stage of final Free Trade. England alone has completely done so.

List wrote his book in the United States, where he was a contemporary with the American economist, Henry Carey, who has met the favourite economic views of the English school with such strong opposition.

Henry Carey, 1793-1879. In his *Principles of Social Science*, 1859, he attacks the theory of population, maintaining that

Henry Carey. numbers regulate themselves sufficiently, and that pressure on the means of subsistence is a mark, not of the more advanced, but of the lower stages of civilisation.

Wealth, meaning thereby the sum of useful things, is the measure of our power over nature, and the value of an object expresses the resistance of nature, which labour has to overcome in order to produce the object.

Carey denies Ricardo's theory of rent, basing his denial on the fact that it is contrary to experience that the most fertile lands are first brought under cultivation. Carey maintains the light and dry lands in elevated situations are *first* cultivated, and afterwards the more unhealthy, though more fertile, lands in the valleys and on the banks of rivers. Rent, as a proportion of the produce, like all interest upon capital, tends to decrease, but as an absolute amount it tends to rise.

Property in land owes its origin to its being a form of investment of capital, as a certain quantity of the fruits of labour is permanently incorporated with the soil; and for this the owner, like any other capitalist, is compensated by a share in the produce. The value of land is due to the labour expended on it in the past, and is measured, not by the sum of that labour, but by the labour necessary under existing conditions to bring new land to the same stage of productiveness.

The present value of the land amounts to only a small portion of the cost expended upon it, as it represents only what it would cost, with agricultural science at its present level and the machinery at present available, to bring land from its primitive condition to its present state of productiveness.

Carey was an ardent Protectionist. All the articles derived from land are separated portions of it, and must be given back to it, if its fertility is not to be exhausted. The producer and consumer must be close together; and the products of the land must not be exported to other countries in exchange for their manufactures, and so go to enrich a foreign soil. This is what the author calls "land-butchery"; but the argument ignores the fact that agricultural manures can be imported. The export of the products of the land may be for the private advantage of individuals, but "the co-ordinating power" must intervene to prevent private advantage being turned into public detriment.

Richard Whately, Archbishop of Dublin, 1789–1863. He was Drummond Professor of Political Economy at Oxford University after Senior, in which capacity he published *Introductory Lectures on Political Economy*. In the same way as Ricardo, who wished to confine the scope of political economy to merely one of its branches—"the determining the division of the produce of industry among the classes who concur in its formation," Whately thought that political economy should be viewed merely as the science of exchanges, and proposed for it the name of Catallactics.

Archbishop Whately.

Sir Travers Twiss, also Professor of Political Economy at the University of Oxford, published his *Lectures on the Progress of Political Economy from the 16th Century down to about 1825*.

Professor Thorold Rogers' *History of Agriculture and Prices*, 1866–82, is an important contribution to the knowledge of the economic condition of past times which may be gained by tracing the prices prevalent in them. His other important works on Economics are *Six Centuries of Work and Wages* and *The Industrial and Commercial History of England*, published *posthumously*.

Sir James Caird's *Letters on Agriculture* treats of the influence of various systems of agriculture upon economics. Hardly any work on subjects bearing upon economics can be compared to this, except, perhaps, Arthur Young's *Travels in France previous to the Revolution*.

J. E. Cairnes, 1824–75, was Whately Professor of Political Economy at Trinity College, Dublin, and afterwards at Queen's College, Galway. His works were: *The Slave Power, The Logical Method of Political Economy, Some Leading Principles of Political Economy Newly Expounded, Essays towards a Solution of the Gold Question, Essays in Political Economy Theoretical and Applied, Political Essays*.

J. E. Cairnes.

The *Logical Method* says that, "if the political economist declines to avail himself of any other path than that of strict induction, he may reason till the crack of doom without arriving at any conclusion of the slightest value." He must employ deduction, "incomparably, when conducted under the proper checks, the most powerful instrument of discovery ever wielded by human intelligence." "The economist, starting with a knowledge of ultimate causes (such as the desire for wealth), is thus, at the outset of his enterprise, at the position which the physicist only obtains after ages of laborious research." Mill, in his *Logic*, insists on verification as an essential part of the discovery of economic laws. Cairnes says: "As they are not assertions respecting the character or the sequence of phenomena, they can neither be established or refuted by statistical or documentary evidence."

Mill and Cairnes showed that the "economic man" (the man only actuated by desire of wealth and dislike of exertion), so far from being in actual existence was only hypothetical, and only, so far as its premises correspond with actual fact, can the conclusions of political economy be depended on in practice.

The *Leading Principles* contains essays on Value, Labour and Capital, and International Trade. Cairnes wished to substitute the term "expenses of production," meaning by it the money wages and profits of different occupations, for Mill's "cost of production," and to confine the term "cost of production" to the actual effort of labour and abstinence from expenditure or postponement of it, for which wages and profits are the money rewards. He points out that wages and profits are the remuneration of sacrifice, not elements of it. Competition is of two sorts: commercial—the competition of dealer with dealer; and industrial—that of producer with producer. When industrial competition is not fully realised, wages and profits in different occupations may not be an equivalent reward for the labour incurred, and the abstinence from expenditure or postponement of it by workmen and capitalists. Non-competing groups are those between which competition is not active, and in which labour does not move readily from the less to the more advantageous trades.

Cairnes concludes that trades unions can only affect the rate of wages by accelerating by their combined efforts the natural rise of wages, which would have come about independently of them owing to increased competition for labour in times of good trade.

The necessaries of the labourers being chiefly articles of food, the raw material is the chief element in their cost, and therefore their cost of production must increase *pari passu* with the increase in the population. The only hope for the labourer is that he should cease to be a labourer, profits being brought to supplement wages by the aid of co-operation.

In international trade the cost of production does not regulate values—it only does so under a *regime* of effective competition, and between two countries effective competition cannot exist. Nations are non-competing groups; and "such a state of relative prices will establish itself amongst the products of non-competing groups, as shall enable that portion of the products of each group which is applied to the purchase of the products of all other groups, to discharge its liabilities towards those other groups." The reciprocal demand of these groups determines the "average relative level" of prices within each group; whilst the cost of production regulates the distribution of price amongst the individual products of each group. The market price is that which most advantageously adjusts the existing supply to the existing demand, pending the coming forward of fresh supplies from the sources of production.

Rise of the Historical or Realistic School of Political Economy in Germany. This school is so called because they regard the economic constitution of society as the result of a definite historical development in the closest connection with the social organisation of the period. It is called Realistic because it aims at considering life as it actually exists, and does not "abstract" man from any of the desires and feelings which animate him. This new way of regarding economic problems was first put forward by Comte in his *Positive Philosophy*, but it is in Germany that it has been most zealously adopted.

William Roscher in 1843 published his *Groundwork to Lectures on Political Economy on the Historical Method*. The historical method is distinguished by the following principles :—

1. It aims at treating economic phenomena according to the order of chronological succession, and tries to discover what nations have thought, willed, and discovered with regard to economics, and the reasons for this.

2. A people is not merely the aggregate of individuals living at any one time, therefore it is not enough to observe merely contemporary facts.

3. All the nations from whom we can learn anything must be studied and compared with regard to economic matters.

4. We must not give unqualified praise or blame to any economic institutions; few of them have been productive of unmixed good or evil to all people and at all stages of national culture.

Bruno Hildebrand wrote *The National Economy of the Present and the Future*, 1848.

Charles Knies wrote *Political Economy from the standpoint of the Historical Method*, 1853, in which he explains that the economic constitution of society at any epoch is the result of a definite historical development in vital connection with the social organisation of the period. The economic system must be regarded as passing through a series of phases correlative with the successive stages of civilisation, and cannot be considered to have assumed an entirely definite form. Neither the present nor any previous economic organisation of society can be regarded as absolutely good and right, but only as a phase in a continuous historical evolution. The body of economic doctrine at present current is not complete and final, but only represents a certain stage in the progressive manifestation of the truth. He insists strongly upon:—

1. The necessity of accentuating the moral element in economic study. Schmoller, in his *Economic Groundworks*, and Schäffle, in his *Social System of Human Economy*, point out that there are three active influences upon the development of society:—

    A. Private economy or personal interest.

    B. Compulsory public economy, or the general interest of society.

    C. The feelings belonging to "the Caritative Sphere," or benevolent impulses.

2. The close relation between economics and jurisprudence which throws light upon the relation of the individual to the community.

3. He takes a different view of the functions of the State from that held by political economicians of the school of Ricardo and Mill. It is not merely an institution for the maintenance of order, but the organ of the nation for all ends which cannot be effected by voluntary effort.

He lays great stress on the evils to society which arise from unlimited competition, and is therefore particularly strong upon the point that distribution is a matter of merely human institution. The present laws of property, inheritance, and contract are "merely historical categories which have changed, and are subject to further change," they are not a fixed order of things on the basis of which the individual creates his own position.

Knies was also the author of two important works on the history of political economy, the *History of English Political Economy*, 1851–52; the *History of Political Economy in Germany*, 1874.

The historical school of political economicians stands in Germany midway between the Free Trade party, or Manchester school, and the Socialists. The former deprecate State interference, except for the protection of individuals, the latter call for it in order to effect an immediate and complete transformation of the State in the interests of the proletariate.

There are, besides, the so-called Katheder Socialisten, or "Socialists of the Chair," a school mostly composed of professors in the Universities, against whom the reproach is sometimes brought that their discussions are too abstract and academical. The most prominent of this school are: Wagner, author of *Speeches on the Social Question*, and *The Building and Life of the Social Body*, in which he endeavours to prove that society has its anatomy, physiology, and psychology, just in the same way as the human body of an individual man; Schäffle, author of *Quintessence of Socialism*; Schonberg, author of *The Question of the Working Man, a problem of the German Kingdom*. These authors are the chief originators of the Verein für Social Politik, or Union for the Discussion of Social Politics, 1873, the majority of which is favourable to a further approach to the realisation of Socialist theories by means of State action on the basis of existing institutions.

Walter Bagehot was a banker and editor of the *Economist*, a financial newspaper, and so well qualified by his training to write upon economic questions.

Walter Bagehot, 1826-77.

His works dealing with economic questions are: *International Coinage, or an Universal Money; Lombard*

Street; *The Depreciation of Silver*, an essay reprinted from the *Economist*, 1877; *Economic Studies* (including Postulates of English Political Economy), published posthumously under the editorship of R. H. Hutton, 1880.

In *Lombard Street* he describes the phenomena of speculation, of times of commercial crisis, and of the other characteristic features of what he calls "the great commerce." He explains why the state of business in Lombard Street is sometimes dull and sometimes unduly excited.

He also traces the history of banking, pointing out that the early banks of the great Italian cities, such as the Bardi and Peruzzi of Florence, who were ruined by our Edward the Third's inability to pay his debts, were merely finance companies for granting loans. The banks of Northern Europe, such as that of Amsterdam, 1609, received foreign and light coin at its worth in good money of the country, after deducting the cost of coinage and management. For the amount so estimated, the bank gave a credit in its books, which was called bank money, and which exactly represented money according to the standard of the mint. All bills above a certain amount were compelled to be paid in bank money, and every merchant therefore kept an account with the bank.

Banks had, therefore, five duties:—

1. To negotiate loans.
2. To supply good money.
3. To remit money.
4. To issue paper currency. The monopoly of this right was given to the Bank of England in 1732.
5. To receive deposits.

In his *Economic Studies* the important service Bagehot has performed for political economy is to point out the essential limitations under which the political economy of Ricardo and Mill labours. It rests upon fundamental assumptions, which, instead of being universally true, are only realised within very narrow limits of time and space. "It is the science of business, such as business is in large trading communities, an analysis of the great commerce by which England has become rich. It will not explain the economic life of earlier times, or even that of other communities in our own time."

"It is a convenient series of deductions from assumed

axioms which are never quite true, which in many times and countries would be utterly untrue, but which are sufficiently near to the principal conditions of the modern English commerce to make it useful to consider them by themselves."

"Political economy is an abstract science labouring under a special hardship," which is that "those who are conversant with its abstractions are usually without a true contact with its facts, and those who are in contact with its facts, have usually little sympathy with, and little cognisance of, its abstractions." Hence the practical men, who have only an empirical knowledge of the affairs of commerce, cannot give a logical account of their conduct in business. Political economy is an hypothetical science, as it deals not with real but with economic men; that is, with men considered merely as money-making animals. The world in which these "economic men" live and act is a "very limited and peculiar one," distinguished by the readiness with which capital and labour transfer themselves from one employment to another.

Bagehot considers that the problems of a complicated and completely organised industrial community must be treated by the abstract deductive method; but the economic phenomena of the human past, and all the rest of the human present, are best investigated by the historic method.

T. E. Cliffe Leslie. T. E. Cliffe Leslie, 1827–82, was Professor of Political Economy at Queen's College, Galway. He wrote *Essays on the Land Systems and Industrial Economy of Ireland, England, and the Continental Countries*, and *Essays, Moral and Political*, 1879. He points out what a variety of wants, desires, and sentiments are included in the expression, "Desire of wealth," which embraces a great variety of economic motors, altruistic as well as egotistic. It is, however, on account of this great variety that the generalisation is broadly that all men are animated by this desire of wealth.

He thus describes the historical method: "The whole economy of every nation is the result of one long evolution, in which there has been both continuity and change, and of which the economical side is only a particular aspect, and the laws of which it is the result must be sought in history and the general laws of society and social evolution. The intellectual, moral, legal, political, and economic sides of social progress are indissolubly connected. Thus juridical facts relating to property, occupation, and trade thrown up by the social movement, are also economic facts. The economic condition of England, or any other society at the present day, is the outcome of the entire movement, which has evolved the political constitution, the structure of the family, the forms of religion, the learned professions, the state of agriculture, manufactures, and commerce. To understand existing economic relations, we must trace their historic evolution, and the philosophic method of political economy must be the one which expounds that evolution."

Leslie considers the cost of production only affects prices in the limited area within which rates of profit and wages are determinate and known. Domestic, as well as international, value generally depends upon demand and supply. Political economy is a department of the science of society, which selects a special class of social phenomena for special investigation, but for this purpose must investigate all the forces and laws by which they are governed. It has not yet reached the stage of a deductive science, the fundamental laws of the economic world are still imperfectly known, and can be fully known only by patient induction.

William Stanley Jevons, 1835–82, Assayer at the Sidney Mint, 1854–59, Lecturer and Professor at Owens College, Manchester, 1863–76, and at University College, London, 1876–80. His first work on economics was a *Statistical Atlas*. In 1863 he wrote an essay *On the Serious Fall in the Value of Gold*, and in 1865 he wrote an essay *On the Coal Question*. In 1871 he wrote his *Theory of Political Economy*. In 1875 his *Money and the Mechanism of Exchange* was published. His other works are, an essay *On the Future of Political Economy*, 1876; *Investigations in Currency and Finance*; and *Methods of Social Reform*, 1883.

William Stanley Jevons.

His *Theory of Political Economy* adopts the method of stating economic laws and problems by mathematical formulæ and figures, which was originated by Cournot, and has since been further developed by Marshall. He was the first to state the law of final utility, that the larger the quantity of any commodity a man possesses, the less the utility of an additional quantity, and the less of other commodities will be given in exchange for it, therefore the larger the quantity the less the price.

Marshall substitutes for final utility the term marginal utility, and denotes by it the utility of that portion for which the buyer will give the price required rather than go without. This determines normal price to the buyers; normal price to the sellers depends upon the expenses of production.

His *Investigations in Currency and Finance* are an "attempt to substitute exact inquiries and exact numerical calculations for guesswork and groundless argument." This is the ground on which he makes use of mathematical methods of statement and figures in discussing economic problems.

He treats of—
1. Periodic fluctuations of price.
2. Currency questions.
    A. An ideally perfect system of coinage.
    B. The condition of the gold coinage in the United Kingdom.

He has discovered the fact that the pressure on the money market recurs at monthly and quarterly periods, when bills are paid and the quarterly dividends are due, and that it also recurs in an aggravated form every autumn, when the harvest is gathered in and large money payments are due. He invented the method of ascertaining the average level of prices by means of index numbers.

Henry Fawcett, 1833–84, wrote *A Manual of Political Economy*, first published in 1863, and which has since passed through seven editions; *The Economic Position of the British Labourer*, 1865; *Pauperism, its Causes and its Remedies*, 1871; *Free Trade and Protection; Indian Finance*, 1880. He was Professor of Political Economy at Cambridge University, 1863–84.

Without troubling overmuch about theoretical niceties, he put the main facts of the science in such a brief and easily intelligible manner that he was justly looked on as one of the best teachers of the subject in modern times.

Arnold Toynbee, 1852–83. He wrote essays *On Ricardo and the old Political Economy* and *On the Industrial Revolu-*

tion in England in the 18th Century. He published addresses which he had given on—
>Wages and Natural Laws.
>Are Radicals Socialists?
>Industry and Democracy.

He contended that political economy cannot stand neutral between contending schemes of social economy, as Cairnes said it should; it must endeavour to guide its disciples to a right choice between them. He held that the opposition between the historical and deductive methods "was due to a wrong use of deduction; to a neglect on the part of those employing it to examine closely their assumptions, and bring their conclusions to the test of fact." The historical method examines the actual causes of economic development, and considers the influence of institutions, such as the mediæval guilds, our present land laws, or the political constitution of any given country in determining the distribution of wealth. It compares the stages of economic development in one country with those which have obtained in other countries and times. He points out that abstract propositions are seen in a new light when studied in relation to the facts which were before the writer at the time when he formulated them.

His opinion is that "the era of Free Trade and free contract is gone, and the era of administration is come." The Government is no longer to abstain from interference, but to claim the power of review of all contracts the parties to which are not on an equality, to enforce on masters the duty of protection of their workmen, to undertake the management of enterprises of public importance now left in private hands, and to represent the collective might of society in doing for individuals what they are unable to do for themselves.

QUESTIONS ON BOOK I.

1. Give the subdivisions of wealth, and explain how it is "an affair of human institution only."

2. Explain the object of political economy, and its relation to the other sciences. To what extent is political economy a hypothetical science?

3. Distinguish the political economy of the school of Ricardo from that of the school of Marshall.

4. What is meant by a law of political economy?

5. Distinguish productive from unproductive labour and circulating from fixed capital. To which kind of capital do the implements and raw materials of a manufacturer belong?

6. What are the chief differences of the mediæval guild system of production from that which at present prevails?

7. How do the moral qualities of the labourer affect the productiveness of his labour?

8. What is meant by "extensive" and "intensive" farming? Compare the respective advantages of both systems.

9. Discuss the effect of Free Trade upon English agriculture. Upon what kind of crops should the English farmer place his dependence for the future?

10. Distinguish the part played by nature in production from that played by man, and explain the law of decreased production from land and the causes which counteract this law.

11. What are the three chief countries, besides America, from which wheat is imported into England? Why is it likely that the amount imported from America must shortly be reduced?

QUESTIONS ON BOOK II.

12. Discuss the origin of private property. Is it just that the State should levy a special tax on the "unearned increment" to the wealth of the landlords?

13. Contrast Socialism with Individualism, and State Socialism with Anarchic Socialism. What advantages to the community are expected to be realised from Socialism?

14. Explain the theories of "surplus value" and of wages upon which Socialism is based.

15. How do Socialists prove that "property is robbery"?

16. What do you know of Louis Blanc's *Organisation of Work*, Lassalle's *Bastiat-Schulze*, the Gotha programme, Bakunin's *God and the State*, Henry George's *Progress and Poverty*?

17. Sketch the history of the International and of the German Socialist Parliamentary Party.

18. Point out the main difficulties in the way of realisation of the Socialist schemes. Show that the mere discussion of Socialistic principles has been of service to the world.

19. How do the cotter tenants of Ireland differ from tenant farmers? What are the faults of this system of tenancy, and how are they to be remedied?

20. What is the fundamental distinction between production and distribution? Show that competition, as a regulator of distribution, is a force of quite modern date. Explain the influence of custom and competition respectively upon the fees of professional men, such as doctors.

21. What are the causes which have prevented wages from increasing in proportion to the increase of the wealth of England?

22. Give Mill's statement of the wages fund theory, and Cairnes' view upon this point.

23. Criticise the statement that "profits vary inversely as wages."

24. Explain the relation between high wages and good trade.

25. State Ricardo's theory of wages.

26. What would be the economical effect of a law fixing the legal duration of a day at eight hours?

27. Explain the operation of
    A. National education;
    B. Emigration,
as remedies for low wages.

28. When the rate of profit rises above or falls below the normal rate, what tendency is put in motion to cause it to revert to that rate?

29. Explain the statement "the cost of labour, and therefore the rate of profit is a function of three variables." Why is the rate of profit higher in Australia than in England, in spite of the rate of wages being also higher?

30. Contrast the changes in profit and rent in a progressive state of society.

31. What parallel can be drawn between profit and rent?

32. Why do profits tend to a minimum? What are the consequences of this tendency, and how is it to some extent counteracted?

33. Define "margin of cultivation." How does its position depend upon the current rate of profit in each country?

34. Distinguish agricultural from monopoly rent. Account for the existence of agricultural rent, and show how it is affected by—
    A. Agricultural improvements.
    B. Increase of population.
    C. Rise in the rate of wages.

35. What objections have been urged against Ricardo's theory of rent?

36. Explain the following sentence: "Given the habits and requirements of the labourers, rent, profits, and money wages are the result of the 'composition of forces,' of the increase of the population, and agricultural improvement."

37. Sketch the history of trades unions. What would be the economic result if their objects were realised?

38. Sketch the history of the co-operative movement, showing how it may be expected to benefit the labourers.

QUESTIONS ON BOOK III.

39. Criticise the statement that "labour is the sole cause of value."

40. Define final or marginal utility, and distinguish normal from market price.

41. Classify commodities in relation to value, and explain how the value of commodities in each class is fixed.

42. How does a rise in general profits affect the value of commodities?

43. Discuss the possibility of an excess of the supply of commodities over the demand.

44. Define money and show how it facilitates exchange. What other functions does it fulfil?

45. How is the amount of money required for circulation in a country regulated, and upon what causes does its purchasing power depend?

46. When the value of money (its purchasing power) is above or below its cost of production, by what means is it restored to its former level?

47. What is meant by the quantitative theory of money? State the main arguments in favour of bimetallism. Can the bimetallists point to any period when the bimetallic ratio was actually maintained?

48. Why has the enormous increase in the amount of gold brought about by the discoveries in Australia and California exercised so little influence upon its value, as compared with silver, or upon prices in general?

49. Explain the effect of the increased production of gold (1) on Australia; (2) on England and America.

50. Explain how the demand for silver has fallen and its supply has been greatly increased.

51. What effect has the depreciation of silver had (1) upon the price of Indian products in India; (2) upon the Indian export trade?

52. What measures have been taken by the Government of India to arrest the fall in the sterling value of the rupee? What amount of success has been gained by these measures, and why have they not met with more? Describe the general effect of these measures upon Indian trade.

53. Compare and account for the difference in the effect on credit of bank notes and bills of exchange or book credits respectively.

54. In times of commercial crisis what form of credit is most used for speculative purchases? Show that the Bank Charter Act of 1844 fails in preventing times of commercial crisis, and is prejudicial in its after effect.

55. Compare the effects of a paper currency (1) if convertible, (2) if unconvertible.

56. Expose the fallacies involved in the expectation of benefit from an unlimited inconvertible paper currency.

57. What causes raise the rate of interest? What effect has a rise in the rate of interest upon the price of the public funds and of land, and why?

58. Why is London the banking centre of the world?

59. What regulates the value of an imported article, and upon what causes does the advantage of a country in foreign trade depend?

60. England trades with France in iron, there is an improvement in production cheapening iron in England. Upon what causes does it depend whether France will participate in this cheapness or not?

61. England trades with France in iron. Examine the effect of the trade :—
    (1.) On the price of iron in England.
    (2.) On the English labourers, who formerly produced that part of the wheat consumed in England which is now imported from France.
    (3.) On the price of home-grown wheat in the English market.

62. Under what circumstances do
    A. The exports of a country permanently exceed the imports?
    B. The imports of a country permanently exceed the exports?

63. In what cases only does a tax on imports fall upon the foreign producer?

64. Upon what causes does underselling depend?

65. Explain the reasons for which bullion is imported and exported, when not an ordinary article of merchandise. What enables a country to import bullion at a cheap rate?

66. What is meant by an unfavourable exchange? Show that it cannot be permanent.

QUESTIONS ON BOOK IV.

67. Distinguish authoritative from permissive State interference, and point out how Mill's views on State interference differ from those of State Socialists. In what cases does Mill consider Government interference justifiable?

68. State Adam Smith's "Canons of Taxation." How are they ambiguous? What provisions are necessary before an income tax can be considered just?

69. What is meant by the "unearned increment" to rent? Is it a proper subject for taxation?

70. Explain the difference in the incidence of a tax on ground rents, (1) when the supply of land for building purposes is unlimited; (2) in exceptionally valuable sites. Show that taxes on commodities fail to satisfy the requisite of "equality of incidence." Why is it more desirable to tax manufactured goods than raw produce?

71. Explain the effect of long-continued taxes upon agricultural produce.

72. Give the arguments for and against Protection. Show that reciprocity is not necessary for Free Trade to be economically desirable.

73. Distinguish the incidence of rates upon manufactories and business premises according as the rate is (1) uniform; (2) higher in some localities than others.

74. Sketch the history of Poor Law legislation.

75. Give the substance of Mill's criticisms on the English Land Law and the Laws of Partnership and Bankruptcy.

QUESTIONS ON BOOK V.

76. How was trade regarded by the ancients?

77. Point out the main differences between ancient and modern industrial life.

78. Estimate the influence on economic progress of the Crusades, the extinction of villeinage, feudalism, the Canon Law, the discovery of America, and the Reformation.

79. Upon what economic theory was the English prohibition of the export of the precious metals justifiable? Why was this prohibition relaxed in favour of the East India Company?

80. Name the early economic authors, and their works dealing with the subject of the English trade with India.

81. Compare Sully and Colbert as financiers. What was Colbert's Ordonnance de la Marine?

82. Give some account of John Locke as an economist?

83. Sketch the history of the Bank of England, and of Chamberlayne's Land Bank.

84. Give some account of Law's theories of paper money, and of the schemes which he carried out in France.

85. Examine Walpole's claims to be considered the first great English Finance Minister.

86. Give as complete an account as you can of the physiocratic school of political economists.

87. In what points were the views of *The Wealth of Nations* erroneous? Estimate the influence of the book. In what respect did Bentham adversely criticise Smith? How did Anderson, West, and Malthus correct Smith's views on rent?

88. How does Smith prove that the interests of the community are best consulted by allowing free play to the selfishness of individuals? What limit is to be assigned to this?

89. What is meant by the "abstract" school of political economy? Under what essential limitations does it labour?

90. Sketch the commercial policy of England towards her colonies and Ireland. Enumerate the steps by which this policy was altered to one of Free Trade.

91. Sketch the history of the Corn Laws.

92. Describe the early training received by J. S. Mill. What logical method does he pursue in argument? Estimate Comte's influence on his writings.

93. Give some account of the theories of Hume, Bastiat, Carey, List.

94. Why does Cairnes find fault with Mill's term, cost of production? What does he propose to substitute for it, and why? What does Cairnes mean by non-competing groups?

95. Account for the name "historic or realistic" school of political economy. Name the chief authors of this school, and contrast its method with that of the school of Ricardo. What English economists belong to the historic school?

96. Enumerate and estimate the value of Bagehot's contributions to economic science.

97. Who originated the method of stating economic problems mathematically? What writers of late years have developed this method, and what is its special advantage?

98. Estimate the use of statistics to political economy. What has Jevons taught us in this respect?

99. Explain "the era of Free Trade and free contract has gone, that of administration has come."

100. What is the meaning of the "ethical factor" in political economy? In the writings of what authors does it find a prominent place?

INDEX.

ABSTRACT method in Economics, 212–223.
Acceptances, 117.
Accommodation Bills, 117.
Agriculture 14 ; small proprietors, 14 ; depression in, 18 ; effect of improvements, 19 ; cost of agricultural labour, 54; improvements in, 57 ; improvements related to rent, 60, 65 ; Eastern Counties Labour Federation of Agricultural Labourers, 74 ; main discoveries in, 195.
Agricultural Holdings Act, 1883, 18.
Allan, William, 69.
Allotment system, 51, 52.
Amana Society, 23, 79.
America, the discovery of, Economic effects of, 196.
American War of Secession, effect on gold appreciation, 106 ; its effect on paper currency, 122.
Anarchism, 26, 28.
Applegarth, Allan, 69.
Applegarth, Robert, 69.
Appreciation of gold, 106.
Apprentices, Statute of, 67, 70.
Arch, Joseph, 72.
Argentina, 17.
Aristotle on political economy, 187.
Army and Navy Co-operative Stores, 80.
Assignments, 117.
Athelstan, 189.
Australia, 13, 54 ; effects of increased production of gold in, 103 ; wool, 104 ; produce in, 104 ; agriculture affected by the gold fields, 104 ; advantages and prices in, 104 ; industrial production in, 104.

Autonomists, 33.
Aveling, Edward, 31.

BACON, Lord, *The New Atlantis*, 187.
Baden-Powell, 1.
Bagehot, 2, 62, 241, 242 ; on money and loans, 242 ; his *Economic Studies*, 242, 243.
Bakunin, 31, 32, 33 ; estimate of his work, 33, 34.
Balance of Trade theory, 200.
Bandini, Sallust, 231.
Banking, co-operative, in Germany, 81 ; in England, 82 ; cheques and bills, 118 ; notes, 119 ; bank credit, 119 ; Bank of England notes, 120 ; increase of bank notes in times of crises, 126 ; discount, 126 ; objections to rise in bank discount, 127 ; working of Peel's Act on, 128, 129.
Bank of England—its formation and history, 203 ; its hoards, 127 ; its procedure, 128.
Bankruptcy, Law of, 182.
Bastiat, Frederic, 232, 233 ; his defence of Free Trade, 233.
Baudeau, Abbé, 211.
Bazard, 27.
Bebel, 29, 34.
Beccaria, Cæsar, 231.
Beehive, The, 70.
Beesley, Professor E. S., 31, 70.
Belfast Trades Union Congress, 1893, 77.
Bequest, 22 ; freedom of, 180, 181.
Bentham, Jeremy, on English Law, 183 ; on Adam Smith, 217, 219.
Berne Socialistic Congress, 34.

Betterment, 23 ; principle of, 158, 159.
Bills of Exchange, 117.
Bimetallism, 96 ; tendency of, 98 ; Locke's case against, 98 ; a quantitative theory of money, 99.
Blanc, Louis, 24 ; failure of his scheme for national workshops, 24.
Bland Act, 96, 97.
Blanqui, 31.
Bois-Guilbert, Seigneur de, 210.
Boot and Shoe Operatives, National Union of, 74.
Bostichi, Bernardo Davanzati, 198.
Bounty system, 174.
Brickmaking, rediscovery of the art of, 194.
Brigg's Co-operative Stores, 78.
Briscoe, John, 203.
Bonded warehousing, 146.
Buckle, T. H., on Adam Smith, 214 ; defence of the abstract method, 233.
Budget, Sir W. Harcourt's, 1894, 156.
Builders' Union, 67.
Bullion, 93 ; removal of restrictions on its exportation from England, 199 ; Ricardo on, 221.
Burns, John, 26.
Burt, Thomas, 72.

CABET, Etienne, 24.
Caird, Sir James, 237.
Cairnes, Prof. J., 3, 41 ; his criticism on Bastiat, 233 ; his works, 237 ; Essays on Value, Labour, Capital, and Free Trade, 238, 239.
California, 75 ; gold v. agriculture, 104.
Callender, W. R., 71.
Capital, definition of, 7 ; its limiting powers, 7 ; how produced, 7 ; of two kinds, 8 ; increase of, 19, 20 ; Socialistic definition of, 32 ; conversion of circulating into fixed, 57 ; effect of loans on, 57 ; its relation to population, 64 ; comparison with credit, 110 ; loanable capital, 130 ; how affected by cheap living, 130 ; Adam Smith on, 213.

Capitalist v. feudalist, 43 ; influence on prices, 44 ; effect on producer, 44 ; effect on buyer, 44.
Carey, Henry, on Ricardo's Theory of Rent, 224 ; his *Principles of Social Science*, 235, 236.
Carpenters' Union, 69.
Carriage, cost of, 136.
Cartels, 40.
Chamberlayne, Hugh, 203.
Chamberlayne's Land Bank, 203.
Charlemagne, 189.
Chartists, 68.
Cheques, 118.
Cherbuliez, A. Elise, 234.
Chevalier, Michael, 234.
Child, Sir Josiah, 201.
Christian Socialism, 37, 69.
Christian Social Union, 37.
Cicero on commercial pursuits, 188.
Civil Service Stores, 80.
Cleveland, President, 97.
Clothworkers' Society (Leeds), 67.
Colbert, his financial measures, 200, 201.
Collective system, 67.
Collectivism, 24.
Colonisation, Wakefield system, 153.
Columella on agriculture, 188.
Combination Acts, 68.
Committees, Herschell's Indian Finance, 112 ; on woollen manufactures, 67.
Commodities, classification according to value, 85-90 ; their market value, 86 ; effect of competition on, 86 ; how their values are affected by supply and demand, 86 ; how prices are affected by over-production and high wages, 86 ; agricultural commodities, 89 ; mineral and sea commodities, 89.
Communism, 23.
Communist League, 31.
Companies, joint-stock, 131 ; price of their shares, 132.
"Company of the West," the, 205.
Competition, 43 ; its effect on value of commodities, 86.
"Composition of forces," 66.
Comte, Auguste, 229, 230.
Conciliation, Boards of, 73, 76.
Condorcet, 220.

Congresses, Belfast Trades Union, 1893, 77; Berne Socialistic, 34; Ghent Universal Socialist, 35; Norwich Trades Union, 1894, 77.
Conspiracy and Protection of Property Act, 72.
"Contracting out," 73.
Contract Law, English, 181, 182.
Contracts for perpetuity, 152; taxes on, 164.
Co-operation, 10; co-operative associations, 52; advantages of, 78; French and English Co-operative Companies, 78; Leclaire's and Brigg's Companies, 78; United Coal-Miners of South Yorkshire, 78; Ouseburn Engineering Factory, 78; how bonuses are distributed, 78; Leeds Flour Mill, 78; Northampton Shoemakers, 79; Oneida Perfectionists, 79; Amana Society, 79; Oldham Sun Cotton Mill, 79; Gurdon's farms, 79; London Co-operative Guild, 79; Shakers, 79; Co-operative Masons and Pianoforte Makers, 79; Rochdale Equitable Society, 80; Zurich Consumers' Union, 80; Milan Co-operative Union, 80; Civil Service Stores, 80; Army and Navy Co-operative Stores, 80; Mulhall on, 80; in Germany, 81; co-operative banking, 81, 82.
Co-operative banking in Germany, 81; in England, 82.
Corn Laws, 15, 18, 168, 227.
Cottier tenants, 42.
Council Drafts, 110, 114.
Courcelle-Seneuil, J. J., 234.
Cournot, Augustine, 234.
Credit, 115-125; Mill's definition, 115; its effect on the resources of a community, 116; distinction from capital, 116; how it affects prices, 116; its creation of purchasing power, 117; book-debts, 117; assignments, 117; bills of exchange, 117; accommodation bills, 117; acceptances, 117; promissory notes, 117; fictitious bills, 117; cheques, 118; how affected by bank or commercial crises, 118; Exchequer bills, 118; bank notes, 119; its influence on prices, 120; how it affects purchasing power, 121; inconvertible paper currency, 121.
Criminal Law Amendment Act, 72.
Crompton, Henry, 73.
Currency, legislation respecting, 125-130; Sir Robert Peel's Act, 125-128; relation of increase of circulating medium to prices, 125; withdrawal of gold from, 127; Bank of England hoards, 127; method of Bank of England procedure, 128; question of monopoly of issue in, 129; objections to plurality of issuers, 129; Act of 1826 abolishing small notes, 130.
Currency reform of India, 1893, its effect, 100.

DAVENANT, Sir William, 208.
Debt, Abolition of Imprisonment for, 182.
Defoe, Daniel, 202, 203.
Demand, definition of, 86; its various uses, 88.
Demonetisation, 108.
Digges, Sir Dudley, 198.
Direct Taxation. See Taxation.
Discount, effects of raising bank rate, 126; objections to its rise, 127; how its rise affects demand for money, 132.
Distribution, 21; influences regulating, 43, 44; distinction between production and distribution, 43.
Double Standard, The, 97; advantages of, 98, 99; its introduction in India, 113.
Duncombe, Thos. Slingsby, 68.
Dunning, T. J., 70.
Dunoyer, Charles, 232.
Dupon de Nemours, 210.

EAST INDIA COMPANY, The, 85, 193; favourable allowances to, 198.
Economics, definition, 186; political, 186; ideas of in ancient times, 186; ideas of among the Greeks, 186, 187; differences between ancient and modern industrial life, 186-188; Xenophon on, 187; Aristotle on, 187; ideas of among

R

the Romans, 188; Varro and Columella on agriculture, 188; Cicero on commerce, 188; ideas of in the Middle Ages, 189; influence of Feudalism on, 189; influence of the Canon Law on, 189; Guilds, 189–191; Rise of woollen industry in England, 191, 192; growth of imports in England, 193; effects of the Reformation and the discovery of America on, 196; royal interference with English trade, 196, 197; the abstract method in, 222, 223; commencement of change in English commercial policy, 225; repeal of the Navigation Laws, 225; Historical or Realistic School of Germany, 239.

Edinburgh Upholsterers' Sewers' Society, 72.

Education, national, 52.

Education, national provision for, 152.

Elcho's Master and Servant Act, 70.

Emigration, 52.

Employers and Workmen Act, 72.

Enfantin, 27.

Engagement, breach of, 72.

Engels, 25, 31.

Engineers, Amalgamated Society of, 69, 74.

Entail, Law of, 24.

Enterprises, private and public, 11.

Escheat, Right of, 189.

Exchange, definition of, 83.

Exchange, its lowness favourable to industrial development, 112; Indian exchange, 112; the results of its low rate on trade in United Kingdom, India, Germany, France and Holland, 112; its law, 132; its effect on a country's money, 148; unfavourable exchange, 148, 149.

Exchange value, 5; Ricardo's doctrine of, 223.

Exchequer, closing of, 201.

Exchequer bills, 118.

FABIAN SOCIETY, 36.

Factory system, 67.

Fair Trade. *See* Reciprocity.

Farming, 13; American system, 16; two systems of, 16.

Fawcett, 23, 38, 50; on farming profits, 53; on depreciation of gold, 106; on credit, 116; on Income Tax, 157; on taxation of commodities; 165; on Protection in Victoria, 168, 169; on Protection and Free Trade, 170–172; on London Poor Law system, 179, 180; his published works, 245.

Feudalism, influence of, on Economics, 189.

Fictitious bills, 117.

Fouquet, 197.

Fourier, Charles, 27.

Fränckel, 32.

Frauds, Statute of, 14.

Free Trade, 15; influence on prices, 101, 102; effect on gold output, 101; international, 132–144; its advantage, 132, 133; import and export, 133; its civilising and peace-making tendencies, 133; examples of Spanish and English trade, 134; how profits are shared, 134; example of French and English trade, 135; cost of carriage, 136; example of English, French, and Belgian trade; 137; cost of commodities, 137; example of English, French, and Russian trade, 137, 138; advantage of increased demand for export, 138; example of English and French trade, 138, 139; consideration of operation of Free Trade, 141; influence of taxation on, 141; equation of international demand in trade, 145; Repeal of Corn and Navigation Laws, 168; Fawcett's summation of its advantages, 170–172; Bastiat's defence of, 233.

Friendly Societies Act, 69, 71.

Fullarton, Mr, on bank issues, 125.

GALIANI, Abbé Ferdinando, 230, 231.

Gasworkers' Union, 77, 78.

George, Henry, 35.

Ghent Universal Socialist Congress, 35.

Giffen, R., 96.

Gilbert's Act, 177.
Gold, the material of money, 92; its price as bullion, 93; effect of depreciation of, 98; effect of increased production of, on prices, 102; on wages, 102; effect of increased production of, in Australia, 103; how appreciated, 105, 106; how its demand is affected by increase in wages, 106; tables of production, 107; reasons for non-falling in value in spite of large production, 108; as a standard value in India, 113; occurrences of gold effluxes, 127; withdrawal from currency, 127. See also Precious Metals.
Glasgow Trades Council, 70.
Goodwin, William, 219.
Goschen, Mr, considerations on appreciation of gold, 105, 106; on export trade, 133.
Government, general functions of, 150-153; considerations on its functions, 150; Mill on, 150; State Socialism, 150; permissive interference of, 151; Mill on Government interference, 151; his exceptions, 152; justifiable cases for Government interference, 152; Mill's estimate of Government value, 153; obligation of a State's subjects, 154; Government interference from mistaken theories, 166-174; attempt to fix price of food, 166; laws against combination of workmen, 167; laws enforcing conformity to religion, 168; Adam Smith on its limitations, 216.
Grave, Jean, 34.
Gresham's Law, 122.
Ground Rents. See Taxation.
Guilds, 189-191.
Gurdon, Mr, 79.

HARCOURT, Sir Wm., Budget of 1894, 156.
Harrington, Sir J., Oceana, 187, 201.
Harrison, Frederic, 70, 71.
Hasenclever, 34.
Herschell Committee on Indian Finance, 112.

Hildebrand, Bruno, 240.
Hill, Frederic, 71.
Historical School, 239.
House Tax. See Taxation.
Houses, investments in, 8.
Hughes, Thomas, 71.
Hume, David, 219.
Hume, Joseph, 67.
Huntingdon, Henry of, 191.
Huskisson, 225, 226.
Hyndman, Henry, 36.

ICARIA, 24.
Income Tax. See Taxation.
India, silver demand in, 109; silver importation in, 109; effect of currency changes in, 110; considerations on gold and silver in, 110; Council Drafts, 110; purchasing power of the rupee, 110; rise in rents, wages, 110; rise in prices, 110; O'Connor's Indian prices and wages statistics, 110; Statistical Atlas, 110; rise in the price of rice, 111; competition of Indian wheat, 111; table of wheat exportation and its dependence on the low rate of exchange, 111; Herschell Committee, 112; gold value of rupee, 112; exchange in, 112; proposals for relief of Government owing to silver depreciation, 113; introduction of double standard, 113; gold standard in, 113; effect of repeal of Sherman Act on its finance, 113; failure of Government plans for finance remedy, 114; results of closing of Indian mints, 115; opium monopoly in, 142.
Indies, the, Trading Company of, 206.
Indirect Taxation. See Taxation.
Industrial and Provident Societies Act, 82.
Inheritance, Laws of, 180.
Insolvency, Laws of, 182.
Insurance against risk, 53.
"International" The, 31.
International Society of Working Men, 70.
Interest, 20; "stationary state" in, 57; rate of, 130-132; its depend-

ence on loans, 130; in Australia, 130; lowering of, 132; how it affects funds, 132.

Jagetzow, 30.
Jevons, Prof. W. S., on money, 92; definition of "standard of value," 96, 101; his works, 244.
Jones, Richard, 227.
Junta, the, 70.

"Katheder Socialisten," 31, 241.
Kemp, John, 192.
Ketteler, Von, 37.
Kidd, Benjamin, on present-day legislation, 150, 151.
King, Gregory, 18.
King's, Lord, Law of Paper Currency, 123.
Kingsley, Charles, 37, 69.
Knies, Charles, 240, 241.
Knights of Labour, 36.
Kolokol, The, 33.
Krapotkine, Prince, 31, 34.

Laborde on Socialistic Corporations, 77.
Labour, productive and unproductive, 6, 9-12; its relation to the labourer, 9; division of labour, 9, 10; its advantages, 10; law of the increase of labour, 12; German Congress, 36; labour v. ability, 39; effect on competition in, 44; wages of, 45; influence of machinery in, 45; its relation to wages and profits, 46-48; eight hours day, 51; cost of agricultural labour, 54; cost of labour, 55; remedies to present condition in, 66-82; labour movement, 66; Royal Commission of 1894, 73; how affected by Trades Unions, 76; Statute of Labourers, 194; Act most prejudicial to, 198; Adam Smith on, 213.
Labour Party, British, 36.
Labourers, Statute of, 70, 194.
Labour Standard, The, 70.
Land, its productiveness, 12-19; its law, 15; comparison of arable and pasture in England, 16; English Nationalisation of, 38; permanent improvements in, 58; its value in a new colony, 90; English land law, 183, 184; uncertainty of title, 183; its transferability, 183, 184; Chamberlayne and Law's Land Banks, 203-205.
Land Law of England, 14; Prussian (Stein & Hardenberg), 15; criticism on, 183.
Lassalle, Ferdinand, 28, 29; his definition of the economic law, 29.
Latin Union, The, 96.
Laveleye, 23.
Lavergne, Leone de, 234.
Lavroff, 33.
Law, John, 204; his theories of paper money, 204; Law's Land Bank, 204, 205; Trading Company of the Indies, 206.
Law's Scotch Land Bank, 124.
Law Taxes. *See* Taxation.
Leasehold Question, 176.
Leclaire, M., 78.
Leeds Flour Mill, 78.
Legal, criticism of English system, 183, 184; Law Courts Procedure, 183; Mercantile Law, 183; Land Law, 183; uncertainty of title, 183.
Lemercier de la Riviere, 211.
Leslie, Cliffe, on Adam Smith, 214; on the deductive method in Political Economy, 215; on the abstract method, 222; his works on the historical method, 243, 244.
Le Trosne, 211.
Levi, Prof. Leone, tables of gold and silver, 100, 101.
Lichfield, Earl of, 71.
Liebknecht, 29, 34.
List, Frederic, 235.
Liverpool Trades Guardian Association, 69.
Loans, 7; capital for, 130; causes influencing supply of, 131, 132; Government loans, 131.
Local Taxation. *See* Taxation.
Locke, against Bimetallism, 98; on theory of value, 202; on debasement of coinage, 202; on taxes, 202.
London Co-operative Guild, 29; Trades Council, 69, 70.

INDEX.   261

MACDONALD, Alexander, 68, 70, 72.
Machinery, 45 ; effect on labour, 45 ; on capital, 45, 58.
Mackintosh, Sir James, on Adam Smith, 218.
Macleod on value, 84 ; on fallen prices, 106 ; on credit, 116.
Mahaffy, Prof., on the Greek idea of trade, 186.
Mallet, Sir Louis, 22, 108.
Mallock, W. H., 39.
Malthus's Law, 5 ; *The Essay on Population*, 219 ; on moral checks and the Poor Laws, 220 ; on rent, 220.
" Margin of Cultivation," 59.
Maritime Situation, Advantages of, 13.
Marshall, Prof., 2, 3, 4, 6, 16, 45, 76 ; on wages and Trades Unions, 77 ; on co-operation, 79, 80 ; on utility, 85 ; on the parts played by nature and man in production, 89 ; development of Jevons's position, 244, 245 ; his works, 245.
Masters and Workmen, 72.
Marx, Karl, 31, 32 ; Socialism of, 32 ; *Das Kapital*, 32, 43.
Maurice, F. D., 37, 69.
M'Culloch, 47, 227.
Merchants, Statute of, 128, 190.
Mercantile Fallacy, The, 198.
Mercantile Theory, The, 200.
Metallic currency, how affected by additions of the precious metals, 122.
Metayers, 41.
Methley Colliery, 78.
Methuen Treaty, the, 218.
Milan Co-operative Union, 80.
Mill, James, 227.
Mill, John Stuart, 1, 5, 22 ; statement of wages fund theory, 46, 47; on retail dealers, 81 ; on credit, 115 ; on commodities, 134 ; on Government, 150 ; his reasons against Government interference, 151 ; his exceptions, 152 ; his estimate of Government value, 153 ; on equality of taxation, 156 ; on Income-tax, 157 ; on unearned increment, 158 ; on House-tax, 161; on taxation of commodities, 165 ;
on Laws of Inheritance, 180 ; Criticism on English law, 183 ; his works, 227, 228 ; his debt to Auguste Comte, 228 ; his debt to Bentham, 228 ; his training, 228 ; alteration in his economic views, 229 ; Mill's review of Comte, 230.
Minerals, 13.
Miners' Union, 68.
Miners' Association, 68.
Mir, 22, 33.
Mirabeau, Victor, 211.
Missenden's *Circle of Commerce*, 191.
Money, definition of, 5 ; its full consideration, 91–96 ; a form of capital, 91 ; a measure of value, 91 ; the medium of exchange, 92 ; summation of the functions of, 92 ; gold and silver, 92 ; its circulation, 92, 93 ; paper substitutes, 93 ; its purchasing power, 93 ; its value, how regulated, 94 ; its circulation, 94 ; the laws of its supply and demand, 95 ; exceptions, 95, 96 ; quantitative theory of, 99 ; Gresham's law, 122 ; debasement of, 195.
Monometallism, 96 ; reasons for a gold standard, 97.
Monopoly, its evil effects, 167 ; how affected by the Declaration of Rights, 197.
Monopoly value, 85.
More, Sir Thos., *The Utopia*, 187.
Morrill Tariff, 168.
Moufang, Canon, 37.
Muller, Adam, 234.
Mulhall, 16, 45 ; on Co-operation, 80 ; comparative tables of imports and exports, 101.
Mun, Sir Thomas, 198.
Municipal Socialism, 25.

NAVIGATION LAWS, effect on gold output, 101.
Navigation Laws in England and France, 197.
Navigation Law, repeal of, 168, 225.
Nebenius, Frederic, 235.
Nevada silver mines, 107.
Newspaper Tax. *See* Taxation.
Nihilist movement, 33.

North, Sir Dudley, 208.
Northampton Co-operative Shoemakers, 79.
Norwich Trades Union Congress, 1894, 77.

O'Connor's Indian prices and wages statistics, 110.
Odger, 31, 69.
Oldham Sun Cotton Mill, 79.
Oneida Perfectionists, 23, 79.
Opium, Indian monopoly, 143.
Oresme, Nicolas, 196; his works on "Money," 196.
Ouseburn Engineering Factory, 78.
Overtime, 75.
Owen, Robert, 23; his social schemes and works, 23, 24, 25; idea of union of productive classes, 68.

PAPER CURRENCY, inconvertible, 121; its effect on metallic currency, 121; its effect on prices, 122; how affected by American Secession War, 122; Lord King's Law, 123; fallacies involved in an unlimited issue of inconvertible, 123, 124; how its depreciation affected holders of the National Debt, 124, 125; Law's theories on, 204.
Paris Commune, 27.
Paris, Comte de, 71.
Parish Councils Act, 52.
Particularism, 24.
Partnership, Law of, 182.
Patents forbidden by Declaration of Rights, 197.
Paterson, William, 203.
Peasant proprietors, 14, 15.
Peasant proprietorship, 38, 41.
Peel, Sir Robert, Act for limitation of Bank-Note issue, 125, 126.
Petty, Sir William, 201.
Phalange, 28.
Phalanstery, 28.
Physiocratic School, the, 210, 211; their first doctrines, 212.
Picketing, 71, 72.
Piecework, 75.
Pierre le Pesant, 210.
Plato on artizans, 186; on community of property and wives, 186; *The Republic*, 186, 187.

Political Economy, definition, 1; its two methods, 2; its three schools, 3, 4; social dynamics, 63; social statics, 63. *See also* Economics.
Pools, American, 40, 44.
Poor Law, 153, 176; origin of, 177; Acts, 177–179; growth of Poor Law charges, 179; Commission of Inquiry, 178; Poor Law Amendment Act, 179; Scotch and Irish Poor Laws, 179; Metropolitan Poor Act, 179; Fawcett on London System, 179; decrease of paupers, 179; circumstances affecting the decrease in paupers, 180.
Population, checks on its increase, 12; effect on rents, 59; effects of wages, profits, and rents on, 63; ratios existing between capital and population, 63.
Potato famine, Irish, 46, 66.
Potosi, 94.
Potter, George, 70.
Prairie cropping, 16.
Precious metals as commodities, 144–149; their difference from other commodities, 144; effect of their importation into England, 144; cheap importation of bullion, 144, 145; equation of international demand in trade, 145; cheap money, 145; causes of their importation, 146; effect of bonded warehousing, 146; disturbances corrected, 147; rise of prices in, 147; Ricardo's Law of their distribution, 148; how exports and imports in, affect international bills, 148.
Price, definition of, 84.
Price, L. L., 73.
Prices, influence of custom on, 43; on what they depend, 48; relation of agricultural prices to rent, 60; causes for differences in, 84, 85; rise and fall in, 85; how related to joint cost of production, 90; how affected by Free Trade, 101, 102; by increased production of gold, 102; animal produce most affected by a rise in, 103; effect of a rise in, on manufactured goods, 103; effect of the use of machinery on, 103; how equality of prices is

realised, 103 ; order in which the countries have been affected by a rise in, 105 ; reasons for this order, 105 ; fall in, affecting value of gold, 105 ; Macleod on fall in, 106 ; how affected by credit, 116 ; high prices dependent on greater use of money, 145 ; decline in, affected by wealth and population, 146.

Primogeniture, Law of, 14 ; the system, 181.

Prisage, 190.

Production, its three requisites, 6 ; its advantages on the large and the small scale, 10, 11 ; Rodbertus's system of its nationalisation, 30 ; nationalisation of the means of, 38 ; guild system, 62 ; industrial system, 62 ; definition of 86 ; parts played by nature and man in, 89 ; a joint cost of 90.

Productive Associations, 30.

Profits, elements of, 53 ; effects of increase of, 54 ; rate of, 54 ; causes of increase in, 55 ; decrease of profits, 56 ; relation to increase of capital, 57 ; how lessening rate is counteracted, 57 ; tendency to a minimum, consequences of, 58 ; how affected by labour, 86 ; its variations, 87 ; how its rise affects value, 87 ; patentees' profits, 89 ; compared to rent, 89.

Prohibitions, Imposition of, 197.

Promissory Notes, 117.

Property, private, 21-42 ; its origin, 21 ; its progressive stages, 22 ; in land, 22 ; socialistic definition of, 32 ; criticism on schemes of substitutes for, 37-40 ; workmen's rights to, 62 ; Conspiracy and Protection of Property Act, 72.

Property, Common, 21, 22.

Protection, an argument for, 139 ; its rationale, 140, 141 ; imposition of duties, 142 ; arguments against, 142, 143 ; its evils, 168 ; Fawcett on Victorian Protection, 168-169 ; Morrill Tariff, 168 ; American prosperity under, 168-170 ; Fawcett's summary of Protectionist arguments, 170-174 ; Bounty system, 174 ; Treaties of Commerce, 174 ; History of the Duties on Corn, 226, 227.

Proudhon, 26, 28.

Public Works, 183.

QUANTITATIVE Theory of Money, 99.

Quesnay, Francis, 210, 211.

RAILWAYS, American, 17 ; Victorian, 26 ; Railway Servants, Amalgamated Society of, 74.

Rates, 175 ; municipal, 176 ; railway, 176.

Raw, Charles Henry, 235.

Rayats, 42.

Realistic School, 239.

Reciprocity, 168.

Recluse, Elisée, 34.

Reformation, the, Economic Effects of, 196.

Registration of Trade, 71.

Rent, Rodbertus's Theory of, 30 ; George's definition, 35, 43 ; reason for its existence, 58 ; its relation to profit, 59 ; relation to the "margin of cultivation," 59 ; relation to increase of population, 60; population effects counteracted, 60 ; relation to value, 60 ; and to prices, 60 ; monopoly rent, 61; objections to theory of rent, 61 ; relation to new colonies, 61 ; agricultural rent, 65; reduction in through cheaper food, 65; Ricardo's Theory of, 220, 221.

Ricardo, 3, 29 ; theory of wage, 47 ; on value, 84 ; his Law of the distribution of the precious metals, 148 ; his theory of rent, 220, 221 ; on bullion, 221 ; his abstract method, 221, 222 ; his doctrine of exchange value, 223 ; drawbacks of Ricardo's School, 223, 224 ; his principles of economics, 224, 225.

Rice, rise in the price of Indian, 111.

Rings, 40.

Rochdale Equitable Pioneers' Society, 80, 81.

Rodbertus, Karl Johann, 30 ; his theory of rent, profit, and wages, 30.

Rogers, Professor Thorold, on retail dealers, 80 ; on guilds, 190 ; his work on "prices," 237.

Roscher, William, 239, 240.

Rupee, value of, 100; its purchasing power, 110; its gold value, 112; effect of its depreciation, 113; proposals for a fixity of its sterling value, 113; effect of Government policy on its value, 114.
Ruskin, 3.
Russia Company, The, 193.
Rutherford, Dr, 82.

St Simon, 27.
Say, Jean Baptiste, 231; Ricardo's opinion of, 231, 232.
Scaruffi, Gaspar, 198.
Schäffle, 24, 27, 30; "Social System," 240, 241.
Schmoller, 240.
Schulze-Delitzsch, 29; co-operative banking, 81.
Schweitzer, 34.
Seigniorage, 93.
Senior, Nassau, 68; on Tithe, 162.
Serra, Antonio, 198.
Settlement, Law of, 178.
Shakers, the, 23, 79.
Sheffield Trades Council, 70.
Sherman Act, 97, 110, 113; the effect of its repeal on Indian finance, 113.
Shipton, George, 70.
Sidgwick, Prof. H., 2; on Ricardo's Theory of Rent, 224; on J. S. Mill, 228.
Silver, the material of money, 92; considerations on as a sole legal tender, 99; opinion of bimetallists on, 99; value of, relatively to gold, 100; tables of silver production, 107, 108; reasons for its depreciation, 108, 109; circulation in Austria and Germany, 108; its demand in India, 109; tables of its importation into, 109; proposals for relief of Indian Government owing to its depreciation, 113. *See also* Precious Metals.
Sismondi, John Charles, 232.
Slaney, Mr, 82.
Slave labour, 41.
Smith, Adam, rates of wages, 49, 50; his Canons of Taxation, 154, 155, 214; contents and summary of *The Wealth of Nations*, 213-218; on wages, 213; on capital, 213; on labour, 213; on the various forms of industry, 214; on the systems of political economy, 214; on the method of *The Wealth of Nations*, 215; interest of the community, how best obtained, 215, 216; on the interference of Government, 216; erroneous views in Smith's book, 217; influence of Smith's writings, 218, 219.
Small proprietors, 14.
Social Democratic Federation, 36.
Socialism, 24; definition and aims, 24, 25; State Socialism, 25, 150; Anarchic Socialism, 25-27, 33; St Simonism, 27; Fourierism, 27; Lassalle's idea of, 29, 30; academic, 31; Marx's Socialism, 32; Principles of the Berne Congress, 34; Universal Congress at Ghent, 35; George's *Progress and Poverty*, 35; attitude of Church to, 37; Christian Social Union, 37; Socialism *v.* Private Property, 39; benefits of Socialism, 40; Theory of Wages, 47; New Unionism, 77; French Socialism, 77; Socialistic Corporations, 77.
"South Sea Company," the, 207.
Spencer, Herbert, 4.
Stafford, William, 198.
"Standard of Value," 96.
Staple, Statute of the, 192.
Statistics, definition of, 2.
Statute of Apprentices, 67, 70; Conspiracy and Protection of Property Act, 72; Criminal Law Amendment Act, 72; Elcho's Master and Servant Act, 70; Employers and Workmen Act, 72; Statute of Frauds, 14; Friendly Societies Act, 69-71; Industrial and Provident Societies Act, 82; Statute of Labourers, 194; Statute of Merchants, 128, 190; Parish Councils Act, 52.
Steuart, Sir James, 210.
Stewart, Dugald, on Adam Smith, 215.
Strikes, 66, 69.
Sully, Duke of, his financial measures, 199.

Supply, definition of, 86; how increased, 86; effects of its excess, 89.
Syndicates, 40.

TAXATION, on imports, 142; on land produce, 143; Adam Smith's canons, 154, 155; certainty and uncertainty of, 154; convenience of levy, 154; ways in which a tax may affect the people, 155; evasion of, 155; equality of taxation, 155, 156; Mill on equality of taxation, 156; Income Tax, 156, 157; Mill on Income Tax, 157; direct taxation, 158-161; definition of a direct tax, 158; incidence of Income Tax, 158; taxation of unearned increment, 158; effect of tax on trade profits, 159; tax on wages, 159; objection to Income Tax, 159; house tax, 160; tax on building rent, 160; tax on ground rents, 160, 161; Mill on house tax, 161; indirect taxation, 161-164; its incidence, 161; evil effects of taxation of necessities, 161, 162; Tithe, 162; Commutation of Tithes Act, 162; Customs duties on land produce, 163; repeal of the Corn Laws, 164; taxes on purchases and sales, 164; taxes on contracts, 164; tax on newspapers, 164; law taxes and fees, 164; Mill on taxation of commodities, 165; taxes on luxuries, 165; on stimulants, 165; on imported articles, 165; Fawcett on taxation of commodities, 165; evil effects of taxing home commodities, 166, 167; local taxation, 175-180; difference of local from Imperial taxation, 175; how to raise local taxes, 175; confusion of present state of local taxation, 175; Poor Law, 176-179.
Tempest, Sir Thomas, 196.
Temple, Sir William, 202.
Tithe. *See* Taxation.
Title. *See* Land.
Todt, Pastor, 37.
Tooke, Mr, on bank issues, 125.

Toynbee, Arnold, his influence and published works, 245, 246.
Trades Council, London, 69, 70.
Trades Guardian Association, Liverpool, 69.
Trades Unionism, 66, 67; Builders' Union, 67; Miners' Union, 68; Combination Acts, 68; Robert Owen's idea of, 68; Nassau Senior's Report, 68; Chartists, 68; National Association of United Trades, 68; Amalgamated Society of Engineers, 69; Carpenters' Union, 69; Glasgow and Sheffield Trades Councils, 70; Royal Commission on, 70; The Commission of 1869, 71; Trades Union Act, 1871, 71; Manchester Meeting, 1868, 72; National Trades Union Congress, 72; Trades Union of Women, 72; Sheffield Congress, 1874, 72; National Federation of Associated Employers of Labour, 72; National Agricultural Labourers' Union, 72; Recommendation of the Royal Commission on Labour of 1894, 72; Boot and Shoe Operatives, 74; Amalgamated Engineers, 74; Amalgamated Society of Railway Servants, 74; Webb's work on *Trades Unionism*, 74; influence of, 74; scope of power, 74; influence on labour and wages, 74; attitude towards labour-saving machinery, 75; influence on hours of labour, 75; attitude to piecework, 75; and to overtime, 75; attitude toward strikes, 76; New Unionism, 77; Belfast Congress, 1893, 77; Norwich Congress, 1894, 77; Gasworkers' Union, 77, 78.
Treaties of Commerce, 174.
Trusts, American, 40.
Tucker, Josiah, 209.
Tull, Jethro, 18.
Turgot, Robert James, 211.
Twiss, Sir Travers, 227.

UNDERSELLING, on what it depends, 143.
Unearned increment, 158.

Union, Boot and Shoe Operatives', 74; Builders', 67; Carpenters', 69; Christian Social, 37; Zurich Consumers', 80; Milan Co-operatives', 80; Miners', 68; Yorkshire Woolcombers', 67.
Unionism, New, 36, 77.
United States, 12.
Upholsterers' Sewers' Society, Edinburgh, 72.
Usury, its laws, 166; and their effect, 166.
Utility, how originated, 83; Marshall on, 85.
Utopias, 186, 187.

Varro on Agriculture, 188.
Vauban, Marshal, 210.
Value, relation to rent, 60; its definition, 83, 84; Ricardo on, 84; Macleod on, 84; of land, 84; of commodities, 84; how affected by labour, 84; monopoly value, 85; how affected by supply and demand, 86; how affected by high wages, 86; how affected by rise in profits, 87.
Verri, Pietro, 231.
Village communities, 42.
Vincent, John Claud Marie, 211.
Voltaire, 211, 212.
Vorwärts, The, 29.

Wages, Socialistic definition of, 32; George's definition, 35, 36; Theory of Wages, 44-52; as interest on capital, 44; as a sinking fund, 44; as an insurance agent, 44; basis of wages, 44; circumstances lessening wages, 45; effect of increase in, 46; wages fund theory, 46; effect on pauperism, 46; wages and manufacturers, 46, 47; relation to profits, 47, 48; differences in the rates of, 49, 50; remedies, for low wages, 51-53; wages of superintendence, 53; effect of increase in, on agricultural labour, 59; ratio to profit, 64; tendency of the rise in, 76; attitude of Trades Unions on, 75; how affected by increased production of gold, 102; of Australian gold, 103; how its increase affects gold, 106; indication of high wages, 144; Adam Smith on, 213.
Wagner, 241.
Walker, General, parallel between profit and rent, 56; definition of money, 91.
Walpole, Sir Robert, his financial work, 209.
Warehousing, bonded, 146.
Wealth, definition of, 5; its classification, 5.
Webb, Sidney, 66, 67, 70, 74.
West Indies, 12.
Westcott, Bishop, 37.
Whately, Richard, 236, 237.
Wheat, 16; American, 17; Canadian, 16; comparison of English and American production of, 17.
Whewell, Dr, 3.
Wool, Australian, 104; rise of English industry in, 191, 192; Statute of the Staple, 192.
Woolcombers' Union (Yorks), 67.
Woollen Manufacturers, Select Committee on, 67.
Workshops, Blanc's Theory of National, 24.

Xenophon on Political Economy, 187.

Yorkshire Woolcombers' Union, 67.
Young, Arthur, 18, 41, 234.

Zemindar, 42.
Zurich Consumers' Union, 80.

PRINTED BY NEILL AND COMPANY, EDINBURGH.

www.ingramcontent.com/pod-product-compliance
Lightning Source LLC
Chambersburg PA
CBHW032123230426
43672CB00009B/1839